# DIPLOMACY
# BY
# DECEPTION

AN ACCOUNT OF THE
TREASONOUS CONDUCT
BY THE GOVERNMENTS
OF BRITAIN AND
THE UNITED STATES

DR. JOHN COLEMAN

For permissions, or serializations, condensations, adaptations, or for our catalog of other publications, write the Publisher at the address below.

Library of Congress Cataloging-in-Publication Data (CIP)

DIPLOMACY BY DECEPTION by Dr. John Coleman
p. cm.
Includes Index
ISBN 0-9640104-8-8
1.  Secret Societies
2.  Conspiracy
I.  Title

HS 150.c59 1993
366 — dc20
for Library of Congress                          93-4441
                                                  CIP

Published by
BRIDGER HOUSE PUBLISHERS, INC
P.O. Box 2208, Carson City,  NV 89702, 1-800-729-4131

Cover design by The Right Type

Printed in the United States of America
10 9 8 7 6 5 4 3 2 1

# DEDICATION.

*Dedicated to my wife Lena and our son John who have stood by me throughout the years of dangerous and trying times, bearing severe hardships, deprivation and the slings of outrageous fortune with fortitude and courage. Without their loyalty and devotion to the cause of truth, this book would never have become a reality. To all of those who so greatly assisted with help of all kinds, your efforts meant the difference between failure and success.*

# TABLE OF CONTENTS

# Foreword.

I decided to write this book because so many people who had read my book "The Conspirators Hierarchy: The Committee of 300" asked me to give specific examples and case histories of how the Committee exercises control on such a vast scale. This book is by way of answering those requests.

When you have read "Diplomacy By Deception" you will have little doubt that the British and United States Governments are the most corrupt in the world and that without their full cooperation in carrying out the designs of the Committee of 300, this supranational body would not be able to go forward with its plans for a One World Government, to which former President Bush, one of its more able servants, referred to as "the New World Order."

It is my earnest wish that "Diplomacy By Deception" will bring about a greater understanding of how secret societies operate, and how their orders are carried out by the very people who are supposed to serve the national interests and guard the national security of their respective countries and their people.

Dr. John Coleman.

DR JOHN COLEMAN

# The Threat of the United Nations.

# I.

The history of how the United Nations was created is a classic case of diplomacy by deception. The United Nations is the successor to the defunct League of Nations, the first attempt to set up a One World Government in the wake of the Paris Peace Conference which gave birth to the Treaty of Versailles.

The peace conference opened at Versailles, France on January 18, 1919, attended by 70 delegates representing the international bankers from the 27 "victorious" allied powers. It is a fact that delegates were under the direction of the international bankers from the time they were selected as delegates until they returned to their own countries, and even long after that.

Let us be perfectly clear, the peace conference was about bleeding Germany to death; it was about securing huge sums of money for the international brigand-bankers who had already reaped obscene rewards alongside the terrible casualties of the five-year war (1914-1919). Britain alone suffered 1,000,000 deaths and more than 2,000,000 wounded. It is estimated by war historian Alan Brugar, that the international bankers made a profit of $10,000 from every soldier who fell in battle. Life is cheap when it comes to the Committee of 300-Illuminati-Rothschilds-Warburg-Federal Reserve bankers, who financed both sides of the war.

It is also worthwhile to remember that H.G. Wells and Lord Bertrand Russell foresaw this terrible war in which millions -- the flowers of the mostly Christian -- nations died needless deaths. The Committee of 300 planned the war so that international bankers would profit greatly. H.G. Wells was known as the "prophet" to the Committee of 300. It is true to say that Wells merely brought up-to-date the ideas of the British East India Company (BEIC) which were carried out by

1

Jeremy Bentham and Adam Smith, to name two of the wreckers used by King George III to undermine and scuttle the economic future of the North American colonists seeking to escape the economic toils of the Venetian Party of the North in the late 1700s.

In an article written by Wells published in the "Banker" (a copy of which I found in the British Museum in London), Wells spelled out the future role of the International Monetary Fund (IMF) and the banker's bank, the Bank of International Settlements (BIS). Once we, the sovereign people, understand the role of international banks in fomenting wars, and then financing both sides, wars may well become a thing of the past. Until then, wars will remain the favorite tool of the international banks for raising revenues and getting rid of unwanted populations, as Bertrand Russell so eloquently put it.

In his book, "After Democracy," Wells stated that once the economic order (social energy), of a dictatorship One World Government is established, a political and social order will be imposed. This was precisely what the Paris Peace Talks that began in 1919 set out to do, based primarily upon a Royal Institute for International Affairs (RIIA) memorandum.

The RIIA drafted a 23-point proposal which it sent to Woodrow Wilson, who handed it to Mandel Huis, (a.k.a. Colonel House), Wilson's Dutch-born controller. Col. House immediately left for Magnolia, his private residence in Massachusetts, where he reduced the number of proposals to 14, creating the basis of the "14 Points" presented to the Paris Peace Conference by President Wilson in December of 1918.

Wilson's arrival in Paris was greeted with wild enthusiasm by the poor and deluded populace who had grown tired of war and who saw in Wilson, the harbinger of eternal peace. Wilson cloaked his speeches in true diplomacy by deception language; a new spirit of idealism -- even while intent on securing control of the world by the international bankers through the League of Nations.

The similarity between the way the League of Nations Treaty and its successor, the United Nations Treaty were floated, should not be lost on the reader. German delegates were kept out of the proceedings until the terms were ready to be submitted to the conference. Russia was not represented, because public opinion violently opposed Bolshevism. British Prime Minister Lloyd George and President Wilson well knew that the Bolshevik Revolution was about to succeed with terrible consequences for the Russian people.

From the start, the Big Ten Supreme Council (forerunners of the U.N. Security Council) took over. The council consisted of Wilson, Lansing, Lloyd George, Balfour, Pichon, Orlando, Sonnino (both representing the Black Nobility bankers of Venice), Clemenceau, Saionji and Makino.

On January 25, 1919, the agenda of the RIIA won out, the conference delegates unanimously adopted a resolution for the creation of a League of Nations. A committee was chosen (whose members were actually nominated by the RIIA) to deal with reparations by Germany. On February 15, 1919, Wilson returned to the United States and Lloyd George went back to London. By March however, both men were back in Paris to work on how best Germany could be financially ripped apart -- and the Council of Ten, having proved too cumbersome, was reduced to the Council of Four.

The British invited Gen. Jan Christian Smuts, a Boer War veteran, to join in the discussions, to add an aura of good faith to the deplorable plot. Smuts was a traitor to his own people. As Prime Minister he had led South Africa into the First World War over the objections of 78 percent of its people who felt they had no quarrel with Germany. Smuts became part of the committee consisting of Wilson, House, Lord Cecil controller of the British Royal Family (see my monograph "King Makers/King Breakers"), Bourgeois and Venizelos.

The League of Nations was born in January of 1920. Housed in Geneva, it consisted of a secretary-general, a Council (chosen from the five major powers) and a General Assembly. The German nation was sold down the river, the terms of peace far exceeding those agreed upon when Germany was persuaded to lay down its arms. The

German Army was not defeated on the battle field. It was defeated by diplomacy by deception.

The international bankers became the big winners, eventually stripping Germany of all major assets and receiving huge "reparation" payments. The RIIA now felt it had "everything in the bag" to quote Wilson. But the RIIA had not reckoned with a large number of U.S. Senators who knew the U.S. Constitution. By contrast, the number of senators and congressman who really know the U.S. Constitution today, number only about twenty.

For example Senator Robert Byrd, an admitted Rockefeller protege said recently that a treaty is the supreme law of the land. Apparently, Sen. Byrd does not know that for a treaty to be valid, it has to be made with a country that has sovereignty, and the United Nations, as we will find, has no sovereignty whatsoever. In any case, a treaty is only a law and cannot override the U.S. Constitution, nor can it stand when it threatens the sovereignty and security of the United States.

If Sen. Byrd holds this view, we wonder why he voted to give the Panama Canal away? When the United States acquired the land for the Panama Canal from Colombia, the land became sovereign U.S. territory. Therefore, the Panama Canal give-away was unconstitutional and illegal, as we shall see in the chapter dealing with the Carter-Torrijos Panama Canal Treaty.

When the League of Nations Treaty was brought before the U.S. Senate in March of 1920, 49 senators understood the immense implications involved, and refused to ratify it. There was much discussion compared to what passed for a debate when the U.N. Charter came before the Senate in 1945. Several amendments to the League treaty were submitted by the RIIA. These were acceptable to President Wilson, but were refused by the Senate. On November 19, 1920, the Senate rejected the treaty with and without reservations by a vote of 49-35.

The international bankers then directed Wilson to veto a joint resolution of Congress, declaring the war with Germany at an end, so that they could go on savaging the German nation for another whole year. It was not until April 18, 1945 that the League of Nations dissolved itself, transferring all of its assets (mainly money taken from the German people after WWI, and war loans not repaid by the allies to the United States) to the United Nations In other words, the Committee of 300 never gave up on its plans for a One World Government and waited until the United Nations was in existence before dissolving the discredited League of Nations.

The money that the League of Nations transferred to the United Nations rightfully belonged to the sovereign people of the United States. The United States had advanced billions of dollars to so-called allies to pull their chestnuts out of the fire after they'd picked a quarrel with Germany in 1914 and were in dire danger of losing the fight.

In 1923, a U.S. observer was sent to the Lausanne Conference of the Allied Powers for discussions on repayment of the $10.4 billion owed to the United States, and splitting up the Middle East oil-producing countries between themselves. The international bankers objected to U.S. intervention at Lausanne on the basis of instructions received from Chatham House, home of the RIIA. The first repayment agreement was reached with Britain, which was to repay war loans over a 62-year period, at interest of 3.3 percent.

In November of 1925 and April of 1926, the United States reached agreements with Italy and France to repay their share of war loans over the same period. By May of 1930, 17 nations who had been loaned money by the United States had signed agreements to repay all of their war loans, amounting to nearly $11 billion.

In November of 1932, Franklin D. Roosevelt was elected the first openly socialist President of the United States. Socialist Roosevelt's arrival at the White House had its beginning in the murder of President Willaim McKinley, followed by the election of the fraudulent "patriot" Teddy Roosevelt, whose job it was to open the doors to socialism which was to be ushered in by Franklin D. Roosevelt. This contrived sequence of events is too long be recounted here. On instructions from Chatham House, Roosevelt lost no time in winking at the horrendous default on the loan agreements signed by the allies. By December 15 1932, all of the nations who owed the United States billions of dollars for war debts were in default. Britain was the largest debtor and the largest defaulter.

A substantial amount of this money, plus much of what was wrenched from Germany after WWI, went into the coffers of the League of Nations, and eventually wound up in the coffers of the United Nations. Thus, not only did America needlessly sacrifice its soldier-sons on the battlefields of Europe, but had its pockets picked as well by the nations that began the First World War. Worse yet, worthless war reparation bonds were dumped into the American financial market, costing taxpayers additional billions of dollars.

If there is one thing that we have learned about the Committee of 300, it is that it never gives up. There is a saying that history repeats itself; certainly this is true of the Committee of 300's intention to force a One World Government body on the United States. H.G.Wells, in his work "The Shape of Things to Come" described this body as "a sort of an open conspiracy -- a cult of the World State" (i.e. a One World Government.)

The world state (OWG), Wells said, "must be the sole landowner on earth. All roads must lead to socialism." In his book, "After Democracy," Wells clearly said that once world economic order is established (through the International Monetary Fund and the Bank of International Settlements), political and social order will be imposed. In the chapter on the Tavsitock Institute for Human Relations, it will be explained how Tavistock's "Operation Research" was to be the engine to bring about drastic reforms in economics and politics.

In the case of the United States, the plan is not to overthrow the U.S. government or its Constitution, but to "make it negligible." This has largely been accomplished by slowly and carefully implementing the socialist manifesto written in 1920 by the Fabian Society, which was based on the Communist Manifesto of 1848.

Isn't this making of the Constitution "negligible" exactly what is happening? In fact when the U.S. government violates the Constitution on an almost daily basis with total impunity, it makes the Constitution "negligible." Executive orders, such as going to war without a declaration of war, as in the Gulf War, have worked to make the Constitution "negligible." There is absolutely no provision in the Constitution for executive orders. Executive orders are only proclamations which the president has no power or authority to make. Only a king can make proclamations.

The warmed over League of Nations was thrust upon the U.S. Senate in 1945, dressed under a new label: the United Nations Treaty. The senators were given only three days to discuss the implications of the treaty, which could not have been fully examined in under least a full 18 months of discussion. Had the senators properly understood what they were discussing, which, apart from a few exceptions, they did not, there would have been a demand for a proper period for discussion. The fact is that the Senate did not understand the document and therefore should not have voted on it.

Had the senators who debated the United Nations treaty properly understood the document, it surely would have been rejected. Apart from any other considerations, the document was so poorly written and, in many instances, so vague, deceptive and contradictory, that it could have been rejected on these grounds alone.

A law, which is what a treaty is, must be clearly written and unambiguous. The U.N. Treaty was far from that. In any case, the United States, bound by its Constitution, could not ratify the U.N. treaty, for the following reasons:

(1) Our Constitution rests upon the bedrock of sovereignty, without which there can be no constitution. U.S. foreign policy is based upon Vattel's "Law of Nations" which makes sovereignty the issue. Although the Constitution is silent on world government and foreign bodies, when the Constitution is silent of a power, and it is not incidental to another power in the Constitution, then it is an inhibition of that power, or a PROHIBITION of that power.
(2) The United Nations is not a sovereign body, having no measurable

7

territory of its own. It is housed on U.S. territory in New York in a building loaned by the Rockefellers. Under the U.S. Constitution, we cannot make a treaty with any nation or body that lacks sovereignty. *The United States could not (and cannot) make a treaty with a body or country having no sovereignty.* The U.S. can make an agreement with a country or body having no sovereignty, but can never enter into a treaty with a body lacking in sovereignty.

(3) For the Senate to have attempted to ratify a treaty with a body, state, or country lacking sovereignty, defined boundaries, demographics, a currency system, a set of laws or a constitution, to whit, the United Nations, was to betray the oath to uphold the Constitution which senators are sworn to do. This is commonly called treason.

(4) In order for the United States to become a member of the United Nations, two amendments to the Constitution would have to be passed. The first amendment would have to recognize that a world body exists. In its present form, the Constitution *cannot* recognize the United Nations as a world body. A second amendment would have to say that the United States *can* have a treaty relationship with an unsovereign world body. Neither amendment was ever offered, much less accepted by the Senate and ratified by all of the States.

Thus, the thoroughly suspect U.N. "treaty" never was a legal law in the United States. As matters stood in 1945, and as they stand in 1993, although the President has the power to have a say in foreign affairs, he does not have the power, nor has he ever had the power, to make an agreement -- much less a treaty -- with a world body. This absolutely means that no other world body, specifically, the United Nations, has jurisdiction to deploy American servicemen and women, or to order the United States to act *outside* of the Constitutional restrictions imposed by our Founding Fathers.

Sen. David I. Walsh, one of the few senators who understood the constitutional dangers posed by the badly flawed U.N. Charter, told his colleagues the following:

"The only acts of aggression or breaches of peace the charter is sure to be geared up to suppress are those committed by small nations, that is to say, by the nations which are least able and unlikely to kindle another world conflict. Even in these cases, Mr. President, investigation and preventative action can be arbitrarily paralyzed by any of the big five powers, which are permanent members of the Security Council..."

"Thus, any small nation which enjoys the patronage, or serves as a tool or puppet of one of the big powers is as immune to interference as the Big Five themselves. Let us face the fact: In the Charter we have an instrument for arresting acts of war by countries which lack the power of making war. The menace of large-scale conflict does not reside in quarrels among themselves. Such quarrels can be limited and isolated."

"The menace lies rather when the small powers act in interest of a great neighbor and are provoked into their act by that neighbor. But in that case the veto privilege which makes the big power immune to United Nations action can operate to make the small satellite nation immune. The preventative machinery works smoothly until the point of real danger is reached, the point where a nation is strong enough to precipitate a world war is involved, and can then go dead."

"We may assume, in fact, that every small country could be under temptation and pressure to seek a big power patron. Only in that way can it obtain an indirect share in the monopoly of control vested in the Big Five. One of the faults of the Charter, Mr. President, is that its punitive and coercive leverage could be applied only against a truly small independent nation." (Iraq is a perfect example of the rottenness of the U.N. Charter).

"At the price of its independence, one of these nations could free itself from coercive authority of the charter, by the simple expedient of making a deal with a veto nation..."

Sen. Hiram W. Johnson, one of the few, apart from Sen. Walsh, who saw through the U.N. Charter, stated as follows:

"In some respects, it is a pretty weak reed. It does nothing to stop a war instigated by any of the big five powers; gives each nation complete freedom to make war. Our only hope, therefore, to maintain world peace is that none of the big five nations will choose to make war..."

That the American people have no protection, and no recourse against the war-making potential of the United Nations, was confirmed by the Gulf War when President Bush ran amok, trampling the provisions of the Constitution underfoot. Had President Bush followed the proper procedures and attempted to obtain a declaration of war, the Gulf War would never have happened, because he would have been turned down. Millions of Iraqis and more than 300 U.S. servicemen and women would not have needlessly lost their lives.

The president is not the Commander-In-Chief of our armed services until a legal declaration of war has been issued by Congress and the nation is officially at war. If the president were the Commander-In-Chief at all times, the office would have the same powers as a King — expressly forbidden by the Constitution. Prior to the Gulf War, CNN accepted the false premise that Bush, as Commander-In-Chief of our armed forces, had the right on his own to commit the military to war. This dangerous interpretation was quickly taken up by the media, and today is accepted as a fact, when it is not.

A gross deception practiced upon the American people is that the President is the Commander-In-Chief of the armed services at all times. Senate and House members are so poorly informed on the Constitution that they allowed President George Bush to get away with sending almost 500,000 troops to the Gulf to fight a war for British Petroleum and to satisfy a personal hatred toward Saddam Hussein. Bush lost the fiduciary relationship he was supposed to enjoy with the American people right there. President Bill Clinton lately used this "Commander-In-Chief" misconception to try and oblige the military to accept homosexuals in the services, which he does not have the power to do. It is less a question of morals than it is of the President overstepping his authority.

The tragic truth about American servicemen being deployed to fight -- as they were by the United Nations in the Korean and Gulf Wars -- is that those who died in these wars did not die for their country, as dying for our country under our flag, *constitutes an act of sovereignty*, which was totally absent in the Korean and Gulf Wars. Since neither the Security Council nor any council of the United Nations has any sovereignty, the U.N. flag is meaningless in every sense.

Not a single U.N. Security Council resolution, affecting either directly or indirectly the United States, has any validity, as such resolutions are made by a body which itself has no sovereignty. The U.S. Constitution is *above any so-called world body, and that, particularly, includes the United Nations, the U.S. Constitution is above and superior to any agreement or treaty made with any nation or group of nations, whether connected with the United Nations or not.* But the United Nations de facto and de jure gives the president of the United States unlimited dictatorial powers not granted by the Constitution.

What President Bush did in the Gulf War bypassed the Constitution by issuing a proclamation (an executive order) directly on behalf of the U.N. Security Council. The House and Senate, meanwhile, failed in their constitutional duty to stop the illegal issuance of such an order. They could have done this by refusing to fund the war. Neither the House nor Senate had the right, nor do they have it now, to fund an agreement (or a treaty) with a world body that sets itself up above the U.S. Constitution, especially where that world body has no sovereignty, and more especially, where that body threatens the security of the United States.

Public Law 85766, Section 1602 states:
"...No part of the funds appropriated in this or in any other Act shall be used to pay...any person, firm or corporation, or any combination of persons, firms or corporations to conduct a study or plan when or how or in what circumstances the Government of the United States should surrender this country and its people to any foreign power"

Public Law 471, Section 109 further states:
"It is illegal to use funds for any project that promotes One World Government or One World citizenship."

11

So how has the United Nations addressed this foundation of law? The Korean, Vietnam and Gulf Wars also violated the U.S. Constitution because they violated Article 1, Section 8, clause 11: "Congress shall have the power to declare war." It does *not* say that the State Department, the President or the U.N. has this right.

The United Nations would have us commit our country to waging war in foreign territories, but Article 1, Section 10, Clause 1 says that no provision shall be made whereby the United States, as a nation, can commit itself to waging wars in foreign countries. Moreover, Article 1, Section 8, Clause 1, permits tax revenues to be spent only for the following purposes:

(1)"...to pay the debts, provide for the common defense, and general welfare of the United States."

It says nothing about paying dues (tribute) to the United Nations or any other world body, and no powers are granted to allow this. In addition, there is the prohibition contained in Article 1, Section 10, Clause 1, which says:

(2)"No state shall, without the consent of Congress...keep troops or ships of war in time of peace...or engage in war, unless actually invaded, or in such imminent danger."

Since there has been no valid Constitutional declaration of war by Congress since the Second World War, the United States is at peace, and therefore, our troops stationed in Saudi Arabia, or anywhere in the Persian Gulf region, Botswana and Somalia are there in breach of the Constitution, and should not be funded, but brought back home forthwith.

*The burning question for the United States should be: "How could the U.N. authorize the use of force against Iraq (i.e.: declare war), when it has no sovereignty, and why did our representatives go with such a travesty and violation of our Constitution? Why have our Representatives gone along with such gross violations of the Constitution they are sworn to uphold?" Moreover, the U.N. does not have sovereignty*

12

*which is necessary to enter into a treaty with the U.S., according to our own Constitution.*

What constitutes sovereignty? It is based upon adequate territory, a constitutional form of money, a substantial population, in clearly demarcated borders which are definitely measurable. The United Nations is totally lacking in these requirements, and no matter what our politicians might say, *the U.N. can never qualify as a sovereign body in terms of the U.S. Constitution's definition of sovereignty. Therefore, it follows that we can never have a treaty with the U.N. Not now, not ever.* The answer could be that, either out of sheer ignorance of the Constitution, or else, as servants of the Committee of 300, the senators, in 1945, went along with the U.N. Charter in breach of their oath of office to defend and uphold the U.S. Constitution.

The United Nations is a shiftless, rootless leech, a parasite feeding off its U.S. host. If there are any U.N. troops in this country, they should be ordered out forthwith, as their presence in our land is a defilement of our Constitution, and should not, indeed, cannot be tolerated by those who have sworn an oath to uphold the Constitution. The United Nations is an ongoing extension of the Fabian-Socialist platform established in 1920, of which, every plank has now been carried out exactly in accordance with the Fabian-Socialist blueprint for America. The United Nations presence in Cambodia, its inaction in Bosnia-Herzegovina needs no amplification.

Some legislators saw through the U.N. agreement. One such wide-awake legislator was Rep. Jessie Sumner, of Illinois:

"Mr. Chairman, of course you know that our government peace program is no peace. The movement is led by the same old warmongers, still masquerading as the princes of peace, who involved us in war while pretending their purpose was to keep us out of war (a very apt description of diplomacy by deception). Like Lend-Lease and other bills which involved us in war, while promising to keep us out of war, this measure (the U.N. Treaty) will involve us in every war hereafter."

13

Rep. Sumner was joined by another informed legislator, Rep. Lawrence H. Smith:

"To vote for this proposal is to give approval to world communism. Why else would it have the full support of all shades of communism elsewhere? This (U.N.) measure strikes at the very heart of the Constitution. It provides that the power to declare war shall be taken from Congress and given to the President. Here is the essence of dictatorship and dictatorial control all else must inevitably tend to follow."

Smith further stated:

"The President is given absolute powers (which the U.S. Constitution does not give), to, at any time he elects, and upon any pretext whatsoever, snatch our sons and daughters away from their homes to fight and die in battle, not only for as long as he pleases, but as may suit the majority members of the international organization. Bear in mind, the United States will be in the minority so that the policies relating to the length of time our soldiers will be kept in foreign lands in any future wars, will rest more with foreign nations than our own..."

Smith's fears proved to be well-grounded, because this is precisely what President Bush did when he snatched our sons and daughters away from their homes and sent them to fight in the Gulf War under color of the United Nations, a world body that has no sovereignty. The difference between a treaty (which the documents passed by the Senate in 1945 purported to be) and an agreement, is that a treaty requires sovereignty, whereas an agreement does not require sovereignty.

In 1945, the U.S. Senate debated for only three days -- if one can call that debating the issue of treaties. As we all know, treaties have a history of thousands of years, and the Senate could not, and indeed did not, examine the U.N. Charter to the full extent of the resources which were available to it. The U.S. State Department sent its most devious characters to lie and confuse the senators. A good example of this was the testimony of the late John Foster Dulles, one of the top 13 American Illuminati, a Committee of 300 member and a One World Government proponent down to his fingertips.

Dulles and his crew, hand-picked by the Committee of 300, were instructed to subvert the Senate, and utterly confuse them, the bulk of whom knew little about the Constitution, as Congressional Record testimony proves rather clearly. Dulles talked a crooked streak, lying blatantly and dissembling when he thought he might be caught in a lie. An altogether treasonous, treacherous performance.

Dulles had the support of Sen. W. Lucas, the banker's agent planted in the Senate. Here is what Sen. Lucas had to say on behalf of his masters, the Wall Street bankers:

"...I feel very strongly about it (the U.N. Charter), because now is the time for senators to determine what the charter means. We should not wait for a year, or a year and a half, when conditions will be different (from immediate post-wartime). I do not want to see any senator withdraw judgment until a year and a half from now..."

Obviously, this tacit admission by Sen. Lucas implied that for the Senate to examine the U.N. Charter properly, it would have taken at least eighteen months to accomplish. It was also an admission that if the documents were studied, the treaty would be rejected.

Why the unseemly haste? Had common sense prevailed, had the senators done their homework, they would have seen that it would have taken at least a year and probably two years, to properly study and vote on the charter before them. Had the senators in 1945 done so, thousands of servicemen would still be alive today instead of having sacrificed their lives for the unsovereign body of the United Nations.

As shocking as the truth sounds, the stark fact is that the Korean War was an unconstitutional war on behalf of an unsovereign body. Our brave soldiers did not, therefore, die for their country. Likewise in the Gulf War. There will be many more "Korean Wars"; the Gulf War and Somalia being the repurcessions of the failure of the U.S. Senate to

15

reject the U.N. Treaty in 1945. The United States has fought in many unconstitutional wars because of this.

In his landmark work on constitutional law, Judge Thomas M. Cooley wrote:

"The Constitution in itself never yields to treaty or enactment. It neither changes with time or does it, in theory, bend to the force of circumstance... The Congress derives its powers to legislate from the Constitution, which is the measure of its authority. And any enactment of the Congress which is opposed to its provisions, or is not within the grant of powers made by it, is unconstitutional, therefore no law, and obligatory upon no one... The Constitution imposes no restriction on power, but it is subject to implied restrictions that nothing can be done under it which changes the Constitution of the country, nor rob a department of government or any of the States of its constitutional authority...Congress and the Senate in a treaty, cannot give substance to a treaty greater than itself, or delegated power of the Senate and House."

Professor Hermann von Holst, in his monumental work, "Constitutional Law of the United States" wrote:

"As to the extent of a treaty power, the Constitution says nothing (i.e. it is reserved-prohibited), but it evidently cannot be unlimited. The power exists only under the Constitution, and every treaty inconsistent with a provision of the Constitution, is therefore inadmissible and, according to the Constitution law, ipso facto null and void."

The United Nations treaty violates at least a dozen provisions of the Constitution, and since a "treaty" cannot override the Constitution, each and every one of its Security Council resolutions, are null and void in so far as they affect the United States. This includes our alleged membership in this parasitical organization. The United States has never been a member of the United Nations, is not now, and can never be, save and except where we, the people agree to have the Constitution amended by the Senate and ratified by all of the States, to permit membership in the United Nations.

16

There are a great number of cases where case law backs up this contention. Since they cannot all be included here, I'll mention the three cases where this principle was established; Cherokee Tobacco vs. the United States, Whitney vs. Robertson and Godfrey vs. Riggs (133 U.S., 256.)

To sum up our position regarding U.N. membership: We, the sovereign people of the United States, are not obligated to obey any U.N. resolutions, because enactment of the United Nations Charter by the Senate, which purported to make the Constitution yield to United Nations law, conflicts with the provisions of the Constitution, and is, therefore, ipso facto, null and void.

In 1945, the senators were suborned into believing that a treaty has powers that surpass the Constitution. Clearly, the senators had not read what Thomas Jefferson had to say:

"To hold the treaty-making power as boundless is to make the Constitution blank paper by construction." If the senators in 1945 had bothered to read the wealth of information contained in the Congressional Record as it pertains to treaty-making and agreements, they would not have acted in ignorance by endorsing the United Nations Charter.

The United Nations is in fact a One World Government body put together with the objective of overriding the U.S. Constitution – clearly the intent of its original framers, Fabianists Sydney and Beatrice Webb, Dr. Leo Posvolsky and Leonard Woolf. A good source of confirmation of the foregoing can be found in "Fabian Freeway, High Road to Socialism in the U.S." by Rose Martin.

The foundation of the socialist plot to subvert the United States can be found in such papers as the "New Statesman" and the "New Republic." Both were published circa 1915, and copies were in the British Museum in London, when I was studying there. In 1916, Brentanos of New York, published the same documents under the title: "International Government," accompanied by fulsome praise from socialists of every stripe in the U.S.

Was the United Nations Charter actually written by traitor Alger Hiss, Molotov and Posvolsky? Evidence to the contrary abounds, but basically what happened is that the RIIA took the Beatrice Webb Fabian Socialist document and sent it to President Wilson to get its provisions drafted into U.S. law. The document was not read by President Wilson, but handed to Col. House for immediate action.

Wilson, and indeed all Presidents after him, always acted with alacrity when addressed by our British masters in Chatham House. Col. House retired to his summer home, "Magnolia" in Massachusetts on July 13-14, 1918, aided and abetted by professor David H. Miller of the Harvard Enquiry Group, to work up the British proposals for a One World Government body.

House returned to Washington with a 23 article proposal, which the British Foreign Office accepted as forming the basis of the League of Nations. This was nothing but an attempt to subvert the U.S. Constitution. The "House" draft was forwarded to the British government for its approval and thereafter reduced to 14 articles.

Thus was born Wilson's "14 Points," actually not Wilson's, but rather those of the British government, helped by socialist Walter Lippman- which then became the basis of a document presented to the Paris Peace Conference. (When dealing with subversive secret societies it should be noted that the word "peace" is used strictly in a communist-socialist sense.)

Had the senators done their homework in 1945 they would have discovered in short order that the United Nations Treaty was nothing but a warmed-over version of the socialist document dreamed up by British Fabianists and supported by their American cousins. This would have sounded the alarm bells. Had the senators discovered who the League of Nations treasonous drafters really were, they would surely have rejected the document without hesitation.

It is clear that the senators did not know what they were looking at, judging from the remarks made by Sen. Harold A. Burton:

18

" We again have the chance to retrieve and establish, not a League of Nations, but the present United Nations Charter, although 80 percent of its provisions (in the U.N. Charter) are, in substance, the same as those of the League of Nations in 1919..."

If the senators had read the Congressional Record about the League of Nations, particularly pages 8175-8191, they would have found confirmation of Sen. Burton's claim that the U.N. Charter was nothing but a refurbished League of Nations Charter. Their suspicions ought to have been aroused about the League transferring its assets to the proposed United Nations. They would also have noticed that the task of reshaping the modern version of the League was carried out by a group of dissolute people with no interest in the well-being of the United States: Alger Hiss, whose mentor was the wrecker of the Constitution, Felix Frankfurter, Leo Posvolsky, and behind them, the international bankers personified by the Rothschilds, Warburgs and Rockefellers.

Former Congressman John Rarick put it very well, calling the United Nations "A creature of Invisible Government." Had the senators even glimpsed into the history of the refurbished League of Nations, they would have found that it was resusticated in Chatham House, and in 1941, was sent with RIIA instructions to Cordell Hull, Secretary of State (chosen by the Council on Foreign Relations, as every Secretary of State has been since 1919), and ordered that it be activated.

The timing was perfect, 14 days after Pearl Harbor, when our British masters deemed it would not receive much public attention, and in any case, what with the horror of Pearl Harbor, public opinion would be favorable. So, on December 22, 1941, at the behest of the Committee of 300's international bankers, Cordell Hull was instructed to brief President Roosevelt on his role in bringing up the "new and improved" version of the League of Nations.

The sister-child of the RIIA, the Council on Foreign Relations (CFR) recommended that Roosevelt give orders for a Presidential Advisory Committee on Post War Foreign Policy to be set up forthwith. Here is how the CFR recommended the action to be taken:

19

"That the Charter of the United Nations become the Supreme Law of the land, and that Judges in every state shall be bound thereby, anything in the constitution of any state to the contrary not-withstanding."

What the senators would have found in 1945, had they bothered to look, was that the CFR directive was tantamount to TREASON, which they could not have condoned and still not violate their oath to uphold the Constitution. They would have discovered that, in 1905, a group of international bankers believed they could subvert the Constitution by using a world body as their vehicle, and that the CFR directive was merely a part of that ongoing process.

A treaty cannot be legally higher than the Constitution, yet the United Nations treaty did take precedence over the Constitution. The Consti-tution, or any part of it, cannot simply be repealed by Congress, but a treaty can be overturned or scrapped altogether. The Constitution says that a treaty is only a law that can be repealed by Congress in two ways:

(I) Pass a law that will repeal the treaty.

(2) Cut off funding for the treaty.

In order to avoid such abuses of power, we, the sovereign people, must demand that our government cut off funding for the United Nations, which is most commonly expressed as "membership dues." Congress must pass enabling legislation to fund all United States obligations, but it is clearly illegal for the Congress to pass enabling funding for an illegal purpose, such as our alleged membership of the United Nations, which has set itself above the Constitution. If the senators in 1945 had done the proper research, and if they had not allowed Dulles to bamboozle, lie, dissemble, deceive and mislead them, they would have found the following exchange between Sen. Henry M. Teller and Sen. James B. Allen and benefited from it. Here is a telling exchange made by two Senators:

Sen. Teller: "There can be no treaty that will bind the government of the United States concerning the raising of revenue."

Sen. Allen: "Very well. That in its very nature, is altogether domestic, and cannot be the subject of a treaty."

Sen. Teller: "It is not because it is domestic; it is because the Constitution has put that business in the hands of Congress exclusively."

Sen. Allen: "No, Mr. President, not necessarily so, because the raising of revenue is purely a domestic matter. It lies at the foundation of the life of the nation, and it must be exercised by government alone, without the consent or participation of a foreign power (or world body)..."

A treaty is not the supreme law of the land. It is only a law, and not even a secure law at that. Any treaty that places the Constitution in jeopardy is ipso facto immediately null and void. Also, a treaty can be broken. This is well established by Vattel's "Law of Nations," on page 194:

"In the year 1506, the states-general of the kingdom of France assembled at Tores engaged Louis XII to break a treaty he had concluded with the Emperor Maximilian and Archduke Philip, his son, because the treaty was pernicious to the kingdom. They also decided that neither the treaty nor the oath that accompanied it, could be binding on the kingdom who had no right to alienate the property of the crown...."

Certainly the United Nations treaty is destructive to the national security and the well-being of the United States. Inasmuch as a constitutional amendment, which is required for the United States to be a member of the United Nations, was not passed nor accepted by the 50 states, we are not a member of the United Nations. Such an amendment would have subjugated the right of Congress to declare war, and would have put the declaration of war in the hands of the United Nations on a superior level to that of the Constitution, placing American servicemen under the control and command of the United Nations.

Additionally, it would take an amendment to the Constitution to include a declaration of war by the United Nations and the United States on the same document, or to even be associated with it, either directly, or by implication. On this one count alone, the United Nations threatens the security of the Constitution and therefore on that count alone, our membership of the United Nations is very definitely null and void and must not be allowed to stand. Sen. Langer, one of two senators who voted against the U.N. Charter, warned his colleagues in July of 1945 that the treaty was fraught with peril for America.

The late U.S. Representative, Larry McDonald, fully exposed the massive sedition and treason of the U.N. treaty as found in the Congressional Record, Extension of Remarks, January 27, 1982, under the title, "Get Us Out":

"The United Nations, for three and a half decades, has been indulging in a gigantic unfettered conspiracy, mostly at the U.S. taxpayers expense, to enslave our republic in a world government dominated by the Soviet Union and its Third World. Having had enough of this free-wheeling conspiracy, more and more responsible officials and thinking citizens are ready to pull out..."

McDonald was right on target, but over the last two years, we have seen a marked change in the way the United Nations is run by principally Britain and the United States, and we shall come to that in due course. Under President Bush, there was an obvious desire to remain in the United Nations, as it suited his style of politics as well as his kingly aspirations.

In 1945, sick of war, the senators thought that the United Nations would be a means of ending wars. Little did they know that the United Nation's purpose was just the opposite. It is now known that only five senators actually read the charter scripted by Alger Hiss, before voting on the treaty.

The goal of the United Nations, or rather, the goal of the men behind the United Nations, is not peace, even in the Communist sense of the

22

word, but is actually world revolution, the overthrow of good government and good order and the destruction of established religion. Socialism and communism are not in themselves necessarily the goal; they are only the means to an end. The economic chaos now being perpetrated against the United States is a much more powerful means to that end.

World revolution, of which the United Nations is an integral component, is another matter entirely; a complete overturning of moral and spiritual values enjoyed by the Western nations for centuries is its goal. As part of that goal, Christian leadership must perforce, be destroyed, and that has already largely been accomplished by placing false leaders in places where they exert tremendous influence. Billy Graham and Robert S. Schuler are two good examples of so-called Christian leaders who are not. Much of this program of revolution was confirmed by Franklin D. Roosevelt in his book, "Our Way."

If one reads between the lines of the treasonous, seditious U.N. Charter, one will find that much of the objectives outlined in the preceding paragraphs are implied, and, even in some instances, are even spelled out in the pernicious "treaty," which, if we, the people do not reverse, will trample our Constitution underfoot and make of us slaves in a dictatorship of the most savage and repressive kind under a One World Government.

Summed up, the goals of the spiritual and moral world revolution now raging -- and nowhere more so than in the United States -- are:

(1) The destruction of Western civilization.

(2) Dissolution of legal government.

(3) Destruction of nationalism, and with it, the ideal of patriotism.

(4) Bringing the people of the United States into penury via graduated income taxes, property taxes, inheritance taxes, sales taxes and so on, ad nausea.

(5) The abolition of the God-given right to private property by taxing property out of existence and targeting inheritance with bigger and bigger taxes. (President Clinton has already taken a giant step down this road.)

(6) Destruction of the family unit via "free love", abortion, lesbianism and homosexuality. (Here again, President Clinton has placed himself firmly behind these revolutionary goals, thereby destroying any lingering doubts about where he stands in relation to the forces of world revolution.)

The Committee of 300 employs a vast number of specialists in diplomacy by deception who make us believe that severely dangerous and often disruptive changes come about through "changing times," as though their direction could change without some force compelling such changes. The Committee has a vast number of "teachers" and "leaders," whose sole task in life is to dupe as many people as possible into believing that major changes "just happen" and so, of course, should just be accepted.

Toward this end, these "leaders" who are in the vanguard of carrying out the Communist Manifesto's "social programs," have cleverly employed the Tavistock Institute for Human Relations methods like "inner directional conditioning" and "Operation Research" to make us accept the changes as if they were our own ideas to begin with.

A critical examination of the U.N. Charter shows that it differs only very slightly from the Communist Manifesto of 1848, an unabridged, unaltered copy of which is kept in the British Museum in London. There is an extract of the manifesto, allegedly the work of Karl Marx (Mordechai Levy) and Friedrich Engels, but was actually written by members of the Illuminati, which is still very active today through their top 13 council members in the United States.

In 1945 absolutely none of this vital information was ever viewed by the senators, who fell all over themselves in their rush to sign the dangerous document. If our lawmakers knew the Constitution, if our Supreme Court would uphold it, then we would be able to echo the words of the late Sen. Sam Ervin, a great constitutional scholar, so much admired by liberals because of his work on Watergate: " There is no way under the noon-day sun we ever joined the United Nations" and force our legislators to recognize the fact that the U.S. Constitution stands supreme over any treaty.

The United Nations is a war-making body. It strives to place power in the hands of the executive branch instead of where it belongs: in the legislative branch. Take the examples of the Korean War and the Gulf War. In the latter, the United Nations, not the Senate and the House, gave President Bush the authority to go to war against Iraq, thereby enabling him to use diplomacy by deception as a means to bypass the mandated Constitutional declaration of war. President Harry Truman evoked the same unauthorized power for the Korean War.

If we, the sovereign people, continue to go on believing that the United States is legally a member of the United Nations, then we must be prepared for more illegal actions by our Presidents, such as we saw in the invasion of Panama and the Gulf War. By acting under color of Security Council resolutions, the president of the United States can take on the powers of a king or a dictator. Those powers are expressly forbidden in the Constitution.

Under the powers vested in the president by U.N. Security Council resolutions, the president will be able to drag us into any future wars he decides we must fight. The groundwork for this method of sabotaging the declaration of war procedures mandated by the Constitution was tested and carried out in the days before the Gulf War, which will no doubt, forever be used as a precedent for future undeclared wars, in furtherance of the strategy of diplomacy by deception. Wars make far reaching changes which are unable to be achieved by diplomacy.

So that we are perfectly clear about the procedures laid down by the Constitution, which must be complied with BEFORE the United States can be engaged in war, let us examine them:

(1) Both the Senate and the House must pass separate resolutions

declaring that a state of belligerency exists between the United States and the other nation. In this connection we need to study the word "belligerent," for without "belligerency" there can be no intent to go to war

(2) The House and Senate then must separately and individually pass resolutions declaring that a state of war exists between the belligerent nation or nations and the United States. This officially places America on notice that it is about to go to war.

(3) The House and Senate then must pass individual and separate resolutions advising the military that the United States is now at war with the belligerent nation or nations.

(4) The House and Senate must then decide if the war is to be an "imperfect" or a "perfect" war. An imperfect war means that only a single branch of the military can become involved, while a perfect war means that every man, women and child in the United States is in a public war with every man, women and child of the other nation or nations. In the latter case, all branches of the armed services are engaged.

If the president does not get a constitutional declaration of war from Congress, any and all U.S. military personnel dispatched to fight the undeclared war *must* return to the United States within 60 days from the date they were dispatched (this vital provision has mostly become null and void). It is easy to see how the Constitution was steamrollered by President Bush; our military are still at war with Iraq and are still being used to enforce an illegal U.N. blockade. If we had a government that actually upholds the Constitution, the Gulf War would never have been started, and our troops would not now be in the Middle East, or for that matter, in Somalia.

Such declaration of war measures were designed specifically to avoid the United States being casually thrust into a war, which is why President Bush did an end-run around the Constitution so that we could be railroaded into the Gulf War. Nor does the United Nations have the authority to impose a rule on the United States that tells us to obey an economic blockade of Iraq or any other nation -- because the United Nations *has no sovereignty*. We shall deal with the Gulf War in the next chapters.

These powers, not given to the president, but to the legislative branch of government, de facto, make the United Nations the most powerful body in the world via Security Council resolutions. Since abandoning the Jefferson form of neutrality, we have been ruled by a series of vagabonds, one after another, who have plundered America at will and continue to do so. It was Thomas Jefferson who issued a stern warning, which our agents in Congress blithely disregarded, that America would be destroyed by secret deals with foreign governments having the desire to divide and rule the American people, so that the interests of foreign governments would be served before the needs of our own people.

Foreign aid, is nothing more that a program for robbing and plundering countries of their natural resources, and handing U.S. taxpayer's money to dictators in those countries, so that the Committee of 300 can reap obscene benefits from the illegal plunder, while the American people, no better than the slaves of the Egyptian Pharaohs, groan under the huge burden of "foreign aid." In the chapter on Assassinations we give the Belgian Congo as good example of what we mean. The Belgian Congo was run for the benefit of the Committee of 300, not the Congolese people.

The United Nations uses foreign aid as a means to plunder the resources of sovereign nations. No pirate or robber ever had it so good. Not even Kubla Kahn had it as good as the Rothschilds, Rockefellers, Warburgs and their kin have it. If a nation should demure in handing over its natural resources, as was the case with the Congo, which tried to protect its natural resources, United Nations troops go in an "compel compliance", even if it means murdering civilians which U.N. troops did in the Congo ousting and murdering its leader, as was the case with Patrice Lumumba. The ongoing attempt to murder President Hussein of Iraq is yet another example of how the United Nations is subverting U.S. law and the laws of independent nations.

The question is, how long will we, the sovereign people, go on tolerating our illegal membership in this One World Government body? Only we, the sovereign people, can order our agents, our servants, in the House and Senate, to repeal forthwith our membership in a world body, which is injurious to the well-being of our United States of America.

# The Brutal, Illegal Gulf War. II.

The most recent of wars carried out under the cloak of diplomacy by deception, the Gulf War, differs from others in that the Committee of 300, the Council on Foreign Relations, Illuminati and Bilderbergers-did not adequately cover their tracks along the way to war. The Gulf War therefore is one of the easiest of wars to trace back to Chatham House and Harold Pratt House, and, fortunately for us, it is one of the easiest to prove the diplomacy by deception thesis.

The Gulf War must be viewed as a single component of the Committee of 300's overall strategy for the Middle East oil-producing Islamic states. Only a brief historical overview can be given here. It is essential to know the truth and to be set free from the propaganda of Madison Avenue opinion-makers, also known as "advertising agencies."

British imperialists, aided by their American cousins, began to implement their plans to seize control of all Middle East oil in or around the mid-1800s. The illegal Gulf War was an integral provision of that plan. I say illegal, because, as explained in the chapters dealing with the United Nations, only the Congress can declare war, as laid down in Article I, Section 8, clauses 1, 11, 12, 13, 14, 15 and 18 of the U.S. Constitution. Henry Clay, a recognized authority on the Constitution, said this on a number of occasions.

No elected official can override the provisions of the Constitution, and both former Secretary of State James Baker III and President George Bush, ought to have been impeached for violating the Constitution. A British intelligence source told me that when Baker met Queen Elizabeth II at Buckingham Palace, he actually bragged about how he got around the Constitution, and then, in the presence of the queen, chastised Edward Heath who had opposed the war. Edward Heath, a former British prime minister was sacked by the Committee of 300 for failing to support the European unity policy and for his strong opposition to the Gulf War.

31

Baker remarked to the gathering of heads-of-state and diplomats that he dismissed attempts to draw him into discussing constitutional issues. Baker also boasted about how his threats against the Iraqi nation were carried out, and Queen Elizabeth II nodded her approval. Obviously Baker and President Bush, who was also present at the gathering, placed their fealty to the One World Government above that of the oath of office they took to uphold the Constitution of the United States.

The land of Arabia existed for thousands of years, and it was always known as *Arabia*. The land was linked to events in Turkey, Persia (now Iran), and Iraq through the Wahabi and the Abdul Aziz families. In the 15th century, the British, under the direction of Black Guelph Venetian robber-bankers saw the possibilities of entrenching themselves in Arabia, where they were opposed by the Koreish tribe, the tribe of the prophet Muhammad, the posthumous son of the Hashemite, Abdullah, out of which came the Fatima and Abbasid Dynasties.

The Gulf War was only an extension of the Committee of 300's attempts to destroy Muhammad and the Hashemite people in Iraq. The rulers of Saudi Arabia are hated and despised by all true followers of Islam, more so since they allowed "infidels" (U.S. troops) to be stationed in the land of the prophet Muhammad.

The essential articles of the Muslim religion consist of a belief in one God, (Allah), in his angels and his prophet Muhammad, the last of the prophets and belief in his revealed work, the Koran; belief in the Day of Resurrection and God's predestination of men. The six fundamental duties of believers are recitation of the profession of faith, attesting to the unity of God, and the firm acceptance of the mission of Muhammad; five daily prayers; total fasting during the month of Ramadan, and a pilgrimage to Mecca, at least once in the lifetime of the believer.

Strict observation of the fundamental principles of the Muslim religion make one a fundamentalist, which the Wahabi and Abdul Aziz families (the Saudi Royal family), are not. The Saudi Royal Family has slowly but surely drifted away from fundamentalism, which has not endeared them to Islamic fundamentalist countries like Iraq and Iran, who now blame them for making the Gulf War possible in the first place. Skipping over centuries of history, we come to 1463, when a great war, instigated and planned by the Black Guelph Venetian bankers, broke out in the Ottoman Empire. The Venetian Guelphs (who are directly related to Queen Elizabeth II of England) had deceived the Turks into believing that they were friends and allies, but the Ottomans were to learn a bitter lesson.

To understand the period, we must understand that the British Black Nobility is synonymous with the Venetian Black Nobility. Under the leadership of Mohammed the Conqueror, the Venetians were driven out of what is today Turkey. The role of Venice in world history has been deliberately and grossly understated. And its influence is today understated, such as the role it played in the Bolshevik Revolution, both world wars and the Gulf War. The Ottomans were betrayed by the British and Venetians, who "came as friends but held a concealed dagger behind their backs" as history records. This was one of the earlier sallies into diplomacy by deception. It was very successfully copied by George Bush in posing as a friend of the Arab people.

With British intervention, the Turks were pushed back from the gates of Venice and an Arab presence firmly established in the peninsula. The British misused the Arabs under Col. Thomas E. Lawrence to bring down the Ottoman Empire, eventually betraying them and setting up the Zionist state of Israel, through the Balfour Declaration. This is a good example of the diplomacy by deception that succeeded. In the period 1909 to 1915, the British government used Lawrence to lead Arab forces to fight the Turks and drive them out of Palestine. The void left by the Turks was filled by immigrant Jews flocking into Palestine under the terms of the Balfour Declaration.

The British government continued its deception by moving British troops into the Sinai and Palestine. Sir Archibald Murray assured Lawrence the move was to forestall Jewish immigration under the Balfour Declaration signed by Lord Rothschild, a top member of the Illuminati.

The terms under which the Arabs agreed to intervene in the Ottoman campaign (to whom the Black Nobility of Britain had sworn undying loyalty), was negotiated by Sheriff Hussein of the Hijaz, and specifically included a provision that Britain would not permit Jewish immigration into Palestine, Transjordan and Arabia to continue. Hussein made this demand the very heart of the agreement signed with the British government.

Of course, the British government never intended to honor the terms of its agreement with Hussein, adding the names of the other countries to Palestine so that they could say, "well, we did keep them out of these countries." It was diplomacy by deception at its finest, because the Zionists had no interest in sending Jews to any Middle East country other than Palestine.

The British government always played the Abdul-Aziz and Wahabis (the Saudi Royal Family) against Sheriff Hussein, secretly entering into an agreement with the two families that "officially" pretended to recognize Hussein as the King of Hijaz (which the British government did on Dec. 15, 1916). The British government agreed to secretly back the two families with enough arms and money to conquer the independent city-states of Arabia.

Of course, Hussein was not privy to the side deal, and he agreed to launch a full-scale attack on the Turks. This prompted the Wahabi and Abdul Aziz families to put together an army and launch a war to bring Arabia under their control. The British oil companies thus succeeded in getting Hussein to battle the Turks unwittingly on their behalf.

Funded by Britain in 1913 and 1927, the Abdul Aziz-Wahabi armies conducted a bloody campaign against Arabia's independent city-states overrunning Hijaz, Jauf and Taif. The holy Hashemite city of Mecca was attacked on Oct. 13, 1924, forcing Hussein and his son, Ali, to flee. On Dec. 5, 1925, Medina surrendered after a particularly bloody battle. The British government, demonstrating once again its grasp of diplomacy by deception, did not tell the Wahabis and Saudis that its true goal was the destruction of the sanctity of Mecca and the overall weakening of the Muslim religion, which was deeply resented by the British oligarchists and their Black Nobility Venetian cousins.

Nor did the British government tell the Saudi and Wahabi families that they were merely pawns in the game to secure Arabian oil for Britain over the claims of Italy, France, Russia, Turkey and Germany. On Sept. 22, 1932, the Saudi-Wahabi armies put down a rebellion in the largely Hashemite territory of Transjordan. Thereafter, Arabia was renamed Saudi Arabia and was henceforth to be ruled by a king drawn from the two families. Thus, by the deceit of diplomacy by deception, the British oil companies gained control of Arabia. This diplomacy by deception and the whole bloody campaign is fully described in my monograph, "Who are the Real Saudi Kings and Kuwaiti Sheiks?"

Once freed from the Ottoman threat and Arab nationalism under Sheriff Hussein to pursue its designs even further, the British government, acting on behalf of its oil companies, entered into a new period of diplomacy by deception. They drew up and guaranteed a treaty between Saudi Arabia, as it was now called, and Iraq, which became the foundation of a whole series of inter-Arab-Muslim pacts, which the British government said it would enforce against Jewish immigration to Palestine.

Contrary to what Britain's leaders told the Arab-Muslim parties, the Balfour Declaration which had already been negotiated, permitted Jews not only to immigrate to Palestine, but to make it a homeland. This agreement, laid out terms of an Anglo-French accord, placed Palestine under international administration. This is just as easily done by today's United Nations, with Cyrus Vance carving up Bosnia-Herzegovina, an internationally-recognized country, into small enclaves so that Serbia can take them over in due time.

Then, on Nov. 2, 1917, came the public announcement of the Balfour Declaration, which said that the British government -- not the Arabs or the Palestinians, whose land it was -- favored establishing Palestine as a national homeland for the Jewish people. Britain vowed to use its best endeavors to facilitate the achievement of that goal, "it being clearly understood that nothing shall be done which may prejudice the civil and religious rights of the existing non-Jewish communities in Palestine."

A more audacious piece of diplomacy by deception is hard to find anywhere. Note that the real inhabitants of Palestine were down-graded to "non-Jewish communities." Also note that the declaration, which was in reality a proclamation, was signed by Lord Rothschild, head of British Zionists, who was not a member of the British Royal Family, nor was he a member of Balfour's cabinet and therefore had even less standing than Balfour to sign such a document.

The gross betrayal of the Arabs so angered Col. Lawrence that he threatened to expose the British government's duplicity, a threat that was to cost him his life. Lawrence had given Hussein and his men a solemn promise that further Jewish immigration into Palestine would not occur. Documents in the British Museum clearly show that the promise relayed to Sheriff Hussein by Lawrence, was made by Sir Archibald Murray and General Edmund Allenby on behalf of the British government.

In 1917, British troops marched into Baghdad, marking the beginning of the end of the Ottoman empire. Throughout this period, the Wahabi and Saudi families were continually reassured by Murray that no Jews would be allowed to enter Arabia, and that the few Jews who would be allowed to immigrate would be settled only in Palestine. On Jan. 10, 1919, the British gave themselves a "mandate" to rule Iraq, which passed into law on May 5, 1920. Not a single government in the world protested Britain's illegal action. Sir Percy Cox was named high commissioner. Of course, the people of Iraq were not consulted at all.

By 1922, the League of Nations had approved the terms of the Balfour (Rothschild) Declaration, which gave the British government a mandate to run Palestine and the Hashemite country called Transjordan. One can only marvel at the audacity of the British government and the League of Nations.

In 1880, the British government formed a friendship with a tame Arab sheik by the name of Emir Abdullah al Salem Al Sabah. Al Sabah was made their representative in the area along the southern border of Iraq where the Rumalia oilfields had been discovered inside Iraqi terri-tory. The Al Sabah family kept an eye on this rich prize while the

British went after another prize in 1899, that of the huge gold deposits in the tiny Boer Republics of the Transvaal and Orange Free State, which we shall come to in succeeding chapters. It is mentioned here to illustrate the Committee of 300's quest to grab natural resources of nations whenever and wherever they could do so.

On behalf of the Committee of 300, on Nov. 25, 1899 -- the same year the British went to war against the Boer Republics -- the British government made a deal with Emir Al Sabah, whereby the land encroaching on the Rumalia oilfields in Iraq was ceded to the British government, notwithstanding the fact that the land was an integral part of Iraq,or that the Emir Al Sabah had no right to it.

The deal was signed by Sheik Mubarak Al Sabah, who traveled to London in style with his retinue, with all expenses paid by the British taxpayers and not the British oil companies who were the beneficiaries of the deal. Kuwait became a de facto undeclared British protectorate. The local population had no say in the setting up of the Al Sabahs as absolute dictators who soon showed cruel ruthlessness.

In 1915, the British invaded Iraq and occupied Baghdad in an act President George Bush would have called "naked aggression," the term he used to describe Iraq's move against Kuwait to reclaim its land stolen by Britain. The British government set up a self-proclaimed "mandate" as we have already seen, and on Aug. 23, 1921, two months after his arrival in Baghdad, self-styled high commissioner Cox, named former King Faisal of Syria as head of a puppet regime in Basra. Britain now had one puppet in northern Iraq and another in southern Iraq.

In order to strengthen their position, not being satisfied with the blatantly rigged plebiscite that gave the British their mandate, an elaborate and bloody plot was hatched. MI6 British intelligence agents were sent in to stir up a revolt among the Kurds in the Mosul. Encouraged to revolt by their leader, Sheik Mahmud, they staged a great insurrection on Jun. 18, 1922. British intelligence agents of MI6 had for months told Sheik Mahmud that his chances of securing an autonomous state for the Kurds would never be better.

Why did MI6 ostensibly act against the best interests of the British government? The answer is found in diplomacy by deception. Yet, even as the Kurds were being told that their age-old quest for an autonomous state was about to become a reality, Cox was telling Iraqi leaders in Baghdad that the Kurds were about to revolt. It was, said Cox, only one of many reasons why the Iraqis needed a continued British presence in the country. After two years of fighting, the Kurds were defeated and their leaders executed.

In 1923, however, Britain was forced by Italy, France and Russia to recognize a protocol that granted independence to Iraq once Iraq joined the League of Nations, or, in any case, not later than 1926. This angered the Royal Dutch Shell Co. and British Petroleum, who both called for renewed action, afraid they would lose their oil concessions which were to expire in 1996. Another severe blow to British imperialists and their oil companies was the League of Nations award of the oil-rich Mosul to Iraq.

MI6 arranged for another Kurdish revolt to take place February through April of 1925. False promises were made to the Iraq government, with accounts of what would happen if the British withdrew protection from Iraq. The Kurds were misled into insurrection. The object was to show the League of Nations that its award of Mosul to Iraq was a mistake that it was bad for the world to have an "unstable" government in charge of a major oil reserve. The other benefit was that the Kurds would probably lose, and would once again have their leaders executed. This time, however, the plot didn't work; the League remained steadfast in its decision on Mosul. But the rebellion again ended in defeat for the Kurds and the execution of their leaders.

The Kurds never realized that their enemy was not Iraq, but British and American oil interests. It was Winston Churchill, not the Iraqis, who in 1929 ordered the Royal Air Force to bomb Kurdish villages, because the Kurds objected to British oil interests over the Mosul oilfields which they fully understood the value of.

April, May and June of 1932 saw the Kurds in yet another M16-inspired and directed insurrection, again aimed at persuading the

League to alter its decision over Mosul oil, but the attempt was not successful, and on Oct. 3, 1932, Iraq became an independent nation with full control over Mosul. The British oil companies hung on for another 12 years, until finally, in 1948 they were forced to leave Iraq.

And even after leaving Iraq, the British did not withdraw their presence from Kuwait on the spurious grounds that it was not part of Iraq, but a separate country. After the murder of President Kassem, the Iraqi government feared another uprising by the Kurds, who were still under the control of British intelligence. On June 10, 1963, the Kurds under Mustafa al-Barzani threatened war against Baghdad, which had its hands full with crushing the Communist menace. The Iraqi government made an agreement granting some measure of autonomy to the Kurds, and issued a proclamation to this effect.

Stoked up by British intelligence, the Kurds resumed fighting in April of 1965, because no progress had been made by Iraq in implementing the provisions of the 1963 proclamation. The Baghdad government charged Britain with meddling in its internal affairs, and Kurdish unrest continued for four more years. On Mar. 11, 1970, the Kurds were finally granted autonomy. But, as before, only a very few of the provisions contained in the agreement were implemented. The arrangement had been disturbed in 1923 when, at the insistence of Turkey, Germany and France, a conference was held at Lausanne, Switzerland, under the auspices of the League of Nations.

The real reason for the 1923 Lausanne Conference was the discovery of the Mosul oilfields in northern Iraq. Turkey suddenly decided it had a claim to the vast oilfield that lay beneath the land occupied by the Kurds. By now America was also interested, with John D. Rockefeller ordering President Warren Harding to send an observer. The American observer went along with the existing illegal situation in Kuwait. Rockefeller had no intention of rocking the British boat just as long as he could get his share of the new oil find.

Iraq lost its rights under the old Turkish Petroleum Company agreement, and the status of Kuwait remained unchanged. The question of Mosul oil was left deliberately vague at the insistence of the British delegate. These questions would be settled "by future negotiations" the British delegate stated. The blood of American servicemen will yet be spilled to secure Mosul oil for British and American oil companies, just as it was spilled over the oil in Kuwait.

On June 25, 1961, Iraqi Premier Hassan Abdul Kassem fiercely attacked Britain over the Kuwait issue, pointing out that the promised negotiations agreed upon at the Lausanne Conference had not taken place. Kassem declared that the territory called Kuwait had been an integral part of Iraq and was so recognized for more 400 years by the Ottoman empire. Instead, the British granted Kuwait independence.

But it was clear that the British ploy of leaving the status of Kuwait and the Mosul oil fields to a later date was almost foiled by Kassem. Hence, the sudden need to grant independence to Kuwait, before the rest of the world discovered the British and American tactics. Kuwait could never be independent, because, as the British well knew, it was a piece of Iraq which had been sliced off at the Rumalia oilfields and given to British Petroleum.

Had Kassem succeeded in getting Kuwait back, the British rulers would have lost billions of dollars in oil revenues. But when Kassem vanished after Kuwait got its independence the movement to challenge Britain lost its momentum. By granting independence to Kuwait in 1961, and ignoring the fact that the land was not theirs to give, Britain was able to fend off the just claims of Iraq. As we know, Britain did the same thing in Palestine, India and later, in South Africa.

For the next 30 years, Kuwait continued as a vassal state of Great Britain, with the oil companies pulling billions of dollars into British banks while Iraq got nothing. British banks flourished in Kuwait, which were administered from Whitehall and the City of London. This continued until 1965, in addition to the cruelty of the Al Sabahs was the fact that there was no "one man one vote". In fact there was *no* vote at all for the people. This was not the concern of the British and United States government.

The British government made this deal with the Al Sabah family, who would henceforth remain the rulers of Kuwait (as that portion of Iraqi territory came to be known), under the full protection of the British government. Thus was Kuwait stolen from Iraq. The fact that Kuwait did not apply for membership in the U.N. at the time Saudi Arabia did, is proof that it was never a country in the truest sense of the word.

The creation of Kuwait was hotly disputed by successive Iraqi governments, who could do little to reclaim the land in the face of superior British military might. On July 1, 1961, after years of protest over Kuwait annexing its territory, the Iraqi government finally moved on the issue. Emir Al Sabah called on Britain to honor the 1899 agreement, and the British government moved military forces into Kuwait. Baghdad backed down, but never gave up its just claim to the territory.

Britain's seizure of the Iraqi land, calling it Kuwait and granting it independence, must rank as one of the most audacious acts of piracy in modern times, and directly contributed to the Gulf War. I have gone to some lengths to explain the background of events that led to the Gulf War in an attempt to show just how unjustly the United States acted toward Iraq, and the power of the Committee of 300.

Here is a summary of the events that led up to the Gulf War:

1811-1818. Wahabis of Arabia attack and occupy Mecca, but are forced to withdraw by the Sultan of Egypt.

1899, Nov. 25. Sheik Mubarak al-Sabah cedes part of the Rumalia oilfields to Britain. Land ceded was recognized for 400 years as Iraqi territory. Very sparsely populated up until 1914. Kuwait becomes a British protectorate.

1909-1915, British use Col. Thomas Lawrence of British intelligence to befriend the Arabs. Lawrence assures the Arabs that Gen. Edmund Allenby would keep the Jews out of Palestine. Lawrence was not advised of Britain's real intent. Sheriff Hussein, the ruler of Mecca, raises an Arab army to attack the Turks. Ottoman empire's presence in Palestine and Egypt is destroyed.

1913. British secretly agree to arm, train and supply Abdul Aziz and Wahabi families to prepare for conquest of Arabian city states.

1916. British troops move into Sinai and Palestine. Sir Archibald Murray tells Lawrence it is a move designed to forestall Jewish immigration, which Sheriff Hussein accepts. Hussein declares an Arab state on June 27; becomes king on Oct. 29. On Nov. 6, 1916, Britain, France and Russia recognize Hussein as head of the Arab people; confirmed on Dec. 15 by British government.

1916. In a bizarre action, British get India to recognize Arab city-states of Nejd, Qaif and Jubail as possessions of the Ibn Saud of Abdul Aziz family.

1917. British troops seize Baghdad. Balfour Declaration is signed by Lord Rothschild who betrays the Arabs and grants homeland to the Jews in Palestine. Gen. Allenby occupies Jerusalem.

1920. San Remo Conference. Independence of Turkey; oil disputes settled. The start of British control of oil rich countries in the Middle East. British government establishes puppet regime in Basra, ruled by King Faisal of Syria. Ibn Saud Abdul Aziz attacks Taif in Hijaz, only able to capture it after four year struggle.

1922. Aziz sacks Jauf and murders Shalan family dynasty. Balfour Declaration is approved by the League of Nations.

1923. Turkey, Germany and France object to British occupation of Iraq and call for summit at Lausanne. Britain agrees to freedom for Iraq, but hangs onto Mosul oilfields in order to create a separate entity situation in northern Iraq. In May, British weaken the rule of Emir Abdullah Ibn Hussein, son of Sheriff Hussein of Mecca, and call the new country "Transjordan."

1924. On Oct. 13, Wahabis and Adbul Aziz attack and capture the holy city of Mecca, burial place of prophet Muhammad. Hussein and his two sons are forced to flee.

1925. Medina surrenders to Ibn Saud forces.

1926. Ibn Saud proclaims himself as King of Hijaz and Sultan of Nejd.

1927. British sign treaty with Ibn Saud and Wahabis, granting complete freedom of action and recognizing captured city-states as his possessions. *This marked the beginning of British Petroleum and the American oil companies battling to outdo each other in obtaining oil concessions.*

1929. Britain signs a new treaty of friendship with Iraq recognizing its independence, but leaves Kuwait's status unresolved. First large-scale attacks are aimed at Jewish immigrants by Arabs at disputed "Wailing Wall."

1930. British government releases the White Paper by the Passfield Commission, which recommends that Jewish immigration to Palestine be halted immediately, and that no more land be awarded to Jewish settlers because of "too many landless Arabs." The recommendation is modified by the British parliament and only token action is taken.

1932. Arabia is renamed Saudi Arabia.

1935. British Petroleum builds pipeline from disputed Mosul oilfields to port of Haifa. Peel Commission reports to British parliament that Jews and Arabs can never work together; recommends partitioning of Palestine.

1936. Saudis sign a non-aggression pact with Iraq, but break it during the Gulf war. The Saudis decided to back the United States and in the process, thereby dishonored the previous agreement with Iraq.

1937. Pan Arab Conference in Syria rejects the Peel Commission's plan for Jewish immigration into Palestine. British arrest the Arab leaders and deport them to Seychelles.

1941. Britain invades Iran to "save" the country from Germany.

Churchill sets up puppet government which takes its orders from London.

1946. Transjordan is granted independence by Britain and is renamed "Hashemite Kingdom of Jordan" in 1949. Widespread and violent opposition by Zionists follows.

1952. Serious rioting in Iraq over continued British presence, outrage over U.S. complicity with oil companies..

1953. New government of Jordan orders British troops out of the country.

1954. Britain and U.S. berate Jordan for refusing to join in armistice talks with Israel, followed by downfall of the Jordanian cabinet. U.S. Sixth Fleet menaces Arab countries by landing Marines in Lebanon (an act of war). King Hussein is not intimidated and responds by denouncing the strong U.S. ties with Israel.

1955. Palestinians on West Bank riot, Israel declares "Palestinians a Jordanian problem."

1959. Iraq protests inclusion of Kuwait in CETAN membership. Accuses Saudis of "aiding British imperialism." British control over Kuwait is strengthened. Iraq's outlet to the sea is cut off.

1961. Premiere Kassem of Iraq warns Britain "Kuwait is Iraqi land and has been for 400 years." Kassem is later assassinated mysteriously. British government declares Kuwait an independent nation. British oil companies are given control over a large part of the Rumalia oilfields. Kuwait signs treaty of friendship with Britain. British troops move in to counter possible attack by Iraq.

1962. Britain and Kuwait terminate defense pact.

1965. Crown Prince Sabah Al Salem Al Sabah becomes Emir of Kuwait.

1967. Iraq and Jordan go to war against Israel. Saudi Arabia avoids taking sides, but sends 20,000 troops who are forbidden to take part in the fighting to Jordan.

By now, the Committee of 300's grip on Middle East oi; was almost total. The road Britain and America had followed was not a new one, but an extention began by Lord Bertrand Russell:

"If a world government is to work smoothly, certain economic conditions will have to be fulfilled. Various raw materials are essential to industry. Of these, at present, one of the most important is oil. Probably uranium, though no longer needed for the purposes of war, will be essential for industrial use of nuclear energy. There is no justification in the private ownership of such essential raw materials- and I think we should include in undesirable ownership, not only ownership by individuals or companies, but also separate states. The raw material without which industry is impossible should belong to the international authority and granted to separate nations."

This turned out to be a profound statement by the "prophet" of the Committee of 300, coming precisely when British-U.S. meddling in Arab affairs was at its height. Note that Russell already knew then that there would be no nuclear war. Russell declared himself in favor of a One World Government, or the New World Order spoken of by President Bush. The Gulf War was a continuation of earlier efforts to wrest control of Iraqi oil from its rightful owners and to protect the entrenched position of British Petroleum and other majors of the oil cartel for the Committee of 300.

The Balfour Declaration is the kind of document for which the British became infamous. In 1899, they had pressed deception against the tiny Boer Republics in South Africa to new levels. While talking peace, already disturbed by the hundreds of thousands of vagabonds and carpet-baggers who flocked to the Boer republics in the wake of the biggest gold strike in the history of the world, Queen Victoria was preparing for war.

The Gulf War was fought for two primary reasons: The first concerns the hatred of all things Muslim by the RIIA and their American cousins of the CFR, in adition to their strong desire to protect their surrogate, Israel. The second was unbridled greed and a desire to control all Middle East oil-producing countries.

As to the war itself, U.S. maneuvering began at least three years before Bush officially went on the offensive. The United States first armed Iraq, and then incited it to attack Iran in a war which decimated both countries: the so-called "meatgrinder war." The war was designed to weaken both Iraq and Iran to the point that they would no longer be a credible threat to British and U.S. oil interests, and, as a military force, they would no longer pose a threat to Israel.

In 1981, Iraq asked the Banco Nazionale de Lavoro (BNL) in Brescia, Italy, for a line of credit buy weapons from an Italian company. That company later sold land mines to Iraq. Then, in 1982, U.S. President Ronald Reagan removed Iraq from the list of countries that sponsor terrorism in response to a State Department request.

In 1983, the U.S. Agricultural Department provided Iraq with loans amounting to $365 million, ostensibly to purchase agricultural products, but subsequent events disclosed that the money was used to purchase military hardware. In 1985, Iraq approached the BNL branch in Atlanta, Georgia, with a request that the bank process its loans from the U.S. Agricultural Department's Commodity Credit Corporation.

In January of 1986, a high-level CIA-National Security Agency (NSA) meeting was held in Washington, DC. Discussed was whether the United States should give intelligence data it had on Iraq to the government in Teheran. Then Deputy NSA Director Robert Gates was against doing so, but was overruled by the National Security Council.

It was not until 1987 that President Bush made a number of public references supporting Iraq, one in which he said: "the U.S. must build a solid relationship with Iraq for the future." Shortly thereafter, BNL's Atlanta branch secretly agreed to a $2.1 billion commercial loan to Iraq. In 1989, hostilities between Iraq and Iran came to an end.

By 1989, a secret memorandum prepared by the State Department Intelligence Agency warned Secretary James Baker: "Iraq retains its heavy-handed approach to foreign affairs...and is working hard at (making) chemical and biological weapons and new missiles." Baker did nothing of any substance about the report, and as we shall see, later actively encouraged President Saddam Hussein to believe that the United States would be even-handed about Iraq's policies toward its Middle East neighbors.

In April of the same year, a nuclear proliferation report by the Department of Energy said that Iraq had embarked on a project to build an atomic bomb. This was followed by a June report prepared jointly by Eximbank, (a U.S. banking agency), the CIA and the Federal Reserve Banks, which said that a joint study revealed that Iraq was integrating U.S. technology "directly into Iraq's planned missile, tank and armored personnel carrier industries."

On August 4, 1989, the FBI raided the offices of the BNL in Atlanta. Some suspect that this was done to preempt any real investigation into whether loans for Iraq were used to buy sensitive military technology and other military know-how, rather than for the purposes extended by the Agricultural Department.

During September, in an effort insiders say was an advance move to absolve itself from blame, the CIA reported to Baker that Iraq was obtaining the ability to make nuclear weapons through a variety of front companies suspected of links with Pakistan at the highest levels. Pakistan had been long suspected, and even accused by the U.S. Atomic Energy Commission of making nuclear weapons, which led to a major rift in relations with Washington, described as being " at an all time low."

In October of 1989 the State Department wrote a "damage control" memo to Baker, recommending that Baker "wall off" the Agriculture Department's credit program from BNL investigators. The memo was initialed by Baker, which some interpret as his approval of the recommendation. It is generally recognized that by initialing a document, approval is given to its content and any course of action laid out.

47

Shortly thereafter, in a surprise turn, President Bush signed National Security Directive 26, which supported U.S. trade with Iraq. "Access to the Persian Gulf and key friendly states in that area is vital to U.S. national security," Bush said. Here then, is confirmation that as early as October, 1989, the President was indulging in diplomacy by deception, acting as though Iraq was an ally of the United States, when in fact, preparations for a war against the country were already underway.

Then, on Oct. 26, 1989, slightly more than three weeks after Bush declared Iraq a friendly state, Baker called Secretary of Agriculture Clayton Yeutter with a request that the agricultural trade credits for Iraq be increased. In response, Yeutter ordered his department to provide $1 billion in insured trade credits for the Baghdad government, even though the Treasury Department expressed reservations.

Deputy Secretary of State Lawrence Eagleburger assured the Treasury that the money was needed for "geopolitical reasons": "Our ability to influence Iraqi behavior in areas from Lebanon to the Middle East peace process (an oblique reference to Israel), is enhanced by expanded trade," said Eagleburger.

However, this was not enough to allay a suspicious and hostile element of the Democrats in Congress, possibly reacting to intelligence information received from Israel. In January of 1990, Congress barred loans to Iraq and eight other countries congressional investigators said were hostile toward the United States. This was a setback for the major plan to go to war against Iraq, which Bush did not trust Congress to know. So, on January 17, 1990, he exempted Iraq from the congressional ban.

Possibly fearing that Congressional intervention might upset war plans, State Department specialist John Kelly fired off a memo to Undersecretary of State for Policy Robert Kimit, in which the Agriculture Department was castigated for its tardiness in moving on the loans to Iraq. This February, 1990 incident is of major importance in proving that the president was anxious to complete stocking Iraq with arms and technology so that the timetable for war would not fall behind schedule.

On February 6, James Kelly, a lawyer for the New York Federal Reserve Bank who was responsible for regulating BNL operations in the United States, wrote a memo which ought to have caused a great deal of alarm: A planned trip to Italy by Federal Reserve criminal investigators was put off. The BNL had cited concerns regarding the Italian press. A trip to Istanbul was put off at the request of Attorney General Richard Thornburgh.

Kelly's February, 1990 memo said in part: "...A key component of the relationship and failure to approve the loans will feed Saddam's paranoia and accelerate his swing against us." If we did not already know about the war planned against Iraq, the latter statement would appear to be an amazing one. How could the United States go on arming President Hussein if it feared that he would "swing against us"? Logically, the proper course of action would have been to suspend the credits rather than arm a nation that the State Department believed might turn against us.

March of 1990 brought some surprising developments. Documents produced in federal court in Atlanta showed that Reinaldo Petrignani, Italy's ambassador to Washington, told Thornburgh that incriminating Italian officials in the BNL investigation would be "tantamount to a slap in the face for the Italians." This conversation was subsequently denied as having taken place by both Petrignani and Thornburgh. It proved one thing: the deep involvement of the Bush administration in the BNL loans to Iraq.

In April of 1990, the Interagency Deputies Committee of the National Security Council, headed by Deputy National Security Adviser Robert Gates, met at the White House for discussions about a possible change in U.S. attitude toward Iraq -- yet another twist in the cyclone of diplomacy by deception.

In yet another unexpected turn of events that same month, apparently not anticipated by Bush or the NSA, the Treasury Department balked at the Agriculture Department's $500 million commodity trade credits, refusing to allow it to go through. In May of 1990, the Treasury Department let it be known that it had received a memo from the NSA objecting to its move. The memo said that NSA staff wanted to prevent Agricultural credits "from being cancelled, as this would exacerbate the already strained foreign policy relations with Iraq."

By July 25, 1990, probably earlier than the Committee of 300 preferred, the trap was sprung. Spurred on by a mounting number of setbacks, President Bush authorized U.S. ambassador April Glaspie to meet with President Hussein. The purpose of the meeting was to reassure President Saddam Hussein that the United States had no quarrel with him and would not intervene in any inter-Arab border disputes, according to a number of as yet unreleased State Department cables which Rep. Henry Gonzalez was able to obtain. This was a clear reference to Iraq's dispute with Kuwait over the Rumalia oilfields.

The Iraqis took Glaspie's words as a signal from Washington that they could send their army into Kuwait, thereby buying right into the plot. As Ross Perot stated during the November 1992 elections: "I suggest that in a free society owned by the people, the American people ought to know what we told Ambassador Glaspie to tell Saddam Hussein, because we spent a lot of money and risked lives and lost lives in that effort and did not accomplish most of our objectives."

Meanwhile Glaspie disappeared from view and was sequestered to a secret location shortly after the news broke about her part in the diplomacy by deception practiced against Iraq. Finally, after much media prodding, and flanked by a couple of liberal Senators, who acted as if Glaspie was a wallflower in need of great chivalry, she appeared before a Senate Committee and denied everything. Shortly afterward, Glaspie "resigned" from the State Department, and no doubt now lives in comfortable obscurity from which she ought to be wrenched, placed under oath in a court of law and forced to testify to the truth of how the Bush administration calculatingly deceived not only Iraq, but also this nation.

On July 29, 1990, four days after Glaspie met with the Iraqi president, Iraq began moving its army toward the border with Kuwait. Continuing with the deception, Bush sent a team to Capitol Hill to testify against imposing sanctions against Iraq, thereby adding to President Hussein's belief that his impending invasion of Iraq would be winked at by Washington.

Two days later, on Aug. 2, 1990, the Iraqi Army crossed the artificially created border of Kuwait. Also during August the CIA, in a top secret report, told Bush that Iraq was not going to invade Saudi Arabia, and that the Iraqi military had not made any contingency plans to do so.

In September of 1990, Italian Ambassador Rinaldo Petrignani accompanied by a number of BNL officials, met with Justice Department prosecutors and investigators. At the meeting, Petrignani said that the BNL was "the victim of a terrible fraud...the bank's good name is of great importance, as the Italian state is a majority owner." This came to light in documents turned over to the House Banking Committee's chairman, Henry Gonzalez.

To experienced watchers, this meant one thing: a plot was in motion to let the real culprits in Rome and Milan off the hook and shift blame to the local fall guy. No wonder a "not guilty" attitude was adopted: subsequently incontrovertible evidence surfaced that the loans made by the BNL's Atlanta branch had the full blessing of the head office of the BNL in Rome and Milan.

On Sept. 11, 1990, Bush called for a joint session of Congress and stated falsely that on Aug. 5, 1990, Iraq had 150,000 troops and 1500 tanks in Kuwait, poised to strike at Saudi Arabia. Bush based his statement on false information relayed from the Defense Department. The claim was that 120,000 Iraqi troops and 850 tanks were in Kuwait. The Defense Department must have known this information was false, otherwise its KH11 and KH12 satellites were malfunctioning, and we know that they were not. Apparently Bush needed to exaggerate to convince Congress that Iraq presented a threat to Saudi Arabia.

Meanwhile, the Russian military released its own satellite pictures showing the exact troop strength in Kuwait. As a cover up for Bush, Washington held out that the satellite pictures were from a commercial satellite company that had been sold to ABC television, among others. By turning the satellite pictures over to a commercial company, Russia engaged in a bit of deception of its own. Clearly, the Defense Department and the president had been lying to the American people, and were now caught out in their lies.

By now, Chairman Gonzalez was asking embarrassing questions about the Bush administration's possible involvement in the BNL scandal. In September of 1990, the assistant attorney general for legislative affairs wrote a memo to the attorney general which said: "Our best attempt to thwart any further congressional enquiry by the House banking Committee into (BNL) loans is to have you contact Chairman Gonzalez directly."

On Sept. 26, a few days after he received the memo was, Thornburgh phoned Gonzalez and told him not to investigate the BNL matter because of national security issues involved. Gonzalez bluntly refused to call off the House Banking Committee investigation of BNL. Thornburgh later denied ever having told Gonzalez to leave BNL alone. Gonzalez soon got hold of a memo written by the State Department dated Dec. 18, which exposed Thornburgh's "national security" plea. The memo also stated that the Justice Department's investigation of BNL didn't raise any national security issue or problems.

Further, the Defense Intelligence Agency announced that its teams in Italy had learned that BNL's Brescia branch loaned Iraq $255 million to buy land mines from an Italian manufacturer. The day the "allied victory" in the Gulf War was announced, the Justice Department indicted the fall guy for the BNL scandal, as expected. Christopher Drogoul was accused of illegally loaning Iraq in excess of $5 billion and accepting kick-backs of up to $2.5 million. Few believed that an obscure loan officer at a small branch of an Italian state-owned bank would have had authority to enter into transactions of such magnitude on his own volition.

From the period January to April of 1990, as more and more pressure built up for the Bush administration to explain the glaring anomalies in the BNL scandal, the National Security Council took steps to close ranks. On April 8, Nicolas Rostow, the NSC's general counsel, organized a top-level meeting to explore ways of fending off the pressing requests for documentation from, among others, House Banking Committee Chairman Gonzalez.

The meeting was attended by C. Boyden Gray, legal counsel to Bush, Fred Green, National Security Agency counsel, CIA general counsel Elizabeth Rindskopf and a whole slew of lawyers representing the Agriculture, Defense, Justice, Treasury, Energy and Commerce Departments. Rostow opened the meeting by warning that Congress seemed intent on probing the Bush administration's relations with Iraq before the war.

Rostow told the lawyers that "the National Security Council is providing coordination for the administration's response to congressional documents requests for Iraq-related material," adding that any congressional requests for documents should be checked for "issues of executive privilege, national security, etc. Alternatives to providing documents should be explored." This information was eventually obtained by Gonzalez.

Cracks were now starting to appear in an otherwise solid administration stonewalling policy. On June 4, 1990, officials at the Commerce Department admitted that they had deleted information on export documents to obscure the fact that the department had indeed granted the export licences for shipments of military hardware and technology to Iraq.

Even larger cracks began to appear in July, when Stanley Moskowitz, the CIA's liaison to Congress, reported that the BNL bank officials in Rome not only were fully aware of what had transpired at the Atlanta branch long before the indictment of Drogoul was handed down, but had in fact signed and approved the loans for Iraq. This was a direct contradiction of Ambassador Petrignani's statement to the Justice Department that the BNL's Rome office knew nothing about the Iraq loans made by its Atlanta branch.

In May of 1992, in yet another a surprising turn, Attorney General William Barr wrote a letter to Gonzales in which he charged Gonzalez with harming "national security interests" by revealing the administration's policy toward Iraq. In spite of the serious charge, Barr provided no confirmation to back the allegation. Clearly, the president was rattled, and the November elections were just around the corner. This point was not lost on Gonzalez, who called Barr's charge "politically motivated."

On June 2, 1992, Drougal pleaded guilty to bank fraud. An unhappy Judge Marvin Shoob asked the Justice Department to appoint a special prosecutor to investigate the BNL case in its entirety. But on July 24, 1992, the attack on Gonzalez resumed with a letter from CIA Director Robert Gates. He criticized the chairman for disclosing the fact that the CIA and a number of other U.S. intelligence agencies knew about the Bush administration's pre-Gulf War relationship with Iraq. Later that month, Gates' letter was released by the House Banking Committee for publication.

By August, the former chief of the Atlanta office of the FBI openly accused the Justice Department of dragging its feet and delaying indictments for nearly a year in the BNL affair. And on Aug. 10 1992, Barr refused to appoint a special prosecutor to investigate the Bush administration's pre-Gulf War relationship with Iraq, as requested by the House Judiciary Committee.

Then, on Sept. 4, Barr wrote a letter to the House Banking Committee stating that he would not comply with the Committee's subpoenas for BNL documents and related information. It soon became evident that Barr must have instructed all government departments to refuse to cooperate with the House Banking Committee, because four days after Barr's letter was released, the CIA, the Defense Intelligence Agency, the Customs Service, the Commerce Department and the National Security Agency all stated that their intention was not to comply with subpoenas for information and documents on the BNL issue.

Gonzalez carried the battle to the floor of the House and disclosed that based on the CIA's own July 1991 report, it was clear that BNL's top management in Rome knew of, and had approved the Atlanta-branch loans to Iraq. Federal prosecutors in Atlanta were floored by the highly damaging information.

On Sept. 17, 1991, in an obvious damage control measure, the CIA and the Justice Department agreed to tell federal prosecutors in Atlanta that the only information they had on BNL had already been made publicly available, which was a blatant and reckless falsehood with shattering ramifications. The scramble to exculpate themselves and their departments is what led to all the finger pointing and internal fighting that showered all the news stations just before the election.

With the knowledge that he had spent most of his last 100 days in office desperately trying to keep the lid on the scandals erupting all around him, Bush got a life-line thrown to him: the media agreed not to report the details of the plot. The "national security" smokescreen had done the job.

In an ongoing effort to put distance between itself and the other parties involved in the BNL-Iraqgate coverup, the Justice Department agreed that it would soon release highly damaging documents showing the CIA's prior knowledge of the BNL's Rome office "green light" for loans for Iraq. The information was subsequently released to Judge Shoob, whose earlier doubts about the indictment of Drougal appeared to be vindicated.

Then, on Sept. 23, 1992, Gonzalez announced that he had received classified documents which clearly showed that in January of 1991, the CIA knew about the BNL's high-level approval of the loans for Iraq. In his letter, Gonzalez expressed concern over Gates' lies to federal prosecutors in Atlanta regarding the BNL's Rome office not being aware of what its Atlanta branch was doing.

The Senate Intelligence Committee also accused Gates of misleading the Justice Department, federal prosecutors and Judge Shoob about the extent of CIA knowledge of BNL events. The Justice Department allowed Drogoul to withdraw his guilty plea on Oct. 1.. The lone battle, waged and won by the chairman of the House Banking Committee against the Bush administration was ignored by the media in deference to the wishes of the Republican election committee and to protect Bush, one of its favorite sons.

Judge Shoob excused himself from the BNL case a few days later. He said that he had concluded that "it is likely that the U.S. intelligence agencies were aware of BNL-Atlanta's relations with Iraq... The CIA continues to be uncooperative in attempts to discover information about its knowledge of or involvement in the funding of Iraq by BNL-Atlanta." The source of this information could not originally be revealed, but the gist of it later appeared in a report published by the New York Times.

A major development occurred when Sen. David Boren accused the CIA of a coverup and of lying to Justice Department officials. In its response, the CIA admitted that it gave the wrong information to the Justice Department in its September report-hardly any great admission, as Gonzalez, among others, already had proof of this. The CIA claimed it was an honest mistake. There was "no attempt to mislead anyone or coverup anything" the agency contended. The CIA also reluctantly acknowledged that it had not released all of the documents it had on BNL.

The very next day, CIA chief counsel Rindskopf (who participated in the 1991 damage control briefing held by Nicolas Rostow of the National Security Agency), picked up the "honest mistake" refrain, calling it a "certainly regrettable mistake" brought on by a faulty filing system. Was it the best excuse that the chief lawyer for the CIA could come up with? Neither Sen. Boren or Rep. Gonzalez were convinced.

It should be recalled that the real purpose of the 1991 meeting called by Nicholas Rostow was to control the access to all government documents and information that would show the true relationship between the Bush administration and the Baghdad government. Obviously those responsible for trying to break through the wall placed around such information had every right to be highly skeptical of Rindskopf's lame excuse about faulty filing.

The damage control efforts instituted by Rostow took another pounding on Oct. 8, 1992, when CIA officials were called upon to testify before a closed-door session of the Senate Intelligence Committee. According to information received from sources close to the Senate Intelligence Committee, the CIA officials had an uncomfortable time of it, eventually trying to pin blame on the State Department, claiming that they withheld information, and then gave misleading information on BNL-Atlanta at the insistence of a senior official of the Justice Department. All they had done, CIA officials said, was what the Justice Department told them to do.

An official denial was issued on Oct. 9,1992, with the State Department refusing to take responsibility for having asked the CIA to withhold relevant BNL documents from the Atlanta prosecutors. The Justice Department then delivered its own broadside, accusing the CIA of delivering some classified documents in a disorganized manner while withholding others. The Senate Select Intelligence Committee agreed to launch its own investigation into these charges and counter-charges.

By now, it was becoming clear that all the parties who attended the April 8, 1991 meeting were scrambling to distance themselves from the matter. Then, on Oct. 10, the FBI announced that it, too, would investigate the BNL-Atlanta case. The CIA denied it had ever admitted to the Senate Intelligence Committee that it had withheld information at the special request of the Justice Department.

These strange events were proceeding in such rapid succession that daily announcements of accusations by one government agency or another continued through Oct. 14, 1992. The Justice Department announced on Oct. 11 that its Office of Professional Responsibility would lead an investigation of itself and of the CIA, and that the FBI would help. Assistant Attorney General Robert S. Meuller III, the Justice Department spokesman for its Public Integrity Section, was placed in charge. Information said to have originated from Sen. David Boren's office appeared to indicate that Meuller was directly involved in withholding information from federal prosecutors in Atlanta.

On Oct. 12, 1992, just two days after the FBI had announced that it would conduct its own investigation of the BNL case, ABC News charged that it had received information indicating that William Sessions, head of the FBI, was under investigation by the Justice Department's Office of Professional Responsibility. The accusations charged Sessions with the improper use of government airplanes, having a fence built around his house at government expense and abuse of telephone privileges -- none of which were in any way linked to the BNL case.

The ABC news report came on the heels of the Oct. 10 announcement by the FBI that it would investigate the BNL case, and was an attempt to pressure Sessions into calling off the promised FBI investigation. Sen. Boren told newsmen: "The timing of the accusations against Judge Sessions makes me wonder if an attempt is being made to pressure him not to conduct an independent investigation."

Others pointed to a statement made by Sessions on Oct. 11 that his investigation would not seek help from Justice Department officials, who themselves, might be the subject of investigation. "The Justice Department will not participate in the (FBI) inquiry and the FBI will not share information," Sessions said. In the final days of his bid for reelection, Bush continued to flatly deny that he had any knowledge of or personal involvement in the Iraq-gate or Iran/Contra scandals.

Things took a turn for the worse for the president when on Oct. 12, 1992, Sen.Howard Metzenbaum, a member of the Senate Select Committee on Intelligence, wrote to Attorney General Barr and asked for a special prosecutor to be appointed: "...Since very high-level officials may well have been knowledgeable of or involved in an effort to absolve BNL-Rome of complicity in the activities of BNL-Atlanta, no arm of the executive branch can investigate U.S. government conduct in this case without at least the appearance of a conflict of interest."

Metzenbaum's letter stated that there were indications of "secret U.S. government involvement in arms sales to Iraq," which came out of court proceedings in Atlanta. Gonzalez fired off a stinging letter to Barr requesting that a special prosecutor be appointed to "address the repeated clear failures and obstruction of the leadership of the Justice Department...The best way to accomplish this is to do the right thing and submit your resignation," Gonzalez charged.

Then on Oct. 14, Sen. Boren wrote to Barr telling him to appoint a special independent prosecutor: "A truly independent investigation is required to determine whether federal crimes were committed in the government's handling of the BNL case." Boren went on to say that both the Justice Department and the CIA had engaged in a coverup of the BNL case. The very next day, the CIA released a cable from its station chief in Rome, which quoted an unidentified source as charging that high officials in Italy and the United States were bribed, apparently to keep them from saying what they knew about the BNL-Atlanta case.

This was followed by a five-day lull in the firestorm surrounding the Bush administration until the Senate Select Committee began its investigation into charges that the CIA and the NSA used front companies to supply Iraq with military hardware and technology in breach of federal law. Some Democrats on the Senate Judiciary Committee also called for Barr to appoint an independent prosecutor, which he again refused to do.

Bush struggled for his political life as special prosecutor Lawrence Walsh handed down an indictment against former Secretary of Defense Caspar Weinberger, accusing him of lying to Congress. Sources in Washington said, "there was pandemonium in the White House." Weinberger, meanwhile, indicated that he would not play the role of fall guy for the president. According to one source, C. Boyden Gray told the president that the only course of action open to him was to pardon Weinberger.

So, on Christmas Eve, 1992, Bush pardoned Weinberger and five other key players in the Iran/Contra scandal: Former national Security Adviser Robert McFarlane, CIA's Clair George, Duane Clarridge and Alan Fiers, and former Assistant Secretary of State Elliott Abrams. The clemency effectively "walled" Bush off from Walsh, thereby killing the Iran/Contra investigation. As for Clinton he has not, as yet, shown any priority interest in appointing a special prosecutor.

Walsh was quick to express his anger to the news media. The presidential clemency "demonstrates that powerful people with powerful allies can commit serious crimes in high office-deliberately abusing the public trust without consequences...The Iran/Contra coverup, which has continued for six years, has now been completed... This office was informed only within the past two weeks, on Dec. 11, 1992, that President Bush had failed to produce to investigators his highly relevant contemporaneous notes (the Bush diary) despite repeated requests for such documents...In the light of President Bush's own misconduct in withholding his daily diary, we are gravely concerned about his decision to pardon others who have lied to Congress and obstructed official investigations."

Perhaps Walsh did not know what he was up against: nor that the coverup had been going for a much longer time than he suspected. The case of the Israeli agent Ben-Menashe is one in point. The House October Surprise Task Force did not see fit to call Ben-Menashe as a witness. Had the committee done so, they would have heard that Ben-Menashe told "Time" correspondent Rajai Samghabadi about a vast "off the books" arms trade going on between Israel and Iran back in 1980.

During Ben-Menashe's trial in 1989, at which Samghabadi testified for him, it came out that the story of a huge illicit arms sale by Israel to Iran was repeatedly offered to "Time" magazine, who refused to print it, even though it had been substantiated by Bruce Van Voorst, a former CIA agent working for "Time." Walsh did not appear to know that the Eastern Liberal Establishment, run by the Committee of 300, is unconcerned about the law, because, they say they are the law.

Walsh came up against the same brick wall that Sen. Eugene McCarthy had run into when he attempted to get William Bundy before his committee and only got as far as John Foster Dulles. It was not surprising that Walsh would come up short, especially in going after a Skull and Bonesman. McCarthy had attempted to get Dulles to testify about certain CIA activities, but Dulles refused to cooperate.

Will R. James Woolsey, the man appointed by Clinton to run the CIA, do anything to bring the guilty to justice? Woolsey has credentials which include membership in the National Security Club, serving under Henry Kissinger as a National Security Council staffer, and as Under Secretary of the Navy in the Carter administration. He also served on numerous commissions and became a close associate of Les Aspin and Albert Gore.

Woolsey has another close friend in Dave McMurdy of the House Intelligence Committee and also a key Clinton adviser. A lawyer by profession, Woolsey was a partner in the establishment law firm of Shae and Gardner, during which time he acted as a foreign agent -- without registering as such with the Senate. Woolsey also long enjoyed a client-attorney relationship with a top CIA official.

One of Woolsey's most notable clients was Charles Allen, a national intelligence officer at the CIA headquarters in Langley, Virginia. Allen was accused by his boss, William Webster, in an internal investigation report of the Iran/Contra scandal of hiding evidence. It seems that Allen never handed over all of his files about dealings with Manucher Ghorbanifar, a go-between in the Iran/Contra affair. Webster threatened Allen, who turned to Woolsey for help saying he had made "a simple mistake." When Sessions discovered that Allen was being represented by Woolsey, he dropped the matter. Those who were close to the issue say that with Woolsey at the helm of the CIA, others who were not pardoned by Bush will find an "open door" in Woolsey.

# Grand Larceny: United States Oil Policies Abroad. III.

U.S. oil policies in foreign countries provides a consistent history of diplomacy by deception. In researching State Department documents for this book, I discovered numerous documents which openly proclaimed support for Standard Oil in Mexico and U.S. petroleum companies in the Middle East. It then became clear to me that the State Department was involved in a gigantic plot of diplomacy by deception in the foreign oil business.

A State Department directive dated Aug.16, 1919 to all consuls and embassies in foreign countries urged massive spying and redoubling of foreign service personnel to assist the major American oil companies, an extract of which follows:

"Gentlemen: The vital importance of securing adequate supplies of mineral oil both for present and future needs of the United States has been forcibly brought to the attention of the Department. The development of proven fields and exploration of new areas is being aggressively conducted in many parts of the world by nationals of various countries and concessions for mineral rights are being actively sought. It is desired to have the most complete and recent information regarding such activities by either United States citizens or by others.

"You are accordingly instructed to obtain and forward promptly from time to time information regarding mineral oil concession, change of ownership of oil property, or important changes in ownership, or control of corporate companies concerned with oil production or distribution.

"Information regarding development of new fields or increased

63

output of producing areas should also be forwarded. Comprehensive data are desired and reports should not be limited to points specifically mentioned above, but should include information regarding all matters of interest affecting the mineral oil industry which may arise from time to time..."

This directive was issued following a long and bitter fight with the Mexican government. As we shall see in the account that follows, A.C. Bedford, chairman of Standard Oil, had demanded that the U.S. government come into the picture: "All proper diplomatic support in obtaining and operating oil producing property abroad should be backed by the government." The Federal Trade Commission promptly recommended "diplomatic support" of such oil ventures abroad.

Charles Evans Hughes also testified before the Coolidge Federal Oil Conservation Board, insisting that State Department and oil company policies be synonymous: "The foreign policy of the government, expressed in the phrase 'Open Door', consistently prosecuted by the Department of State, has made it possible for our American interests abroad to be intelligently fostered and the needs of our people, to no slight extent, to be appropriately safeguarded." This really meant that a merging of government and private oil interests was necessary. It was not by accident that Evans just happened to be counsel of the American Petroleum Institute and Standard Oil.

A Case History: Exploitation of Mexican Oil.

The history of exploitation of Mexican oil also serves as an example of how diplomacy by deception attains its desired ends. The conquest of Mexico's main natural resource -- its oil -- remains an ugly, open blot in the pages of American history.

Oil was discovered in Mexico by British construction magnate, Weetman Pearson, whose company was part of the global network of Committee of 300 companies. Pearson was not in the oil business but was backed by the British oil companies, particularly the Royal Dutch Shell Company. He soon became the leading producer in Mexico.

Mexican President Porfirio Diaz officially gave Pearson sole rights to prospect for oil, after he had already given the "sole right" to Edward Dahoney of Standard oil, who was known as "the czar of Mexican oil." As we shall see, Diaz fought for the interests of his elitist backers. He was also firmly under the influence of Dahoney and President Warren Harding.

One must go back to the Treaty of Guadalupe Hidalgo in 1848, in terms of which Mexico ceded Upper California, New Mexico and northern Sonora, Coahuila and Tampaulis to the United States for $15 million. Texas had been annexed by the United States in 1845. One of the main reasons for annexing Texas was that geologists knew of the vast oil fields that lay beneath its lands.

In 1876, Diaz overthrew Leordo de Tejada, and on May 2, 1877, was declared president of Mexico. He remained in office until 1911, except for four years (1880-1884.) Diaz stabilized finances, undertook industrial projects, built railways and increased commerce during his dictatorial rule while remaining true to those who put him in power. Mexico's "royalty" was closely linked to the royalty of Britain and Europe.

It was the promulgation of a new mining code on Nov. 22, 1884, that opened the door for Pearson to get into the oil business. Contrary to the old Spanish law, the new law provided that a title to land carried ownership of subsoil products. It also permitted the communal lands belonging to the Indians and mestizos to pass into the hands of the 1.5 million "upper class" of Mexico. It was against this background that Diaz started giving concessions to foreign investors.

The first to receive a concession was Dahoney, the close associate Secretary of the Interior Albert Fall and President Harding, to whom Dahony had donated large amounts of campaign money. In Harding's cabinet were no less than four oilmen, notably Fall. In 1900, Dahoney bought 280,000 acres of Hacienda del Tulillo for $325,000. By "rewarding" President Diaz, Dahoney was literally able to steal land, or buy it at ridiculously low prices.

After four years of operations, Dahoney was producing most of the 220,000 barrels of oil coming out of Mexico. Thinking he was well established, Dahoney, on instructions from the United States government declined to increase "reward" payments to President Diaz, although the Potrero and Cero Azul fields were producing in excess of $1 million a week. This was rather typical of the selfish greed of John D., a streak that ran through the entire Rockefeller brood. At this point, Diaz, upset with Dahoney, gave Pearson a "sole concession." By 1910, Pearson's Mexican Eagle Company had acquired 58 percent of the total Mexican production.

In response, Rockefeller ordered Pearson's wells dynamited and his workers fired upon by peasants his money had armed for the purpose. Large bands of brigands were armed and trained to smash Mexican Eagle pipelines and oil installations. All of the dirty tricks taught by William "Doc" Avery Rockefeller, surfaced in John D. Rockefeller's war on Pearson.

But Pearson proved to be more than a match for Rockefeller, fighting back with similar tactics. Calculating that there was not enough oil in Mexico to continue fighting over (a grave error as it turned out), Rockefeller backed off and left the field to Pearson. Later, John D. regretted his decision to pull out of the struggle and pledged Standard's resources to create bloody chaos in Mexico. In this country we called the unrest "Mexican revolutions" which no one understood.

In recognition of his services to British oil interests, Pearson was granted the title of "Lord Cowdray," and was henceforth known by that title. He was also made a permanent member of the Committee of 300. Lord Cowdray was on good terms with President Wilson, but behind the scenes, John D. was working to undermine the relationship and get back into the business of exploiting Mexico's oil. Lord Cowdray, however, was determined to keep the bulk of Mexican oil profits in the coffers of the British government.

Oil diplomacy in London and Washington differ little in aggression. Motives and methods have remained remarkably unchanged. After all, international power remains, above all, economic. On Jan. 21,

1928, Rear Admiral Charles Plunkett, commander of the Brooklyn Navy Yard, let the cat out of the bag, defending President Calvin Coolidge's $800 million navy program when he said: "The penalty for commercial and industrial efficiency inevitably is war." This was in reference to the great demand for oil for oil-fired navy ship. Plunkett had his eye on Mexico's oil.

Logically, the nation that is in control of raw material assets of the world, rules it. When Britain had a large navy which it needed to guard its world trade, diplomacy by deception was the key to British operations in oil-producing countries. America learned fast, especially after the advent of the Dulles Illuminati family, as we shall see.

Let us return to Mexico, where, in 1911, Diaz was ousted by Francisco Madero, and uncover the role played by Standard Oil in that endeavor. Gen. Victoriano Huerto alarmed British oil interests by declaring his intention to regain control of Mexico's oil, and the British asked Lord Cowdray (who by that time had sold his Mexican operation to Shell) to get President Wilson to help them unseat Huerta.

This was a fine piece of diplomacy by deception, because the British knew that Standard Oil was behind the 1911 Madero revolution that downed President Diaz. It was a revolution Standard oil thought was necessary to stop British rape of "their" Mexican oil. Francisco Madero, who became president of Mexico on Nov. 6, 1911, had little understanding of the forces who were pulling his strings, and played the political game, not realizing that politics is based solely on economics. But Huerta, who replaced him, knew how the game was played.

Standard Oil was very much involved in the downfall of Porfirio Diaz. Testimony given by a number of witnesses at the 1913 Senate Foreign Relations Committee hearing, implicated Dahoney and Standard Oil for financing the 1911 Madero revolution. One witness, Lawrence E. Converse, told the committee members a lot more than Standard wished them to hear:

"Mr. Madero told me that as soon as the rebels (Madero's forces) made

67

a good showing of strength, several leading bankers in El Paso (Texas) stood ready to advance him. I believe the sum was $100,000, and that Standard Oil interests had bought over the provisional government of Mexico...They (Gov. Gonzalez and Secretary of State Hernandez) said Standard Oil interests were backing Madero in his revolution..."

The Wilson government, anxious to curb Cowdray's concessions, established diplomatic relations with the Madero government, ordering an arms embargo against any counter-revolutionists. Cowdray was cast in the role of villain by Col. House, (Woodrow Wilson's controller) when Francisco Huerta overthrew Madero. "We do not love him (Cowdray), for we think that between him and Carden (Sir Lionel Carden, British Minister to Mexico), are large part of our troubles are made," said House.

Col. House correctly charged that Huerta was brought to power by the British so that Standard's concessions could be crimped by expanding Lord Cowdray's oil exploitation. President Wilson refused to recognize the Huerta government, although Britain and the other major powers did so. Wilson said: "we can have no sympathy with those who seek to seize the power of government to advance their own personal interests or ambitions."

A Committee of 300 spokesman told President Wilson "you talk just like a Standard Oilman." The question was posed, "...what does the oil or commerce of Mexico amount to, in comparison with the close friendship between the United States and Great Britain? The two countries should agree on this primary principle -- to leave their oil interest to fight their own battles, legal and financial."

Those close to President Wilson said he was visibly shaken by British intelligence MI6 having uncovered his direct links with Standard's Mexican enterprises, which was starting to tarnish his Democratic president image. House warned him that the example set by Huerto in defying American power might be felt all across Latin America if the United States (read Standard Oil), did not assert itself. Here was a fine conundrum for a "Liberal Democrat" to confront.

Secretary of the Interior Fall urged the U.S. Senate to send American military forces into Mexico to "protect American lives and property." This rationale was also used by President Bush to send American troops to Saudi Arabia to "protect the lives and property" of British Petroleum and its employees, not to mention his own family's business, Zapata Oil Company. Zapata was one of the first American oil companies to become friendly with the Al Sabahs of Kuwait.

In 1913, the U.S. Senate Foreign Relations Committee convened hearings on what it called "Revolutions in Mexico." The American public, then as now, had no idea what was going on, and were led by the newspapers to believe that a whole lot of "crazy Mexicans were running around shooting at each other."

Mr. Dahoney, appearing as an expert witness was quite lyrical in his veiled request that the Washington government use force to restrain Huerta. He said:

"...it seems to me that the United States must avail itself of the enterprise and ability and the pioneer spirit of its citizens to acquire and to have and to hold a reasonable portion of the world's petroleum supplies. If it does not, it will find that supplies of petroleum not within the boundaries of the United States territory will be rapidly acquired by citizens and governments of other nations..."

Seems like we have heard a similar quote in more recent times, where "madman" Saddam Hussein was supposed to be a threat the world's oil supplies. Secretary Fall added to his appeals in the Senate for armed intrusion into Mexico: "...and lend their assistance (i.e. U.S. military forces) to the restoration of order and maintenance of peace in that unhappy country and the placing of administrative functions in the hands of capable and patriotic citizens of Mexico."

The resemblance between the deception perpetrated against the Senate and the people of the United States by Dahoney of Standard Oil and Secretary Fall bears an eerie resemblance to the rhetoric of Bush prior to and during his illegal war against Iraq. Bush said it was necessary for American soldiers to "return democracy to Kuwait."

The real truth was that democracy was a totally alien concept to the Al Sabah dictators of Kuwait.

Once America succeeded in reclaiming Kuwait for British Petroleum (an example of the special friendship between The United States and Britain talked about by the Committee of 300 messenger during his visit to President Wilson), Bush turned his attention to "the sad and unhappy country of Iraq."

Like Wilson, who believed that "tyrant Huerta" had to be removed and Mexico restored to "order and maintenance of peace in that unhappy country by placing the administrative functions in the hands of capable and patriotic citizens of Mexico," Bush, using a similar form of diplomacy by deception said that America has got to get rid of the "tyrant Saaaddam." (Misspelling intentional.)

American were soon convinced that President Hussein was the cause of all of Iraq's problems which is what Colonel House through Wilson told the American people about President Huerta of Mexico. In both cases, the common denominator is diplomacy by deception, in Mexico and Iraq is oil and greed. Today, Council on Foreign Relations Secretary of State Warren Christopher, has replaced Dahoney, Fall and Bush, and is perpetuating the pretence that Hussein must be brought down to save the people of Iraq.

Christopher is merely continuing to use falsehoods in order to cover the Committee of 300's goal for total seizure of Iraq's oilfields. It is no different than Wilson's policy toward Huerta.

While in 1912, Wilson presented the "Huerta menace" as a danger to the Panama Canal, Bush presented Hussein as a threat to U.S. oil supplies out of Saudi Arabia. In neither case was this the truth: Wilson lied about the "threat" to the Panama Canal, and Bush lied about a "pending invasion" of Saudi Arabia by the Iraqi military. In both cases, there was no such threat. Wilson's verbal assault on Heurta was made public in an address to the Inter-Allied Petroleum Council.

In a speech prepared for him by Col. House, Wilson told Congress that

Mexico was an "ever-present danger to American interests:"

"The present situation in Mexico is incompatible with the fulfillment of international obligations on the part of Mexico, with the civilized development of Mexico herself, and with the maintenance of tolerable political and economic conditions in Central America," Wilson said. "Mexico lies at last where all the world looks on. Central America is about to be touched by great routes of the world's trade and intercourse running from Ocean to Ocean at the Isthmus..." In effect Wilson was announcing that, henceforth, the politics of American petroleum companies would become the policies of the United States of America.

President Wilson was completely in the grip of Wall Street and Standard Oil. Notwithstanding the fact that on May 1, 1911, the Supreme Court had ordered an anti-trust action against Standard Oil, he instructed U.S. consuls in Central America and Mexico to "convey to the authorities an intimation that any maltreatment of Americans is likely to raise the question of intervention." The quote is taken from a long State Department document, and from hearings held by the Senate Foreign Relations Committee in 1913.

Following up on this message, Wilson instructed Secretary of State William Bryan to make it plain that he desired an early removal of President Huerta: "It is the clear judgment that it is the immediate duty of Huerta to retire from the Mexican government, and that the United States government must now proceed to employ such means as may be necessary to secure this result."

In the best style of an imperialist designed United States, Wilson followed up with yet another broadside at President Huerta on Nov. 12, 1912:

"Huerta has to be cut off from foreign sympathy and aid and from domestic credit, whether moral or material, and to force him out. If General Huerta does not retire by force of circumstances, it will become the duty of the United States to use less peaceful means to put him out." Wilson's belligerent statement is all the more shocking when we consider that it followed a peaceful election in which

71

President Huerta was returned to office.

One wonders why if that was the case concerning Panama, John D's heir, David Rockefeller, fought so hard to give the Canal at Panama away to Colonel Torrijos, but that is the subject of another chapter under the heading of Panama and the fraudulent Carter-Torrijos treaty.

One should not be amazed that at the time the American people accepted Wilson's belligerent attack on Mexico, thinly disguised as "patriotic" and in the best interests of the United States. After all, didn't the bulk of the population, and I believe it was 87 percent of Americans, fully support Bush in his attack on Iraq, and aren't we guilty of allowing to stand, the inhuman and totally unjustified embargo against Iraq?

We ought not to be amazed at the similarity of Wilson and Bush rhetoric, for both were controlled by our upper-level, parallel secret government, even as Clinton is controlled from Chatham House in London, through the person of Mrs. Pamela Harriman. No wonder then that Warren Christopher is continuing the big lie against Iraq. Oil and greed is the driving factor in 1993, even as it was in 1912. The charges I make here against Wilson are well documented by author Anton Mohr in his book "The Oil War."

It was America that hurt Mexico the most in 1912, plunging it into a civil war falsely labeled as "revolution", even as we are the nation that hurt Iraq the most in 1991, and continue to do so, in defiance of our Constitution, which those in Congress who swore an oath to uphold, have lamentably and miserably failed to do.

Secretary Bryan, told European powers who did not like what they saw happening in Mexico, that "there is a more hopeful prospect of peace, of security of property and early payment of foreign obligations if Mexico is left to the forces now reckoning with one another there."

This was classic diplomacy by deception. What Bryan did not tell the Europeans was that, far from leaving Mexico "to the forces now

72

reckoning with one another there," Wilson had already begun to isolate Huerta using a financial and armament embargo. At the same time, he armed and financially supported the forces controlled by Venustiano Carranza and Francisco Villa, and urged them to overthrow Gen. Huerta.

On April 9, 1914, a stage-managed crisis was arranged in Tampico by the U.S. Consul which resulted in the arrest of a group of American Marines. The United States government demanded an apology, and, when it was not forthcoming, broke contact with the Huerta government. By April 21, the incident had been blown out of all proportion, to the point that U.S. troops received their orders to march on Vera Cruz.

By capitalizing on the Tampico incident, Wilson was able to justify ordering American naval forces into Vera Cruz. An offer by Huerta to submit the Vera Cruz affair to the Hague Court was refused by Wilson. Like his successor, Bush, in the case of President Hussein, Wilson did not let anything stand in the way of ending the rule of Gen. Huerta. In this, Wilson was ably assisted by Dahoney of Standard Oil, who advised Wilson and Bryan that he had given the rebel Carranza $100,000 in cash and $685,000 in fuel credits.

By mid-1914, Mexico was reduced to utter chaos by President Wilson's interference in its affairs. On July 5, Huerto was elected president by popular vote but resigned on July 11, when it became apparent that Wilson would foment trouble as long as he held the reins of Mexico's government.

A month later, Gen. Obregon gained control of Mexico City and installed Carranza as president. But in the north, Francisco Villa became a dictator. Villa opposed Carranza, but the United States recognized Carranza anyway. By now, Latin American countries feared U.S. intervention, which was heightened by fighting between Villa's troops and U.S. forces at Carrizal.

As a result of the clamor raised in Latin America, and especially heeding the feedback from his consultants on Latin America, Wilson ordered U.S. forces withdrawn from Mexico on Feb. 5, 1917. Carranza disappointed his American backers in that he did nothing to help their cause. Rather, he tried to justify the 1911 revolution, which he said was necessary to preserve Mexico's integrity. This was not what the American oil companies had ordered him to say.

By January of 1917, the new Mexican Constitution was ready, and it came as a shock for Standard Oil and Cowdray's companies. Carranza was elected for four years. The new constitution which, in effect declared oil an inalienable natural resource of the Mexican people, took effect on Feb. 19, 1918 and a new tax was also levied on oil lands and contracts made before May 1, 1917.

This additional tax, covered by Article 27 of the document said the United States was "confiscatory" and in essence urged American companies in Mexico not to pay taxes. The Carranza government told Washington that taxation was a matter for "the sovereign state of Mexico." Try as it did, the U.S. State Department was unable to budge Carranza from his position that Mexican oil belonged to Mexico and, while foreigners could still invest in it, they could only do so at a price – taxation. The oil companies woke up to find that Carranza had turned the tables on them.

At this point, Cowdray went to the American president with a request "to face the common enemy (nationalization) together." Carranza was now persona non grata and Cowdray tried to sell his shares because he saw more confusion coming as the three leading Mexican generals vied for power. Cowdray's offer to sell was taken up by the Royal Dutch Shell Company. Although the conditions were uncertain, Cowdray made a handsome profit from the sale of his shares.

After much fighting, in which Carranza was killed and Villa assassinated, Gen. Obregon was elected president on Sept. 5, 1923. On Dec. 26, Huerta led a revolt against Obregon but was defeated. Obregon was supported by Washington on the condition that he restrict application of the constitution found so objectionable by foreign oil companies. Instead, Obregon slapped a 60 percent tax on oil exports. The U.S. government and the oil companies were angered by what they considered to be Obregon's defection.

For nearly five years, Washington kept up its attack on the Mexican Constitution, while hiding its real motivations. By 1927, Mexico was in civil uproar and its treasury almost empty. The Mexican government was forced to capitulate. There is no better description of what the Mexicans felt about being plundered of the oil than an editorial in "El Universal" of Mexico City, Oct. 1927:

"American imperialism is a fatal product of economic evolution. It is useless to try and persuade our northern neighbor not to be imperialistic; they cannot help being so, no matter how excellent their intentions. Let us study the natural laws of economic imperialism, in the hope that some method may be found, by which instead of blindly opposing them, we mitigate their action and turn it to our advantage."

What followed was a complete and utter retreat from the Mexican Constitution by President Plutarco Calles. The retreat was continued by successive Mexican governments. Mexico paid for the rapprochement, retreating from the principles for which she had fought for in 1911 and 1917. On July 1,1928, Gen. Obregon was reelected president, but was assassinated 16 days later. Foreign oil companies were accused of the crime and of keeping Mexico in a state of flux.

The U.S. government was acting in an alliance with Standard Oil and Lord Cowdray to force the Mexican government to roll back the Feb. 19, 1918 decree which declared oil an inalienable natural resource of the Mexican people. On July 2, 1934, Gen. Lazaro Cardenas was chosen by Calles to be his successor. Cardenas then turned on Calles, calling him "too conservative," and, under pressure from British and American oil interests, had Calles arrested when he returned from the U.S. in 1936. State Department documents leave no doubt about the hand of the U.S. government in these events.

Cardenas showed sympathy for the American and British oil companies, but was vigorously opposed by Vincente Lombardo Toledano, leader of the Confederation of Mexican Workers. Cardenas was forced to bow to demands from this group, and on Nov. 23, 1936, a new expropriation law empowered the government to seize property, especially oil lands. This was the reverse of what the U.S. government and oil companies were expecting, and panicked the oil companies.

By 1936, there were 17 foreign companies busily engaged in pumping the oil that rightfully belonged to Mexico. The situation was something akin to South Africa, where, ever since the Anglo Boer War (1899-1902), the Oppenheimer family of the Committee of 300 drained South Africa of its gold and diamonds, shipping them to London and Zurich, while the South African people got little benefit. The Anglo-Boer War was the first open demonstration of the might and the power of the Committee of 300.

Both with "black gold" and "yellow gold," the national resources of Mexico and South Africa, which really belong to the people, were plundered. This was accomplished under cover of diplomacy by deception, which fell apart only when national leaders of strength emerged, such as Daniel Malan, of South Africa and Lazaro Cardenas, of Mexico.

But unlike Malan, who was unable to hold back the robbing conspirators by nationalizing the gold mines, Cardenas promulgated a decree on Nov. 1, 1936, in which the subsoil rights of Standard Oil and other companies was declared nationalized. The net effect of the decree deprived the oil companies of operating in Mexico and repatriating their profits to the United States. For years, Mexican oil workers had lived on the edge of poverty while Rockefeller and Cowdray added to their bloated profit coffers. Cowdray became one of the richest men in England; Americans know all to well the magnitude of the Rockefeller empire.

The blood of thousands of Mexicans had needlessly been shed because of the greed of Standard Oil, Eagle, Shell, et al. Revolutions were deliberately caused by the manipulators in the United States, always backed by the appropriate U.S. government officials. While Cowdray lived in absolute luxury and frequented the best clubs in London, Mexican oil workers were worse off than the slaves of the Pharaohs, living in squalor and huddled together in misery in shantytowns that beggared description.

On Mar.18,1938, the Cardenas government nationalized the properties of American and British oil companies. Diplomacy by deception then took a back seat to the iron fist. The United States retaliated by halting the purchase of silver from Mexico. The British government broke off diplomatic relations. Secretly, Standard Oil and the British oil companies funded General Saturnino Cedillo, urging him to revolt against Cardenas. However, a massive show of support for Cardenas by the populace, ended the attempted revolt within weeks.

The United States and Britain soon instituted a boycott of Mexican oil, which devastated the national oil company known as PEMEX. Cardenas then arranged for barter agreements with Germany and Italy. Such deceitful conduct by both governments -- which most people considered to be pillars of Western civilization -- continued still when the Communists tried to gain control of Spain and the Mexican government attempted to break the oil boycott by sending oil to Gen. Franco's government.

In the Franco-Communist War, known as the "Spanish Civil War," Roosevelt backed the Communist side, and allowed them to recruit men and munitions in the United States. Washington adopted an official policy of "neutrality," but this piece of deception was ill-concealed, and came out when Texaco was hauled onto the carpet.

PEMEX decided to supply Franco with oil, using Texaco tankers to ship it to Spanish ports. Sir William Stephenson, head of MI6 intelligence, reported Texaco to Roosevelt. As it is custom where right-wing anti-communist governments battle for the existence of their countries, the secret upper-level parallel government of the United States ordered Roosevelt to halt Mexican oil shipments to Franco. But that did not stop the Bolsheviks from recruiting in the United States, or from obtaining munitions and financing from Wall Street. Texaco did not act out of sympathy for Franco or Mexico: its motive was profit. This demonstrates what happens when a Fabian Socialist such as Roosevelt, directs a country that is opposed to socialism.

It was not until 1946 that a semblance of good order came to Mexico with the election of President Miguel Aleman. On Sept. 30, 1947, the

Mexican government made a final settlement of all American and British expropriation claims. This cost the Mexican people dearly and still left control of the oil de facto in the hands of American and British oil companies. Thus, the 1936 expropriation decree signed by Cardenas was only partially successful.

In 1966, when several writers exposed the greed and corruption of Lord Cowdray, he hired Desmond Young to write a book whitewashing and playing down his involvement with Diaz and Huerta. In 1970, President Richard Nixon, at the behest of the Council on Foreign Relations, signed an agreement with President Diaz Ordaz which called for peaceful settlement of future border and other (meaning oil) disputes.

This agreement still holds good today, and, while the methods of plundering Mexican oil have changed, the intent and motivation has not. There is a common misconception over Nixon's agreement, namely, that it represented a change in Washington policy. It was meant to convey the impression that we now recognize Mexico's right to its natural resources. This is a repeat of the period when Morrow negotiated a settlement with Calles-Obregon in what the people of America were told was a "large concession by the United States," when in fact, it was hardly any concession at all as far as Washington was concerned. Such is diplomacy by deception.

# Rockefeller: The Evil Genie. IV.

No other industry has been corrupted as much as the mighty, powerful petroleum industry, and no other industry has as justly earned the epithets hurled against it. When the American Indians led Father Joseph de la Roche D'Allion, a French Franciscan missionary, to the mysterious pool of black waters in Western Pennsylvania, they could not have imagined what horrible results would come from it.

The oil industry has survived all attempts to breach its walls, whether by government or by private citizens. The U.S. oil industry has survived personal vendettas by the late senators Henry Jackson and Frank Church, and has emerged from numerous investigations with aplomb and its secrets intact. Not even anti-trust suits could break its power.

The petroleum industry cannot be mentioned without naming John D. Rockefeller, who created Standard Oil of New Jersey. The Rockefeller name is also synonymous with greed and an unwavering lust for power. The hatred the majority of Americans feel for the Rockefellers started when the "Big Hand" surfaced in the Pennsylvania oil regions. It began among the descendants of the pioneer drillers who flocked to Titusville and Pit Head when the black "gold rush" was getting into its stride in 1865.

John D. Rockefeller's ability to rob prospectors and drillers of their oil claims is strangely reminiscent of the "pioneering" efforts of Cecil John Rhodes, Barny Barnato and other Rothschild-Warburg agents who provided the money for daylight robbery and chicanery practiced by these con artists on the Kimberly diamond and the Rand gold claims owners. Nelson Rockefeller once claimed that the family fortune was "an accident," but the facts speak otherwise.

The paranoia and need for secrecy that surrounded John D. Rockefeller was handed down to his sons and adopted as a successful defense against outside prying into oil matters. Today, the Committee of 300 accounting firm of Price Waterhouse does the accounts in such a way that even the best accountants and various Senate committees have not been able to unlock the Rockefeller finances. Such is the nature of the beast. The question is often asked: "Why was Rockefeller so profoundly crooked?" One can only surmise that it was inherent in his nature.

John D. Rockefeller did not believe in letting friendship stand in the way of his progress, and warned his sons never to let "good fellowship get a hold of you." His favorite dogma concerned the wise old owl who said nothing and heard much. Early photographs of John D. show a long, grim face, small eyes, without a trace of any human qualities.

In view of his appearance, it is all the more wonder that the Clark brothers allowed John D. in as their bookkeeper, and then, as a partner in their refinery. The brothers soon found out that Rockefeller was not to be trusted. In a short space of time, they were forced out; "bought out" according to John D. Ida Tarbell's book "The History of the Standard Oil Company", which is rich with examples of Rockefeller's cast-iron ruthlessness and his inhumanity to all, except himself.

The Standard Oil Company was the most secretly run company in the history of the United States, a tradition carried on by Exxon and its affiliates today. It is said that Standard oil was bolted down and barricaded like a fortress. Rockefeller's image became so tarnished that he hired Ivy Lee, a public relations man to help him remake his image into one of a philanthropist. But in spite of his best efforts, Lee was unable to remove the legacy of hatred left by John D. The tarnished image of Standard and the Rockefellers has carried over into the 1990s and will probably be there forever. Standard Oil was to be the standard bearer for the oil industry in its conduct toward nations with oil and gas reserves beneath their soil.

The Rockefellers have always been a law unto themselves, and very early on, they decided that the only way to escape taxation was to place the bulk of their funds and assets outside of the United States. Already by 1885, Rockefeller had established markets in Europe and the Far East, which accounted for a staggering 70 percent of Standard Oil's business.

But Rockefeller's march across the continents did not go unchallenged. Public resentment of Standard reached new levels after to writers like Ida Tarbell and H.D. Lloyd exposed the fact that Standard was a company with an army of spies above local, state and federal government "who have declared war, negotiated peace, reduced courts, legislature and sovereign states to an unequaled obedience to its will."

Angry complaints poured into the Senate when the American people were told about Standard's monopoly practices which resulted in the Sherman Anti-trust Act. But so deliberately vague was the law, which left several issues unaddressed, that compliance was easily avoided by Rockefeller and his brood of lawyers. Rockefeller once described it as "an exercise in public relations with no teeth to it." Never was John D. Rockefeller's influence in the Senate more keenly felt than during the Sherman Anti-trust debates. It was a time when individual senators were subjected to great pressure by Rockefeller lobbyists.

Rockefeller suffered a temporary setback when, on May 11, 1911 Chief Justice Edward White handed down his decision in an anti-trust case brought against Standard by Frank Kellogg: Standard was to shed all of its subsidiaries within 6 months. Rockefeller responded by employing an army of writers who explained that the "special nature" of the oil trade did not lend itself to normal business methods; it had to be treated as a special entity, to be handled just as John D. Rockefeller had done.

To dilute Judge White's ruling, Rockefeller set up his own form of government. The new "government" took the form of foundations and philanthropic institutions, modeled after the patronage system of the royal courts of Europe. These institutions and foundations would shield the Rockefeller fortune from income tax, which his paid hirelings in the Senate had warned him would be coming in the years ahead.

This was the beginning of the petroleum industry's "government within government," power which is still in place today. No doubt the CFR owes its rapid rise to power to Rockefeller and Harold Pratt. In 1914, a member of the Senate called Rockefeller's empire, "the secret government of the United States." Rockefeller's strategists called for a private intelligence agency, and following their advice, Rockefeller literally bought the personnel and equipment of Reinhardt Heydrich's SS intelligence service, which today is known as "Interpol."

With intelligence likened to the best of Heydrich's SS intelligence behind them, the Rockefellers were able to infiltrate countries, virtually take over their governments, change their tax laws and foreign policies and, then pressure the U.S. government to fall in. If taxation laws became tougher, the Rockefellers would simply get the law changed. It is this bacillus in the oil industry that closed out local production that would have made America totally independent of foreign oil. The net result? Higher prices for the American consumer and obscene profits for the oil companies.

The Rockefellers were soon on the scene in the Middle East, but their efforts to gain concessions were blocked by Harry F. Sinclair. It seems that Sinclair was able to beat out the Rockefellers at every turn. Then came a dramatic reversal, the Tea Pot Dome Scandal in which Sinclair's close friend, Secretary of the Interior Albert Fall, and Fall's friend Dahoney were indicted for grabbing the Tea Pot Dome and Elk Hills Naval Oil Reserves for private gain. There were many who voiced concern that the Tea Pot Dome Scandal was set up by the Rockefellers to discredit and remove Sinclair as an unwelcome competitor.

The scandal shook Washington, and cost Fall his job, (the origin of the term "fall guy"). Sinclair was barely able to stay out of prison. All of his lucrative contracts with Persia and Russia were canceled. To this day it is widely suspected, but not proved, that the Tea Pot Dome scandal was a Rockefeller "sting" operation. Eventually, most of Sinclair's concessions in the Middle East, with the exception of those held by Britain, passed into Rockefeller hands.

Events in Iran were soon to prove the power of Rockefeller and his

British associates. In 1941, when Reza Shah Pahlavi of Iran refused to join the so-called "allies" against Germany and expel its nationals from the country, Churchill flew into a rage and thereupon ordered an invasion of Iraq, in which he was joined by his Bolshevik Russian allies. By permitting Russian troops to enter Iran, Churchill opened the door to a Russian presence in the region, one of Stalin's longed-for goals. This was a shocking betrayal of the Iranian people and the West in general, and showed that the Rockefeller influence was international.

Such is the power of the petroleum companies, especially those controlled by the Rockefellers. The representatives of Standard Oil and Royal Dutch Shell oil companies advised Churchill to arrest and expel Reza Shah, which he promptly did, sending him first to Mauritius and then to South Africa, where he died in exile. Documents I examined in the British Museum in London show extensive intervention by the Rockefellers in Middle East politics.

In the British parliament, Churchill crowed: "We (the oil companies), have just chased a dictator into exile and installed a constitutional government pledged to a whole catalog of serious-minded reforms.". What he did not say, was that the "constitutional government" was a puppet government selected by the oil companies, and its "whole catalog of reforms" was for the sole purpose of further entrenching American and British oil interests to get even bigger cuts of oil revenues.

But by 1951, the nationalistic mood sweeping the Middle East, which had begun in Egypt where Col. Gamal Abdel Nasser was bent on ousting the British from control of the country, spread to Iran as well. At this time, a genuine Iranian patriot, Dr. Mohamed Mossadegh, emerged to challenge Churchill's puppet government. Mossadegh's main thrust was to break the power of the foreign oil companies. He judged the mood of the Iranian people as ripe for such a move.

This deeply alarmed the Rockefellers, who appealed to Britain for help. Mossadegh told Rockefeller and British Petroleum that he would not abide by their concession agreements. David Rockefeller is said to have developed a personal hatred of Mossadegh. Because of this, British Petroleum appealed to the British government to "put an end to the nuisance Mossadegh was creating." Churchill, eager to comply with the demands of the Seven Sisters oil cartel (made up of the seven major British and American oil companies in the Middle East), asked the U.S. for help.

A talented, well-educated and astute politician from a wealthy background, Mossadegh's desire to help the Iranian people benefit from their national resource was genuine. In May of 1951, Dr. Mossadegh nationalized Iranian oil. An international advertising campaign was launched against Mossadegh, who was depicted as silly little man running around Teheran in his pajamas, immersed in emotion. This was far from the truth.

Led by the Rockefeller oil companies and backed by the U.S. State Department, an international boycott of Iranian oil was ordered. Iranian oil soon became unsalable. The State Department declared its support for Churchill's puppet government in Teheran, which was installed when the Shah refused to join the allies in the war against Germany.

At the same time, the CIA and MI6 launched a joint operation against Mossadegh. It was code-named "Operation Ajax".What followed was a classic example of how governments are subverted and toppled through diplomacy by deception. Churchill, who had lost the election after the war ended, was returned to power by a thoroughly brainwashed British public. He used his office to wage war against Dr. Mossadegh and the Iranian people through highwayman and pirate tactics as the following example shows:

The "Rose Marie," which sailed in international waters carrying Iranian oil, was not in breach of any international laws or treaties when it was ordered by Churchill to be intercepted by the Royal Air Force, and was forced to sail for Aden, a port under British control. The hijacking of a ship at sea had the full backing of the U.S. State Department, at the Rockefeller family suggestion.

My source in London whose job it is to monitor the oil industry, told me in 1970 that Churchill was restrained by his cabinet only with difficulty from ordering the RAF to bomb the "Rose Marie." A year passed, in which Iran suffered great financial losses. In 1953, Dr. Mossadegh wrote to President Dwight D. Eisenhower asking for help. He might as well have written to Rockefeller. Eisenhower, playing a game of nerves, did not respond.

The tactic had the desired effect of frightening Mossadegh. Finally, Eisenhower did reply, and in the classic style of diplomacy by deception, advised the Iranian leader to "abide by Iran's international obligations." Mossadegh continued to defy both the British and American governments. The oil companies sent a deputation to see Eisenhower to ask that immediate measures be taken to remove Mossadegh.

Kermit Roosevelt, who headed the CIA's covert operation against Mossadegh, worked tirelessly to establish forces inside Teheran that could be used to cause unrest. Large sums of money, said by my source to have amounted to $3 million, changed hands. In April of 1953, Shah Mohammed Reza Pahlavi, under intense pressure from the international bankers, tried to dismiss Dr. Mossadegh, but the attempt failed. The CIA and MI6-equipped army of agents, started to attack the military. Fearing assassination, the Shah fled, and Mossadegh was toppled in August 1953. The cost to American taxpayers was almost $10 million.

It is worth noting that even while Kermit Roosevelt was preparing the CIA's covert operation against Dr. Mossadegh in 1951, his Rockefeller partners were facing judicial proceedings in Washington that should have caused a halt to operations in Iran. The fact is that the all-powerful petroleum industry knew it could beat back the challenge as it had done with all others. Justice Department proceedings were launched against Exxon, Texaco, Standard Gulf, Mobil and Socal. (No effort was made to go after Shell and BP).

Standard Oil immediately commissioned Dean Acheson to blunt the inquiry. Acheson proves a good example of how Rockefeller used important people in government and the private sector to override the government of Washington. Early in 1952, Acheson went on the attack. Citing the interests of the State Department in protecting America's foreign policy initiatives, thereby tacitly admitting that the major oil companies were running State's foreign policy, Acheson demanded that the investigation be shelved in the interest of not weakening "our good relations in the Near East."

Acheson failed to mention the uproar and instability being created at that very moment in Iran by Rockefeller, the CIA and MI6. The Attorney General responded with a sharply-worded attack on the oil monopolists, warning that petroleum should be freed "from the grip of the few; free enterprise can only be preserved by safeguarding it from excess of power, both government and private." He then accused the cartel of acting in a way that endangered national security.

Rockefeller immediately ordered that damage control efforts put in place through his contacts inside the State and Justice Departments. (To this day, both are infested with CFR-Rockefeller agents.) Acheson publicly denounced the investigation as an action "by police dogs from the antitrust who want no truck with mammon and the unrighteous." His tone of voice was at all times belligerent and threatening. Acheson lined up support for Rockefeller from the Defense and Interior Departments, who vouched for the Seven Sisters in a most astounding manner:

"The companies (the major oil companies) play a vital role in supplying the free world's most essential commodity. American oil operations are for all practical purposes instruments of our foreign policy." Dean Acheson then attempted to raise the bogeyman of Soviet interference in the Middle East, which was nothing more than a red herring to distract attention away from how the oil companies operated. Eventually, all criminal charges against the cartel were dropped

To show their utter contempt for U.S. law, the representatives of the major oil companies met in London in 1924 to avoid possible conspiracy charges at the request of Sir William Fraser. The letter that Fraser wrote to the top executives of Standard, Mobil, Texaco, BP,

Socal and Shell, said that they needed to meet in order to settle accounts with a now thoroughly aroused Shah Reza Pahlavi.

The conspirators met again in London one month later, where they were joined by the CEO of the French company, Francias de Petroles. An agreement was reached to form a consortium that would control the Iranian oil. The new body was called a "consortium" as the use of the word "cartel" in America was deemed to be injudicious. Success was guaranteed, American executives told their foreign counterparts, because the State Department had given its blessing to the London meeting.

As far as the State Department was concerned, the Seven Sisters played a key role in the Middle East in fending off Communist penetration in an area of vital concern to the United States. Given the fact that in 1942, the very same oil companies backed Churchill in bringing Soviet Bolshevik troops to invade Iran, thereby giving Stalin his greatest opportunity to get a foothold in the Middle East, this was not exactly the truth.

Throughout the Justice Department proceedings, which began in October of 1951, State Department witnesses kept referring to the petroleum industry as " the so-called cartel." The State Department is densely populated with Rockefeller agents, perhaps more so than any of the other government institutions which David Rockefeller controls.

It remains my firm conviction to this day that a way has not yet been found to break the Rockefeller chains that bind the oil companies and this nation to the Council on Foreign Relations, which controls every facet of our foreign policy toward the oil nations of the world. It is a situation that we, the people, will have to confront, hopefully sooner rather than later.

In Washington, civil proceedings against the petroleum cartel fizzled out in the face of threats by the Council on Foreign Relations, which was backed by its puppet, President Eisenhower. Eisenhower said that the national security interests of the United States were being threatened by the proceedings. CFR puppet Eisenhower instructed his Attorney General Herbert Brownell Jr. to tell the court that the "anti-trust laws must be deemed secondary to the national security interests."

While Kermit Roosevelt was going at it hammer and tongs in Teheran, Eisenhower and Dulles offered the court a compromise that would, in Eisenhower's words, "protect the interests of the free world in the Near East as a major source of petroleum supplies." No wonder that the Ayatollah Khomeini decades later, would call the United States "the great Satan." Khomeini was not referring to the people of the United States, but to their government.

Khomeini knew full well that the ordinary American was the victim of a conspiracy, that they were lied to, cheated, robbed and forced to sacrifice the blood of millions of their sons in foreign wars in which they had absolutely no reason to take part. Khomeini, an avid student of history, knew all about the Federal Reserve Act which he said "kept the people in the grip of slavery." When the U.S. embassy in Teheran was seized by revolutionary guards, several compromising documents fell into Khomeini's hands which clearly showed CIA involvement with British Petroleum, Standard and the other major oil companies.

Once the coup was declared a success, the Shah returned to his palace. Little did he know that two decades later he would suffer the same fate as Mossadegh, at the hands of the petroleum industry and its surrogate governments in Washington and London: the CIA and MI6. The Shah thought he could trust David Rockefeller, but like many others, it was not long before he realized that his trust was sadly misplaced.

Having access to the documents Mossadegh had dug up, which showed the extent of the plundering of Iran's national resource, the Shah quickly became disenchanted with London and Washington. Upon hearing the news of revolts in Mexico and Venezuela against Rockefeller and Shell, and coupled with the news about Saudi Arabia's "Golden Gimmick," the Shah began to pressure Rockefeller and the British for a larger share of the Iranian oil revenues which, at that time, amounted to only 30 percent of the total amount of oil revenues enjoyed by the oil companies.

Other countries had felt the lash of the petroleum industry as well. Mexico is a classic case of petroleum companies foreign policy-making ability which transcended national boundaries and cost American consumers a huge fortune. Oil, it seemed, was the foundation of a new economic order, with undisputed power in the hands of a few people hardly known outside of the petroleum industry.

The "majors" have been referred to a number of times. This is shorthand for the major oil companies that form the most successful cartel in the history of commerce. Exxon (called Esso in Europe), Shell, BP, Gulf, Texaco, Mobil and Socol-Chevron. Together they form part of a major network of interlocking, interfacing banks, insurance companies and brokerage houses controlled by the Committee of 300, which are hardly known outside their circle.

The reality of the One World Government, or New World Order upper level government, brooks no interference from anyone, no matter who it might be -- even powerful national governments -- the rulers of nations great and small, corporations or private people. These supranational giants have expertise and accounting methods that have flummoxed the best brains in government, out of whose reach they remain. Through diplomacy by deception it seems the majors were able to induce governments to parcel out oil concessions to them, no matter who opposed it. John D. Rockefeller would very much have approved this closed shop, run for the last 68 years by Exxon and Shell.

It is evident from the vastness and the complexity of their operations, most often carried out like clockwork and often involving activities in several countries at the one time, that the petroleum industry is one of the most powerful components that make up the economic operations of the Committee of 300.

In secret, the Seven Sisters club has plotted wars and decided amongst themselves which governments must bow to their depredations. When trouble arises, such as in the case of Dr. Mossadegh, and later

President Saddam Hussein of Iraq, it is only a matter of calling upon the right airforce, navy, army, intelligence service to solve the problem and get rid of the "nuisance." It can be no more trouble than swatting a fly. The Seven Sisters became a government within a government, and nowhere is this more the case than with Rockefeller's Standard Oil (SOCO- Exxon-Chevron.)

If one would like to know American and British foreign policies for Saudi Arabia, Iran or Iraq, one need only study the policies of BP, Exxon, Gulf Oil and ARAMCO. What is our policy in Angola? It is to protect Gulf Oil properties in that country, even though it means supporting an avowed Marxist. Who would have imagined that Gulf, Exxon, Chevron and ARAMCO have more say about American foreign affairs than members of Congress? Indeed, who would imagine that, Standard Oil would one day control the foreign policy of the United States and have the State Department acting as if it were run for its own economic benefit?

Is any other group so exalted, so favored with showers of tax concessions thar run into billions of dollars per annum? I am often asked why it is that the American domestic petroleum industry, once so bustling and full of promise, went into a steep decline. The answer, in one word, is greed. For this reason, domestic production of oil had to be curtailed, in case the public should ever discover what was going on. This knowledge is much more difficult to obtainwhen dealing with foreign operations. What does the American public know about what goes on in the oil politics of Saudi Arabia? Even while making record profits, the petroleum industry demands and gets additional tax breaks, both open -- and hidden -- from public view.

Have the citizens of the United States benefited from the huge profits made by Exxon, Texaco, Chevron and Mobil (before it was sold?) The answer is no, because most of the profit was made "up-stream," that is, outside of the United States, which is where the profits were kept, while the U.S. consumer paid ever-rising prices for gas at the pumps.

Rockefeller's main area of concern became Saudi Arabia. The oil companies, by various stratagems, had entrenched themselves with

King Ibn Saud. The king, worried that Israel would one day threaten his country and strengthen the Israeli lobby in Washington, needed something that would give him an edge. The State Department, at the urging of the Rockefellers, said it could only follow a pro-Saudi policy without upsetting Israel by using Exxon (ARAMCO) as a front. This information was given to the Senate Foreign Relations Committee. It was so sensitive that committee staffers were not even allowed to see it.

Rockefeller had in fact paid only a small fee, $500,000, to secure a major oil concession from Ibn Saud. After considerable diplomacy, a deception was worked out, a deception which cost American taxpayers at least $50 million in its first year. What came out of the discussions between Exxon and Ibn Saud is known as "the Golden Gimmick" in the inner sanctums of Rockefeller board rooms. The American oil companies agreed to pay a subsidy to the Saudi ruler of not less that $50 million a year, based on the amount of Saudi oil pumped. The State Department would then allow the American companies to declare such subsidy payment as "foreign income tax," which Rockefeller, for example, could deduct from Exxon's U.S. taxes.

With production of cheap Saudi oil soaring, so did the subsidy payments soar. This is one of the greatest scams perpetrated upon the American public. The bottom line of the plan was that huge foreign aid payments were made annually to the Saudis under the guise of "subsidies." When the Israeli government uncovered the scheme, it too, demanded "subsidies" which today amount to $13 billion per annum -- all at the expense of American taxpayers.

Since the American consumer actually helps pay for cheaper imported crude oil than domestic crude oil, shouldn't we benefit from this arrangement through cheaper gasoline prices at the pumps? After all, Saudi oil was so cheap, and in view of the production subsidies, wouldn't this translate into lower gasoline prices at the pumps? Does the American consumer derive the slightest benefit from footing this huge bill? No way. Apart from geopolitical considerations, "the majors" are also guilty of price fixing. The cheap Arab oil for instance, was fixed at the higher domestic crude oil price when imported into the United States by a subterfuge known as "phantom freight rates."

According to hard evidence presented to the Multi-national Hearings in 1975, the major oil companies, led by Rockefeller companies, made 70 percent of their profits abroad, profits which could not be taxed at the time. With the bulk of their profits coming from "up stream," the petroleum industry was not about to make a major investment in the domestic oil industry. As a consequence, the domestic oil industry began to decline. Why spend money on the exploration and exploitation of domestic oil when it was theirs for the asking in Saudi Arabia -- at a cheaper price than the local product and at a far bigger profit?

The unsuspecting American consumer was and is being shafted, without knowing it. According to secret economic data, which a contact of mine who is still in the economic intelligence monitoring business showed me, gas at the pumps in America, given all local, state and federal taxes piled on the price, should not have cost the consumer more than 35 cents per gallon by the end of 1991. Yet, we know that prices at the pumps were three to five times greater without any justification for such excessively high prices.

The immorality of this gross deception is that had the big oil companies, and again I must emphasize the leadership of the Rockefellers in this, not been so greedy, they could have produced domestic oil which would have made our gasoline prices the cheapest in the world. In my opinion, the manner in which this diplomatic deception was set up between the State Department and Saudi Arabia, makes the State Department a partner to a criminal enterprise. For, in order not to have a falling-out with Israel and at the same time keep the Saudis happy, the American consumer was loaded with a huge tax burden, from which this country derived absolutely no benefit. Isn't that tantamount to the involuntary servitude forbidden by the U.S. Constitution?

The rulers of Saudi Arabia then demanded that fixed prices be posted by the oil companies (ARAMCO), meaning that the country would not suffer a decline in income if prices for oil dropped. When they heard of the arrangement, Iran and Iraq demanded and received the same fixed pricing agreement. The bottom line here is that the oil companies led by the Rockefeller companies, paid taxes on an artificially higher price, not the real market price, which was offset by the lower taxes they paid in the United States -- a major benefit not enjoyed by any other industry in America.

This made it possible for Exxon and Mobil (and all the ARAMCO companies) to pay an average tax rate of 5 percent, notwithstanding the huge profits they were making. Not only were the oil companies gouging the American consumer, and still are, but they are also making and carrying out U.S. foreign policy to the extreme detriment of the American people. These arrangements and actions place the petroleum industry above the law, giving it a position from where the companies can, and do, dictate foreign policy to the elected government, free of any control by our representatives in Washington.

The policies of the petroleum companies cost the American taxpayer billions of dollars in additional taxation and billions of dollars in excess profits at the pumps. The petroleum industry, and, in particular, Exxon, has no fear of the U.S. government. Thanks to the control exercised by the permanent upper-level parallel secret government of the Council on Foreign Relations (CFR), Rockefeller is untouchable. That enabled ARAMCO to sell oil to the French Navy at $0.95 per barrel, while at the same time the U.S. Navy was charged $1.23 per barrel.

One of the few in the Senate who dared tackle the awesome power of the Rockefellers was Sen. Brewster. He disclosed some of the "slippery conduct" of the petroleum industry during hearings in 1948, accusing the industry of bad faith "with an avaricious desire for enormous profits while at the same time constantly seeking the cloak of United States protection and assistance to preserve their vast concessions,". The Rockefellers drafted a memo signed by the bigger U.S. oil companies, the gist of which was that they did not owe "any special obligation to the United States." Rockefeller's blatant internationalism was finally flaunted for all to see.

As an example of the foregoing, M.J. Eaton in an article published by "The Oil Industry" stated: "The oil industry is at present confronted with the question of government control." When the U.S. government invited the American Petroleum Institute to name three members to a committee it had set up to consider conservation legislation, API's president E.W. Clarke said:

"We cannot undertake to pass upon, still less accede to, any suggestion that the Federal government may directly regulate the production of crude oil in several states."

The API argued that the Federal government did not have authority to control oil companies under Article 1 of the U.S. Constitution. On May 27, 1927, the API said the government could not tell the industry what to do -- even where the common defense and the general welfare of the nation was concerned.

One of the best and most far-reaching exposes of the petroleum industry is a 400-page report entitled "The International Petroleum Cartel." This great report has disappeared from view, and it is my understanding that Rockefeller and the CFR bought up every available copy shortly after it was published, and prevented any more copies of the report from being printed.

Inspired by the late Sen. John Sparkman and put together by Professor M. Blair, the history of the petroleum cartel was traced back to a conspiracy that took place at Achnacarry Castle, a remote fishing preserve in Scotland. Sparkman pulled no punches in a slashing attack on Rockefeller's oil empire. Professor Blair meticulously built up a case which proved that the major oil companies had entered into a conspiracy to achieve the following goals:

1) To control all oil production in foreign countries in so far as production, sale and distribution of oil was concerned.

2) To strictly control all technology and patents related to oil production and refining.

3) To share pipelines and tankers between the Seven Sisters.

4) To share world markets among themselves only.

5) To act jointly to maintain artificially high prices for oil and gasoline.

Professor Blair charged that particularly ARAMCO had been guilty of keeping oil prices at a high level when it was getting Saudi oil at incredibly low prices. In response to Sparkman's charges, the Justice Department began its own investigation in 1951, which was dealt with earlier herein.

Nothing has changed. The Gulf War is a good example of "business as usual." The occupation of Somalia also has oil overtones. Thanks to our newest spy satellite, the La Crosse Imager which can relay images of what lies underground, very substantial oil and gas reserves were detected in Somalia about 3 years ago. The find was kept absolutely secret. This led to the U.S. mission ostensibly to feed starving Somali children shown on television night after night for 3 months.

A "starving children" rescue mission was staged by the Bush administration as a means of providing protection for Aramco, Phillips, Conoco, Cohoco and British Petroleum drilling operations coming under threat from Somali leaders who were becoming aware that they were about to be plundered. The American operation had little to do with feeding starving children. Why didn't the U.S. mount a similar "rescue" mission in Ethiopia, where starvation is a real problem? Obviously, the answer is that Ethiopia does not have any known oil reserves. However, securing the port of Berbera is the chief goal of U.S. forces. There is great discord in Russia over oil. The Kurds will have to suffer again and again over Mosul oil. Rockefeller and BP are still the greedy oil grabbers they always were.

# Israel In Focus.
# V.

Perhaps more than any other country in the Middle East, with the exception of what is now called Saudi Arabia, diplomacy by deception was seen at its height during the formative years of the State of Israel. As I have done throughout this book, I have made every effort to be absolutely objective in dealing with the background to the formation of Israel, given the propensity of the majority to regard almost anything said about the country as "anti-semitic."

This account of how the State of Israel came into being does not take religious matters into consideration, but is based purely and simply on political, geographical, geopolitical and economic factors. It is difficult to arrive at a starting point when dealing with the history of any country, but after almost fifteen years of research, I have pinned down Oct. 31, 1914 as the beginning of events that led to the founding of Israel.

The history of one country cannot be separated from that of its neighbors, and this applies especially when it comes to an historical account of Israel. Lord Horatio Kitchener, fresh from his success in putting an end to the sovereign independent Boer Republics in South Africa, was turned loose on the Middle East by the Committee of 300 acting through the British Foreign Office.

The British government had been scheming and plotting against the Turkish Ottoman Empire since 1899, and by 1914, was ready to make its final move to bring down the 400-year old dynasty. The Committee of 300 plan was to involve Arabs through false promises, and use Arabian forces to do Britain's dirty work, as we saw in the chapter which showed how Col. Thomas Lawrence was used for this purpose.

The first step in this direction was a meeting between Hussein, the grand Sherif of Mecca, bastion of the Hashemites, and Lord Kitchener. Hussein was offered a guarantee of independence for his assistance against the Turks. Full negotiations began in July of 1915. At these meetings, the British government repeatedly assured Sherif Hussein that Jewish immigration to Palestine would never be allowed, which, as I detailed in earlier chapters, was the only thing that would guarantee Hussein's participation.

Even before the negotiations for complete independence for Mecca got under way, emissaries of the British government met secretly with members of the Abdul Aziz and Wahabi families to discuss British cooperation in helping these two families subjugate the city-states of Arabia.

The strategy was to get Hussein and his military forces to help drive the Turks out of Egypt, Palestine, Jordan and Arabia by promising Hussein and the leaders of Arabia's city-states that Jewish immigration into Palestine would not be permitted. The second part of the strategy called for the Abdul Aziz and Wahabi forces (armed, trained and financed by Britain) to bring all independent city-states in Arabia under their control while the city-state's leaders alongside Hussein were busy fighting Britain's war against the Turks.

The overall plan, proposed by Lord Kitchener, was discussed by the British government on July 24, 1914. But it was not until Oct. 24, 1914 that the British government gave its answer. The Arab territories, with certain exceptions in Syria, "in which Great Britain is free to act without detriment to her ally, France," would be respected. On Jan. 30, 1916, Britain accepted Hussein's proposals, which, in essence were that in return for his help, Hussein would be declared king of Hijaz and would rule the Arab people.

On June 27, 1916, Hussein proclaimed the establishment of the Arab State, and was proclaimed king of the Hijaz on October 29. On Nov. 6, 1916, Britain, France and Russia recognized Hussein as the head of Arab peoples and the king of Hijaz. Were the Abdul Aziz and Wahabi families disturbed by the contradiction in the terms of their agreement with Great Britain? Apparently not, for the simple reason that they were informed in advance of these developments, and knew that they were no more than a needed deception to be played out on Hussein.

100

The years 1915 and 1917 saw the British government meeting with leaders of the World Zionist Congress to determine how best to implement its long-planned Jewish immigration into Palestine. An agreement was reached to send MI6 agents to Arabia to help train the Abdul Aziz and Wahabi armies.

Britain, France and Russia held a secret meeting on April 26, 1916, agreeing that Palestine would be placed under international administration. None of the Arabs were informed, although British Foreign Office documents infer that leaders of the World Zionist Congress were notified in advance of the meeting and advised on its purpose.

Previously, in March of 1915, France and Britain had also promised Constantinople to the Russians. In return, Russia agreed that it would recognize the independence of Arab states. Britain would control Haifa. France would get Syria. Russia would get Armenia and Kurdistan (oil was not yet a factor). What is amazing, is that not once were the inhabitants of these lands ever informed. How the governments could trade in lands that did not belong to them speaks to the tremendous power exercised by secret societies under the control of the Committee of 300.

This perpetual agreement, known as the Sykes-Picot Agreement, was concluded between Britain and France on May 9, 1916. All zones of influence in the Middle East were specifically spelled out, even where Arab states were ostensibly recognized as "independent." The means of control here was through secret societies particularly through a planned Freemason Lodge in Salonika.

Unaware of what had been arranged, M16 operative Col. Lawrence ("Lawrence of Arabia") led the Arab forces of Sherif Hussein to one spectacular victory after another, eventually capturing the key Hijaz rail line, driving the Turks into full retreat. The key element in persuading the Arabs to attack the Turks (both were Islamic nations) was the British statement that the Ottoman empire had befriended the Jews expelled from Spain by Ferdinand and Isabella in 1492, and had made Constantinople a haven for Jews. This, the British negotiators (MI6 agents) told Hussein, guaranteed that the rulers in Constantinople would look with favor upon Jewish immigration to Palestine, which was under Turkish control.

Affectionately known as "Orrenz" by his Arab soldiers, looked up to and idolized, it was impossible for Col. Lawrence to accept the gross betrayal of Hussein and his army. When it became apparent that Jews were being allowed into Palestine in large numbers, Lawrence was subsequently murdered to stop him from disclosing the machinations of the British government. British War Office records show that Lawrence received personal guarantees from Gen. Edmund Allenby, commander of British forces in the Middle East, that Jewish immigration to Palestine would not be allowed under any circumstances.

Let us return now to the Balfour Declaration, a remarkable document in the sense that it was neither drafted nor signed by British Prime Minister Arthur Balfour, but by Lord Rothschild, as head of the British branch of the World Zionist Federation. Britain promised land in Palestine to Jews that really belonged to the Arabs, in breach of the pledge to Sherif Hussein and solemn promises made to Col. Lawrence by Gen. Allenby.

What is more striking is that although Lord Rothschild was not a member of the British government, his proposals for Palestine were accepted by the League of Nations on April 25, 1920 as an official British government document. The League of Nations accepted the Balfour Declaration and gave a mandate to Britain to administer Palestine and Transjordan. The only alteration made was that a Jewish national home would not be established in Transjordan, which, in any case, the Zionists did not want.

Once the Turks were defeated by Arab forces under Lawrence's command, and later the Arabs under Hussein, were defeated by the British-trained and equipped Abdul Aziz armies, the way was clear for Jewish immigration to Palestine to begin in earnest. Arrangements were confirmed at a conference of allied prime ministers held at San Remo, Italy on April 18, 1920. No Arab delegates were invited. In May of 1921, serious anti-Jewish rioting broke out in Palestine over the sudden influx of Jewish immigrants and the large number of Jewish settlements springing up.

Sir Herbert Samuel, British high commissioner for Palestine, attempted to appoint a legislative council, but the Arabs would have no part of it. Unrest continued from 1921, and a dispute at the Wailing Wall in 1929 erupted and rapidly escalated into large scale attacks on Jews, 50 of whom were killed.

A British government report issued in March of 1931 cited the cause of the rioting as "Arab hatred of Jews, and the disappointment of the Arab hopes for independence." The British government then issued a decree restricting Jewish immigration, which led to a Jewish strike that caused wide disruption in Palestine.

British foreign office documents indicate that in June of 1931, "complaints were filed with the League of Nations Commission on Mandates, which blamed the problems on an inadequate security force." Although the papers did not indicate who originated the complaints, notations in the margins of these papers point to Lord Rothschild.

As a result of League of Nations pressure, the British government appointed Sir John Hope-Simpson to track and report on the unrest in Palestine. His report, known as The Passfield White Paper was presented to Parliament in 1930. The White Paper stressed the plight of the landless Arabs and their increasing desire to own land. It strongly advocated that Jews be forbidden to acquire more land if any Arabs were landless, and that Jewish immigration be stopped for as long as any Arabs were unemployed.

The confidence of the Jews badly shaken, the World Zionist Congress went on the offensive and forced a debate in Parliament on the Passfield paper. The "London Times" in Nov. of 1930 said debates in Parliament were "heated and acrimonious." After two years of intense pressure on the British government, the Zionist World Federation was able to obtain a relaxation of restrictions on the number of Jews allowed into Palestine.

In 1933, Sir Arthur Wauchope, British high commissioner, rejected

Arab demands that the sale of Arab land to Jews be declared illegal, and that Jewish immigration be halted. By now, talk of war in Europe was in the air, alongside daily reports of Jews being persecuted in Germany. This worked against the Arabs. The Zionists organized large-scale protests and riots against restricted immigration, and newspapers in London reported unfavorably on their activities. This, however, did little to further the Palestinian people's cause.

It became clear in 1935, why Britain had demanded control of Haifa with the opening of the Mosul-Haifa oil pipeline. In April of 1936, the Arab High Committee united Arab opposition to the Jews in Palestine, and near civil war erupted. The British government responded with more troops and appointed a commission to investigate the causes of the unrest. The Arabs boycotted the commission, "because the British already know what the problem is but hide behind commissions and do nothing to stop the causes."

The Peel Commission took evidence in Palestine in 1936, and just before leaving for London in January 1937, heard from an Arab delegation which had previously boycotted commission meetings. On July 8, 1937, the Peel Commission Report was made public. It dealt a devastating blow to Jewish aspirations, flatly stating that Jews and Arabs could not live together, and recommended that Palestine be split into three states:

(a) A Jewish state to occupy about one third of the land. In it, would reside 200,000 Arabs, with the land being held by Arabs.

(b) A British mandated territory comprising a strip of land from Jaffa along the railway to Jerusalem. It would include Bethlehem and Jerusalem.

(c)The remainder of the land to be an Arab state united with Trans Jordan.

The Peel Commission report was adopted by the World Zionist Federation, but it was denounced by the Arab world and several European countries, especially France. The Peel Commission recommendations were adopted by the League of Nations on August 23, 1937.

The assassination of High Commissioner Yelland Andrew on August 2, 1937 was attributed to the Zionists, which the Palestinians and Arabs said was arranged to engender hatred among the British people for the Arabs. By 1937, pitched battles between Jews and Arabs took on the semblance of all-out war.

This led to a postponement of the Peel Commission recommendations and the appointment of a new commission under Sir John Woodhead. It is important to know that the diplomacy by deception tactics of the British government were leading up to one objective, the total abandonment of the Arab cause in Palestine. Secret MI6 documents of the period were not disclosed even to the British parliament. They suggested that the "Palestinian problem" was impossible to solve, and gave suggestions for dissembling to prevent further Arab unrest. When the Arab leaders spoke of the problem as being a "Zionist problem", Lord Rothschild issued orders to the British press that the problem was always to be expressed as a "Palestinian problem."

A horrible massacre of 20 Jews occurred at Tiberias and Arab forces took Bethlehem and the old city of Jerusalem; the two cities only being recaptured by British troops with considerable difficulty. British foreign office documents, while not clearly expressing an opinion, nevertheless seemed to indicate that attacks on the cities and towns, and the murder of Jews was the work of agent-provocateurs who did not wish to see any agreement reached that would accommodate further Jewish immigration.

The Woodhead Commission report, expressing the view that partitioning Palestine was not a practical solution, was released in Nov. 1938. It called for an immediate conference of Arabs and Jews. Talks commenced in London in February 1939, but a stalemate arose that was not resolved and the meeting broke up one month later without any results being achieved.

Then, on May 17, 1939, the British government announced a new plan which provided for an independent Palestine state by 1949. It would have a treaty relationship with Great Britain; Arabs and Jews were to share in the government "in such a way as to ensure that the essential interests of each community are safeguarded," the report said.

The plan was for Jewish immigration to be halted for five years unless the Arabs agreed to let it continue, but, in any case, by 1949, 75,000 Jews were to be allowed enter the country. The aim of the British government was to arrange matters in such a way that Jews would make up about one-third of the population. The transfer of Arab land to Jews was to be prohibited.

The plan was approved by the British Parliament, but violently denounced by the World Zionist Congress and American Jewish leaders. The Palestinians also rejected the plan, and fighting between Jews and Arabs erupted across the land. But Palestine took a back seat a few months later when Britain declared war on Germany and was promptly backed by the World Zionist Congress.

Once Britain declared war on Germany, a flood of Jewish refugees from Europe went to Palestine, and in May of 1942, a conference of American Zionists adopted the Biltmore Program, which repudiated the modified Woodhead plan which called for an independent Palestine, demanding in its place a Jewish state, with a Jewish army, and a distinctly Jewish identity.

Three years later, the World Zionist Congress demanded that one million Jews be admitted to Palestine as refugees from war-torn Europe. Egypt and Syria warned President Truman in October of 1945 that war would follow attempts to create a Jewish state in Palestine. By July 1946, Zionist pressure was at a fever pitch, culminating in a bombing of the King David Hotel in Jerusalem that took 91 lives. The United Nations report stated that the bombing was the work of Irgun terrorists. The Arabs accused the United States and Britain of arming and training both the Irgun and Haganah as the forerunner to establishing an Israeli army.

The British abandoned Palestine in February of 1947 and handed it

106

over to United Nations, which was their way of admitting that they had betrayed Lawrence and the Arabs, and finally reneging on their responsibilities toward Palestine. In so doing, they abandoned their own agreement to hold the line until 1949. The U. N. General Assembly voted to partition Palestine on November 29, 1946. There was to be a Jewish and an Arab state, with Jerusalem under U.N. trusteeship. The vote was approved by the World Zionist Congress but rejected by the Arab states and Palestine.

The Arab League Council announced in December of 1947 that it would stop the partition of the country by force, and began attacking Jewish communities all across Palestine. 1948 saw the open rise to power of the MI6-trained and American armed Irgun and Haganah counterforce. Terror reigned and hundreds of thousands of Arabs left their lands. In the final act of betrayal and the abdication of its responsibilities toward the Arabs, the last of the 30,000 British troops were withdrawn.

In defiance of U.N. resolutions, on May 14, 1948, Zionist leader David Ben Gurion announced a provisional Jewish government for the State of Israel. The United Nations, unwilling or unable to stop Ben Gurion, let the declaration stand. On May 16, the United States and Russia both recognized the newly formed Ben Gurion government, brushing aside cries of betrayal emanating from Palestinians, all the Arab nations and at least eight European governments.

Later in the same month, the Arab League declared war against the newly created state of Israel. The Israeli forces, illegally equipped and armed not by the British, but by U.S. military supplies from stockpiles for American forces in Europe, gained the upper hand. Count Folke Bernadotte, a U.N. mediator was assassinated by Irgun terrorists on Sept. 17 while trying to bring about a truce. This eventually led to a U.N. brokered armistice and a temporary halt to hostilities. Bernadotte was accused of favoring the Arab cause, although the record shows he tried to be neutral.

Israel joined the United Nations in May of 1949, and was recognized by the U.S., Britain, the USSR and France. Arab countries protested to the United Nations and blamed Britain, France and the U.S. for helping Israel open a pipeline from the Sea of Galilee to the Negev Desert, which made possible extensive irrigation for Jewish settlements and agriculture at the cost of unilateral tapping into the waters of the River Jordan at the expense of the Arab population. The Arabs were not consulted about this extensive project "to make the desert bloom" and considered it a breach of a May, 1939 agreement that called for administering the country "in such a way as to ensure that the interests of each community are safeguarded."

On May 9, 1956, Secretary of State John Foster Dulles, a member of one of the top 13 families of the American Illuminati, went before Congress to practice his own diplomacy by deception, explaining that the U.S. would not supply Israel with arms because we wanted to avoid a U.S.-USSR war by proxy. The fact that Israel was already fully armed and equipped by the U.S. was not brought out. What the Dulles declaration accomplished provided a reason for the USSR to halt arms supplies to the Arab nations on the basis of the U.S. position of "neutrality." At that point, there was a glaring imbalance of arms in favor of Israel.

Another point worth noting in the game of deception was that in spite of its alleged friendship with the Arab countries, in response to a U.S. initiative in 1956, the Soviet Union signed a secret deal which called for stepping up oil supplies to Israel, fearing that an Arab oil embargo might hurt Israel's defense capabilities.

Dulles, in another change of face, told members of Congress to get around restrictions by offering aid to any Middle Eastern nation desiring it. On March 9, 1957, a joint congressional resolution empowered the president to use up to $200 million for economic and military assistance to any Middle Eastern nation desiring it. According to the Eisenhower Doctrine, this was supposed to "assure vital U.S. interest in the integrity and independence of all Middle East countries."

President Eisenhower embarked on what was billed as "a goodwill tour" in December of 1959, which took in several Arab countries, including Tunisia and Morocco. Both of these Arab countries later tried to tone down Arab resistance to Israel, efforts which, however, were only partially successful, as was Eisenhower's tour. Syria in particular condemned the tour as "an attempt to disguise the outright support of Israel by the United States."

During the next 10 years, the arms build-up of both the Arabs and the Israelis continued to grow until war broke out again. Israeli forces took Jerusalem and refused to return the city to U.N. control in spite of several Security Council resolutions calling upon the government of Israel to comply. In a transparent move on June 10, 1967, the Soviet Union announced it was breaking off diplomatic relations with Israel although it did not cancel a 1956 agreement made which stepped up oil supplies to Israel. As the two main French newspapers pointed out, had the USSR been genuine in its opposition to Israel, it could have vetoed Israel's membership in the United Nations, but it did not.

By breaking off diplomatic relations with Israel, the Soviets opened the way for the U.S. to supply Israel with 50 F-4 Phantom jet fighters. This so angered President Charles De Gaulle, that he signed a decree forbidding any further financial or military assistance to Israel by France. The decree was rigidly enforced for about two years.

The U.N. Security Council met on July 3, 1969 and censured in the strongest terms Israel's continued occupation of Jerusalem and deplored Israel's failure to respect previous resolutions which demanded that Israel withdraw from the city. According to a former general assembly member from Pakistan, "the Israeli delegation was not at all perturbed, having met earlier that day with the U.S. ambassador to the United Nations, who gave the Israeli delegates absolute assurances that the resolution 'has no teeth,'" and that "any active attempt to punish Israel will be blocked by the United States and the Security Council." But when the Security Council met, the United States joined in the condemnation of Israel. Of such stuff is diplomacy by deception made.

In closing this chapter, it seems fitting to give a summary of the diplomatic treachery of Britain toward its Arab ally, Sherif Hussein of Mecca:

In August, 1920, Ibn Saud ben Abdul Aziz conquered and annexed Asir.

On Nov. 2, 1921, Ibn Saud captured Hali, ending the ancient dynasty of the Rashids.

In July, 1922, Ibn Saud overran Jauf and ended the ancient Shalan dynasty.

On Aug. 24, 1924, the Wahabis and Ibn Saud attacked Taif, in the Hijaz, and overran it on Sept. 5.

On Oct. 13 1924, Ibn Saud took Mecca. Sherif Hussein and his son, Ali, were forced to flee. This is how Saudi Arabia usurped the holy city, an act which remains, to this day, deeply resented by millions of Moslems in Iran, Iraq and elsewhere. Without British help, Ibn Saud would not have been able to subdue Mecca. The British oligarchical structure had long expressed hatred of the prophet Muhammad, and no doubt took great satisfaction in the Saudi victory.

Between January and June of 1925, the Wahabis laid siege to the city-state of Jiddah.

On Dec. 5, 1925, Medina surrendered to Ibn Saud, and on Dec. 19, Sherif Ali, son of Hussein, was forced to abdicate.

On Jan. 8, 1926, Ibn Saud was proclaimed King of the Hijaz and Sultan of Nejd.

On May 20, 1927, the Abdul Aziz and Wahabi families, represented by Ibn Saud, signed a treaty with Great Britain, which recognized the complete independence of all territories held by the two families, and allowed them to become known as Saudi Arabia.

Without the help of the Arab nation-states under Hussein, and without the conquest of Arabian city-states by the Wahabi and Abdul Aziz families, the Turks would not have been driven out of Egypt and Palestine, and Jewish immigration into that country would have been strictly curtailed or possibly halted altogether. As President Hafez el Assad of Syria said in 1973, "the British planted a Zionist dagger in the heart of the Arab nations."

It is said by friends of the late Col. Lawrence that his ghost walks the corridors of Whitehall, unable to find peace because of the manner in which diplomacy by deception succeeded in undercutting his firm promise to the Arab armies of Sherif Hussein, and because of his culpability in accepting Allenby's and Whitehall's false promises that Jewish immigration to Palestine would not be permitted.

# Tavistock and "Operation Research": Undeclared War. VI.

The founder for the Tavistock Institute for Human Relations, John Rawlings Reese, was to perfect a system that would subvert and then control the thinking of human beings so that they could be channeled in any direction so desired by the Committee of 300, also known as the Olympians. It must be said that to do this, one must introduce an automated mentality into the bulk of the targeted population. This is an objective with very far-reaching implications nationally and internationally.

The end result of Reese's objectives were and remain, control of all human life; its destruction when deemed desirable, whether it be through mass genocide or mass slavery. We are witnessing both today. One is the Global 2000 genocidal plan, which calls for the deaths of more of 500 million people by the year 2010; the other is slavery by an economic means. Both systems are fully operational and working side-by-side in today's America.

Reese began his Tavistock experiments in 1921; it soon became clear to him that his system could be applied both domestically and militarily. Reese said that the solution to the problems he foresaw needed a ruthless approach, without concern for religious or moral values. He later added another area to his list: that of nationalism.

Reese is known to have studied the work of the Nine Unkown Men, as referred to in 1860 by the French writer Jacolliot. Among Jacolliot's remarks were that the Nine Unknown Men knew about the liberation of energy, sterilzation by radiation, propaganda and psychological warfare, all of which were absolutely unheard of in that century. Jacolliot said that the technique of psychological warfare was "the most dangerous of all sciences, in moulding mass opinion, because it would enable anyone to govern the whole world." This statement was made in the year 1860.

When it became obvious that British politicians were bent on solving the country's economic problems by means of another war, Reese was given 80,000 British Army recruits to use as guinea pigs. Operation Research was the name given to his project, and basically, it was designed to develop a methodology (logistics) in military management that would make the best use of limited military resources sea, air and land defense systems against Britain's foreign enemies.

Thus, the original program was a military-management one, but by 1946, Reese had developed Operation Research to the point that it could be applied as a civilian management program. Reese had "arrived," insofar as social engineering was concerned, but his work is concealed in top secret files at Tavistock. Technically, the Reese Tavistock manual, of which I have a copy, is a full declaration of war against the civilian population of any targeted country. Reese said that it had to be understood that "whenever any government, groups, persons in positions of power" use his methods without the consent of the people, it is understood by these governments or groups of people that conquest is the motive, and that domestic warfare exists between them and the public.

Reese discovered that with social engineering comes the greater need for information that can be rapidly collected and correlated. One of the earlier statements attributed to Reese was the necessity to stay ahead of society and predict its moves by engineering situations. A big breakthrough for Reese and his social tinkerers came with the discovery of linear programming by George B. Danzig in 1947. This came at a time when Reese was engaged in a war with the American nation, a war which is still ongoing, and which was greatly facilitated by the invention of the transistor by Bardeen, Brittain and Shockley in 1948.

Enter the Rockefellers, who gave a huge grant to Tavistock to enable Reese to press ahead with a study of the American economy, using Operation Research methods. Simultaneously, the Rockefeller Foundation gave Harvard University a four-year grant to create its own American economy model. The year was 1949, and Harvard pressed ahead with its own economic model, based on Tavistock's.

The only stipulation Reese made as a condition of his cooperation with Harvard, was that Tavistock methods be followed throughout. These were based upon the Prudential Assurance Bombing Survey Study, which led to saturation bombing of German worker housing as a means of bringing about the capitulation of the German war machine. These methods were now ready to be applied in a civilian context.

Reese made a detailed study of America's entry into WWI, which he deemed to be the beginning of the 20th century. Reese realized that for America to be seduced away from so-called "isolationism," American thinking would have to be drastically changed. Woodrow Wilson had dragged America into European affairs in 1916 with corruption and corrupting policies. Wilson sent American forces to fight on Europe's battlefields, in spite of the warnings issued by the Founding Fathers, to stay out of foreign entanglements. The Committee of 300, was determined to keep the United States entangled in European and indeed world affairs forever after.

Wilson did not change Europe, but Europe changed America. The banishing of power politics, which is what Wilson thought he could do, was not possible, because power is politics and politics is economic power. This has been so since the earliest recorded history of politics: those of the city-states of the Sumer and Akkad of 5,000 years ago, right down to Hitler and the USSR. Economics is only an extension of a natural energy system, but that system, the elitists have always said, belongs under their control.

In order for an economy to be under the control of elite body, it has to be an economy that is predictable and totally manipulatable. This is what the Harvard model set out to accomplish, backed by the social dynamics of the Reese Operation Research. Reese had discovered that to achieve total predictability in population groups, the elements of society had to be brought under control under a yoke of slavery, and dispossessed of the means of discovering their predicament, so that not knowing how to unite or a joint defense, they would not know where to turn to for help.

That Tavistock methodology is at work can be found everywhere in the United States. People, not knowing where to turn to understand the predicament they find themselves in, turn to the worst place of all for supposed help: the government. The Harvard Economic Research Project, which began in 1948, embodied all the Reese principles, which, in turn, came out of the Prudential Bombing Survey and Operations Research. By joining forces, the elite felt that a means of controlling a nation's economy and the population was now available with the coming of the computer age -- both a blessing and a terrible curse for mankind.

All science is only a means to an end, and man is knowledge (information), which ends in control. Who the beneficiaries of that control are was decided by the Committee of 300 and its antecedents 300 years ago. The war waged against the American people by Tavistock is now 47 years old and shows no signs of letting up. As energy is the key to all life on this planet, through diplomacy by deception and outright strong-arm methods, the Committee has gained control of most energy resources.

The Committee, by deception and dissembling, has also gained control of social energy, which is expressed in economic terms. Provided that the ordinary citizen could be kept ignorant of the real economic methods of bookkeeping, then the citizens would be doomed to lead a life of economic slavery. This is what has happened. We, the people, gave our consent to the economic controllers of our lives and became slaves of the elite. As Reese once said, people who will not use their intelligence have no better rights than dumb animals who have no intelligence at all. Economic slavery is essential if good order is to be maintained, and the ruling class may enjoy the fruits produced by slave labor.

Reese and his team of social scientists and social engineers went to work on the American public by learning first, then understanding, and then attacking, the social energy (economics) and the mental and

116

physical weaknesses of the nation. Earlier, I said that the computer is both a blessing and a curse for mankind. On the positive side, there are many emerging economists who, through the use of computers, are starting to wake up to the fact that the Harvard model is a blueprint for economic slavery.

If this new breed of economic programmers can get its message out to the American people fast enough, the New World Order (of slavery) can still be stopped. This is where diplomacy by deception plays such a vast role in subverting through the media, education and influencing the way we think by distracting us with issues of absolutely no importance, while the truly important issues are glossed over. In a major policy study meeting ordered by the Committee of 300 in 1954, it was made clear to economic experts, high-ranking government officials, bankers, and leaders of commerce and industry, that the war against the American people was to be stepped up.

Robert McNamara was one of those who said that, because peace and good order was being threatened by an out-of-control population, the wealth of the nation had to be moved away from the undisciplined masses and into the control of the self-disciplined few. McNamara savagely attacked overpopulation, which he said threatened to change the world in which we live and make it ungovernable:

"We can begin with the most critical problems of population growth. As I have pointed out elsewhere, short of nuclear war itself, it is the gravest issue that the world faces in the decades ahead. If current trends continue, the world as a whole will not reach replacement level fertility-in effect, an average of two children per family-until about the year 2020. That means that the world's population would finally stabilize at about 10 billion, compared with today's 4.3 billion.

"We call it stabilized, but what kind of stability would be possible? Can we assume that the levels of poverty, hunger, stress, crowding and frustration that such a situation could cause in the developing nations -- which by then would contain 9 out of 10 human beings on earth -- would be likely to assure social stability? Or, for that matter, military stability?

117

"It is not a world that any of us would want to live in. Is such a world inevitable? It is not, but there are only two possible ways in which a world of 10 billion people can be averted. Either the current birthrate must come down more quickly, or the current death rates must go up. There is no other way.

"There are, of course, many ways in which the death rates can go up. In a thermonuclear age, war can accomplish it very quickly and decisively. Famine and disease are nature's ancient checks on population growth, and neither one has disappeared from the scene."

In 1979 McNamara repeated his message to the leading bankers from around the world, and Thomas Enders, a high-ranking State Department official, made the following statement:

"There is a single theme behind all of our work. We must reduce population growth. Either they do it our way, through nice, clean methods, or they will get the kind of a mess that we have in El Salvador, or Iran, or Beirut. Once population growth is out of control, it requires authoritarian government, even fascism, to reduce it. Civil war can help things, but it would have to be greatly expanded. To reduce population quickly, you have to pull all males into the fighting and kill significant numbers of fertile, child-bearing-age females."

The solution to the problem of a world in which the elite would not want to live is mass genocide. The Club of Rome was ordered to produce a blueprint that would wipe out 500 million of excess population. The plan was called Global 2000, and it was activated by spreading the AIDS virus throughout Africa and Brazil. Global 2000 was officially accepted as U.S. policy by President James Carter.

The conference members agreed that the "low-class element of society must be brought under total control, trained and assigned to duties at an early age, which can be accomplished by the quality of education, which must be the poorest of the poor. The lower-classes must be trained to accept their position, long before they have an opportunity to query it."

"Technically, children must be 'orphaned' in day care centers under government control. With such an initial handicap, the lower-classes will have little hope of upward mobility away from their assigned positions in life. The form of slavery we have in mind is essential for good social order, peace and tranquility.

"We have the resources to attack the vitality, options and mobility of the individuals in society by knowing through our social scientist, understanding and manipulating and attacking their sources of social energy (income), and therefore, their physical, mental and emotional strengths and weaknesses. The general public refuses to improve its own mentality. It has become a herd of proliferating barbarians, and a blight on the face of the earth.

"By measuring the economic habits by which the sheep try to run from their problems and escape from reality via the medium of 'entertainment', it is absolutely possible, applying Operation Research methods, to predict the probable combination shocks (created events) which are necessary to bring about complete control and subjugation of the population by subverting the economy. The strategy includes the use of amplifiers (advertising), and when we speak on television in the manner that a ten year old can relate to, then because of the suggestions made, that person will purchase that product on impulse, the next time he comes across it in a store.

"The balance of power will provide the stability that the world of the 21st century is likely to achieve, rent as it will be, by passionate tribalism and by such seemingly insoluble issues like that posed by mass migration from the South to the North, and from farm to city. There may be mass transfers of population, such as those between Greece and Turkey in the aftermath of the First World War; really mass murders. It will be a time of troubles, in need of a unifier; an Alexander or Mohammed.

"A great change that will come about as a result of emerging conflicts between peoples who live side by side -- and which will, by their intensity, take primacy over their other conflicts -- is that political rivalry will be within regions, rather than between them. This will

119

bring about a turning back from global politics. After a decade in which the U.S. and the Soviet Union dueled across oceans, the powers will focus on protecting themselves against forces on their frontiers -- *or within them.*

"The American people do not know economic science and care little about it, hence, they are always ripe for war. They cannot avoid war, notwithstanding their religious morality, nor can they find in religion the solution to their earthly problems. They are knocked out of shape by economic experts who cause shockwaves that wreck budgets and buying habits. The American public is yet to realize that we control their buying habits."

There we have it. Split up nations into tribal factions, keep the populace struggling to make a living and concerned with regional conflicts so that they will never have an opportunity to get a clear view of what is going on, let alone challenge it, and at the same time, bring about a drastic lowering of the world's population. We see this happening in the former Yugoslavia, where the country is being forced into small, tribal entities, and we see it in America, where the average family has both parents working, and yet cannot make ends meet. These parents do not have time to pay careful attention to how they are being deceived and led into economic slavery. *It is all a set-up.*

Today, we observe -- if we have the time -- that the United States stand at the threshold of progressive dissolution as the result of Tavistock's silent "control" war against the American nation. The Bush presidency was a total disaster, and the Clinton presidency will be even more of a shock. This is the way the blueprint is drawn, and we, the people, are fast losing faith in our institutions and our ability to remake America into what it was intended to be -- a very far cry from what it is now -- overrun by foreign people who threaten to engulf the nation -- a South-North invasion right here in our own country.

We have surrendered our real wealth for a promise of greater wealth, instead of compensation in real terms. We have fallen into the toils of the Babylonian system of "capitalism," which isn't capitalism at all, but an appearance of capital, as typified by currency which is in fact negative capital. This is deceptive and destructive. The U.S. dollar has the appearance of currency, but it is in fact a token of debt and indebtedness.

Currency as we know it will be balanced by war and genocide—which is what is happening in front of our very eyes. Total goods and services is real capital, and currency can be printed up to this level, but not beyond it. Once currency is printed beyond the level of goods and services, it becomes a destructive, subtractive force. War is the only way to "balance" the system by killing those creditors, which the people docilely gave up true value in exchange for inflated currency.

Energy (economics) is the key to all earthly activities. Hence the oft-repeated statement I have made that all wars are economic in origin. The thrust of the One World Government-New World Order must, of necessity, be to obtain a monopoly of all goods and services, raw materials, and control over the manner in which economics is taught. Only in this framework can the New World Order gain full control. In the United States, we are constantly helping the One World Government to obtain control of the world's natural resources by being tricked into giving part of our income for this purpose. It is called "foreign aid."

Tavistock's Operation Research project states as follows:

"Our research has established that the simplest mode of gaining control of people is to keep them undisciplined and in the dark of basic systems and principles while at the same time keeping them disorganized, confused and distracted by issues which are of relatively little import.

"In addition to our less direct long-range penetration methods, this can be accomplished by a disengagement of mental activities and providing low quality programs of public education in mathematics, logic, system designs and economics and by discouraging technical creativity.

"Our mode calls for emotional stimulus, increased use of amplifiers which induce self-indulgence, whether direct (television programs) or advertising. We at Tavistock have found that the best way to accomplish the goal is through an unremitting and unrelenting emotional affrontation and attack (mental rape) through a constant barrage of sex, violence, wars, racial strife both in the electronic and print media. This steady diet could be called 'mental junk food'.

"Of primary importance is the revision of history and law and subjecting the populace to the deviant creation, thus shifting thinking from personal needs to constructed, fabricated outside priorities. The general rule is that there is profit in confusion, the greater the confusion, the greater the profit. One of the ways in which this can be accomplished is to create problems and then offer solutions.

"It is essential to divide the people, keep the adults' attention away from real issues and overcome their thinking with matters of relatively little importance. The young must be kept ignorant of mathematics; the proper teaching of economics and history must never be made available. Keep all groups so occupied with an endless round of issues and problems that they have no time to think clearly, and here, we rely on entertainment which should not reach beyond the mental capacity of a child in the sixth grade.

"When government is able to seize private property without just compensation, it is certain that people are ripe for surrender and consenting to slavery and legal encroachment. Energy sources which support a primitive economy are a supply of raw materials, the consent of people to labor, and assume a certain place, position, level in the social structure viz., provide labor at various levels of the structure.

"Each class, therefore, guarantees its level of income and hence controls the class immediately below it, thereby preserving the class structure. One of the best examples of this was found in the caste system in India, in which rigid control was exercised, ensuring that upward mobility which could threaten the elite at the top, was constrained. In this method is security and stability attained, and also a government from the top.

"The sovereignty of the elite is threatened when the lower classes, through communications and education become informed and envious of the power and possessions of the class above them. As some of them become better educated, they seek to rise higher through a real knowledge of economics-energy. This presents a real threat to the sovereignty of the elite class.

"It follows that the rise of the lower classes must be postponed long enough for the elite class to achieve energy (economic) dominance, labor by consent becoming a lesser economic source. Until such economic dominance is achieved to the fullest extent possible, the consent of people to labor and let others handle their affairs has to be taken into account. Failure to achieve this goal would result in interference in the final transfer of energy sources (economic wealth) to the control of the elite.

"Until such times, it is essential to recognize that public consent is still the essential key to the release of energy in the process of economic amplification. A consent of energy release system is therefore vital. *Artificial security must be provided in the absence of the mother's womb,* which can take the form of withdrawal, protective devices and shelters. Such shells will provide a stable environment for stable and unstable activity, and provide a shelter for the evolutionary processes of growth, that is to say, survival in a shelter that gives defensive protection against offensive activities.

"It applies equally to the elite and the lower classes, but there is a definite difference in the manner in which both these classes approach the solution of the problem. Our social science scientists have made out a very compelling case that the reason why individuals create a political structure is because they have a subconscious desire to perpetuate their childhood-dependency relationship.

"In the simplest of terms, what the subconscious longing demands is an earthly god to eliminate risks from their lives, put food on the table and pat them on the back in a comforting way when things don't go well. The demand for an earthly problem-solver-risk-eliminator is insatiable, which has given rise to a substitute earthly god: the

123

politician. The insatiable public demand for `protection' is met by promises, but the politician actually delivers little or nothing on his promises.

"Ever present in humans is a desire to control or subdue others who disturb their daily existence. However, they are unable to cope with the moral and religious issues such actions would raise, so they give the task to professional `hit men', which we collectively call politicians.

"The services of politicians are engaged for a number of reasons, which, in the main are listed in the following order:

1) To obtain the longed-for security without managing it.
2) To obtain action without the need to act, and without having to give the desired action thought.
3) To avoid responsibility for their intentions.
4) To obtain the benefits of reality without exerting the necessary discipline of learning.

"We can readily divide a nation into two sub-categories, the Political Sub Nation and the Docile Sub-Nation. The politicians hold quasi-military jobs, of which the lowest is the police force, next come attorneys. The presidential level is run by the international bankers. The docile sub-nation finances the political machine by consent, that is to say, through taxation. The sub nation remains attached to the political sub-nation, the latter feeding off it and growing stronger, until the day comes when it is strong enough to devour its creator, the people."

When read in conjunction with the systems outlined in my book, the "Committee of 300", it is relatively easy to see just how far Tavistock's Operation Research project has succeeded, and nowhere more so than in the United States. Recent statistics show that 75 percent of sixth grade school children were unable to pass what was called " the maths test." The maths test consisted of elementary simple arithmetic, which ought to tell us something. Mathematics did not come into the test at all. Cause for alarm? You be the judge.

# Covert Operations.
# VII.

Covert operations -- the stuff that "James Bond" was made of. As I have often said, James Bond was a fictitious character, but the organization portrayed in the movie series is very real, only it is known as "C" and not "M." Britain's Secret Intelligence Service and Security Service was what "James Bond" portrayed. These are known as and MI5 (internal security) and MI6 (external security). Together they are the oldest of the world's secret intelligence agencies. They also lead the world in the development of techniques and new technologies of spying. Neither service is responsible to the British people through Parliament. and both operate in the utmost secrecy behind a wide variety of fronts.

The beginnings of these agencies date back to the time of Queen Elizabeth I, the founder being recognized as Sir Francis Walsingham, Elizabeth's Secretary of State, and have existed since then under different names. It is not the intention to write a history about these supersecret espionage agencies, but merely to give a background to the main thrust of this chapter, which is covert action and assassinations for economic and/or political reasons.

The cardinal thing to remember that in almost all cases, covert actions are forbidden by international law. Having said that, I should also point out that it is one thing to have laws against covert actions, but it is another, very difficult thing to enforce such laws, because of the extreme lengths which the parties will go to keep the operation secret. America is no exception when it comes to disobeying laws. President Gerald Ford's executive order banning "engaging in, or conspiring to engage in political assassination" is largely ignored by the CIA.

The excuse that Bush didn't know what was going on in the Iran/ Contra covert operation cannot be sustained because of the Hughes-Ryan Amendment, which was tailor-made to knock the supports out from under such a defense. The amendment was meant to make the

CIA and other U.S. intelligence agencies accountable: "...unless and until the President finds that each such operation is important to the national security of the United States and reports in a timely fashion to the appropriate committee of the Congress, including the Senate Foreign Relations Committee and the House Foreign Affairs Committee ," the covert operation would become unlawful. So if either President Reagan or President Bush knew about the Iran/Contra operation, or, if they did not, then those who engaged in it were acting in an illegal manner.

In the Iran/Contra covert operation, Admiral John Poindexter was the "fall guy" for President Reagan and President Bush, both of whom claimed to have no knowledge of it. This is shocking, because it implies that here are two presidents who had no control over their military and intelligence departments. Had Poindexter not taken the stand to say that he never informed Bush about the specifics of the Iran/Contra operation, impeachment proceedings would have followed, which Bush with all of his powerful protection would not have been able to avoid. In this, Bush was ably assisted by Congressman Lee Hamilton, whose investigation of the covert action was so poorly carried out as to amount to a total whitewash of the guilty parties, including Reagan and Bush.

Apart from "James Bond," perhaps the best known MI6 operatives were Sydney Reilly, Bruce Lockhart and Captain George Hill, who were seconded to Russia to help the Bolsheviks overcome their enemies and at the same time, secure vast raw material and economic concessions for the British Black Nobility, with a slice of the pie going to the Wall Street financiers. Perhaps the least known MI6 agent (but one of its most effective), was Somerset Maugham, the distinguished British author, well known in the literary world by this "sheepdipped" name.

Like most MI6 officers, Maugham's real name was not disclosed during his service years, and indeed remained undisclosed up until close to his death. Sydney Reilly had 3 secret names, and eight others (he had eleven passports), his real name being Sigmund Georgievich Rosenblum.

Setting aside all the diplomacy by deception of name tags such as Bolshevism, Socialism, Marxism, Communism, Fabianism and Trotskyism, the fact is that the Bolshevik Revolution was a foreign ideology forced upon the Russian people by the Committee of 300 for economic gain and the control of Russia.

It is that simple, and when stripped of all the rhetoric and terminology, makes the whole concept of "Communism" easier to understand. We should never, ever, lose sight of the fact that, as Churchill put it, before he was irretrievably turned and lost, "Russia was seized by the hair of its head," and dragged kicking and screaming into a dictatorship straight out of hell, set up primarily to exploit and control its vast resources, which even today, far exceed those of the United States, not to mention Great Britain, which, apart from coal and some North Sea oil, has none worth mentioning.

Just as in the days of Queen Elizabeth I, when the Cecils, her controllers, set up Sir Francis Walsingham in a spy system to guard her assets in England, and to watch over trade in the far corners of the world, so did the modern kings and queens of England carry on the tradition. One might say that these spy organizations were motivated first by economics, and then by national sovereignty. Nothing much has changed in the intervening centuries.

That was what Sydney Reilly's now legendary mission to Russia was about; it was to secure a lock on Russia's oil and its other huge treasures of minerals for the British Black Nobility, led by Lord Alfred Milner; the City of London's merchant bankers and the American Boston Brahmins, Wall Street financiers and tycoons, among the better-known of whom are the Rockefellers, J.P. Morgan and Kuhn Loeb. Sharing Britain's plunder, gained through diplomacy by deception and backed by military might, became a tradition during the golden era of the vast, unbelievably lucrative opium trade with China.

The oldest American equivalent of "noble" families were up to their eyebrows in this unspeakable trade. Today, one would never know this as they are judged on their outward facade of attending the best schools and colleges, joining the finest private clubs, becoming lead-ing lawyers and bankers, philanthropists, religious leaders, and of course, leading politicians, that this brood is smeared all over with, and mired in the stench and filth of the China opium trade, which brought death and misery to millions while filling the banks they owned with obscenely vast wealth.

The rogues gallery of the China opium trade reads like a page out of the American social register: John Perkins, Thomas Nelson Perkins, Delano, Cabot, Lodge, Russell, Morgan, Mellon. Hardly a single one of our "elite" families is not tainted by opium riches.

Lord Alfred Milner sent Sydney Reilly of MI6 to secure the Baku region oilfields for British investment and for Rockefellers. Bruce Lockhart was Lord Milner's personal representative who controlled Lenin and Trotsky. "Hansard" of the time, which is the equivalent of our Congressional Record, is filled with expressions of outrage and frustration as Parliament began to glean a little information about the exploits of Reilly. There were furious exchanges in private between Prime Minister Lloyd George (Earl of Dwyfor) and his cabinet col-leagues, and in open debate with members of Parliament on the floor of the House. All demanded that Reilly be brought back and forced to give an account of his doings in Russia.

But to no avail, Reilly remained untouchable and unaccountable. For perhaps the very first time, the British public became dimly aware that some unseen force was above Parliament. The British public did not know, and could not know, that Reilly represented MI6, which had a much greater power than that of their elected representatives in Parliament. Those who were trying to break down the wall of secrecy got nowhere, so they waited for Reilly's return to England, which came only after it was all over.

Reilly and his close friend, Count Felix Dzerzinsky, (they both came from the same part of Poland) head of the dreaded Bolshevik secret police terror apparat, staged Reilly's death by shooting as he was allegedly trying to escape across the border. The cover story was that Reilly's name was discovered among the papers of a group of Latvian officers who planned to assassinate Lenin. Reilly lived in secret opulence and splendour in Soviet Russia until, to round out the plan, he "escaped" aboard a Dutch freighter. Reilly was recruited by Sir William Wiseman, head of British MI6 in Washington, in 1917. Reilly was described by his superior, Sir Mansfield Smith Cumming as "a sinister man I felt I could never really trust."

Somerset Maugham's mission to Petrograd on behalf of MI6 in 1917 was a classic example of diplomacy by deception. Lockhart was dispatched to Petrograd to back the provisional government of Alexander Kerensky, who was supposed to run the "interim" government opposed to the Bolsheviks. (De Klerk, the South African turncoat leader has quite properly been described as the "Kerensky of the Whites in South Africa, because his task is to form an "interim" government which will allow Mandela and his gang of murderers to take the country.)

What neither the British Parliament nor the public knew was that the government of Kerensky was programmed to fail; its job to make it look as if real opposition to a Bolshevik government was coming from Britain and the United States, when in fact, the opposite was true. In an elaborately stage-managed plot, Maugham, who was also selected by Sir William Wiseman, went to meet Kerensky, traveling via Japan with $150,000 (yes, it was mainly American money) to spend on Kerensky. Maugham left on June 17, 1917, and met with Kerensky on October 31, 1917.

Kerensky asked Maugham to deliver a note to Prime Minister Lloyd George, which contained a desperate appeal for guns and ammunition. It is interesting that Kerensky completely by-passed the British consul in Petrograd, having sniffed out that something was going on behind his back, fired off angry complaints to Lloyd George, but got no apology or explanation. As Captain Hill himself once said, "those who believe that the Bolshevik Revolution was Zionist-inspired and run, may have had some truth on their side." Wiseman, Maugham, Hill and Reilly were Jews; but Lockhart was pure Anglo-Saxon.

The British Prime Minister's response to Kerensky's note was a very brusque "I cannot do that." Maugham never went back to Russia and Kerensky was overthrown by the Bolsheviks on Nov. 7, 1917. Capt. Hill was drafted into MI5 and then to MI6. He was sent to Petrograd to advise Trotsky on how to set up an airforce, although Russia was still technically an ally of the British.

The object lesson in this diplomacy by deception maneuvering was to ensure that Russia remained at war against Germany, which Britain wanted defeated because of its great commercial and financial successes. At the same time, Russia was to be weakened to such an extent, that it would not be able to resist the Bolshevik hordesfor long. As we know, the deception worked perfectly. Capt.Hill played a big role in helping to set up the CHEKA, the dreaded Bolshevik secret police apparat and military intelligence, forerunner of the GRU.

One of Hill's exploits was the "transferance" of the crown jewels of Rumania. Hill, a weapons and training specialist, was very active in diplomacy by deception in aiding the grand design to make the world believe that Britain and the United States were really fighting the Bolshevik takeover. (Only France, of all the nations, was not deceived.) In documents I read years later, Allen Dulles, head of the OSS, was denounced by De Gaulle, who bluntly reminded him of the great diplomacy by deception successfully pulled off against Czar Nicholas II and the Russian people.

An integral part of the deception was to land a combined British, French and American force at Murmansk on June 23, 1918, under the command of American Major General Frederick Poole, ostensibly to help the Russians in their struggle against the Bolsheviks. The French truly believed that they were there to attack the Bolsheviks, when the allied force moved into Archangel on August 2nd, in which there was some fighting. Actually, the expeditionary force had three objectives: (a) to make it look as if Britain and America were battling the Bolsheviks (b) to protect the large cache of Russian Army weapons and munitions in the region, and (c) to help convert a doubtful populace to support Lenin by making it look as if he was the savior of the motherland, struggling to repel a foreign military force.

In reality, the British-American force was actually there to help Lenin, and not fight the Red Army. The allied troops were to see that the munitions dump was turned over to the Bolsheviks, and to prevent it being taken over by the advancing Germans. Years later, Secretary of State George Marshall repeated the trick against China's Marshal Chiang Kai Shek, leaving a huge arsenal for Mao Tse Tung to use in the struggle to turn China into a Communist nation. The third objective was to convert those Russians wavering in their support of Lenin into full-blown supporters. Lenin used the Murmansk landing to tell the Russian people, "look, British and American imperialists are trying to steal Russia from you. Join us in our struggle to defend Mother Russia!"

When White Russian Generals Denekin and Wrangel were having sweeping successes against the Red Army, pushing it out of the Baku region and threatening the work done by Sydney Reilly for British and American oil interests (especially Rockefeller oil interests), the same Lloyd George who in 1917 plotted with Kerensky was joined by a "private American citizen", William Bullit actually an emissary for Rockefeller and the Wall Street bankers. Together, they committed treachery and treason against their respective countries.

In January 1919, Gen. Peter Denekin defeated the Bolsheviks in Georgia, Armenia, Arzebaijan and Turkestan (the oil regions), and later that month drove the Bolsheviks right out of the Caucuses, advancing almost to the gates of Moscow. Thereupon, Bullit and Lloyd George pulled the rug out from under the White Russians, cutting off supplies of arms, munitions and money. Upon a signal from Lloyd George, sent through MI6 in September, the American-British force abandoned Archangel and sailed from Murmansk on October 12, 1919.

Please note the perfect timing of the operation. The only thing the expeditionary force had done, apart from slight fighting at Archangel and some other skirmishes against the Bolshevik forces, was march through the streets of Vladivostok in support of Lenin's contention that here were British and American imperialist soldiers bent on taking over mother Russia. By Nov. 14, 1920, it was all over as the last

White Russian forces embarked for Constantinople.

One of the greatest pieces of diplomacy by deception had been successfully pulled off without the American and British people having the slightest notion of what was going on. A more or less similar procedure is being carried out in Russia today with "ex-Communist" Boris Yeltsin being touted by the West as a sort of a Russian folk hero, trying to "save" Russia from a revival of Communism. As it was in 1917, so it is now: the American public has no inkling of what is really transpiring in Russia.

There is much more to the plot: the attempted assassination of Lenin, when he began kicking over the traces controlled by Bruce Lockhart; Lockhart's arrest and later exchange for Bolshevik Maxim Litvinov, complete with a sentence of death in absentia handed down by a Bolshevik court in Moscow. In this manner, MI6 plays its games in the most masterly of fashions, even as it still does today. Incidentally, Lenin died of syphilis of the brain, and not from wounds received at the hands of Dora Kaplan.

It might be in order to expand upon the doings of Capt. Hill. Documents I was able to examine in the archives of Whitehall, London tell a great deal about the activities of Hill, a second generation MI5 officer. Hill's father was apparently very active in Jewish merchant circles with connections to Salonika in the time of Czar Nicholas II.

Hill's son, George, who lived in London, was an MI5 courier for Wall Street and the City of London financiers backing the Bolsheviks; the money was channeled through Maxim Gorky, the darling of the theater set in London. In 1916, he was promoted to MI6 and sent to Salonika by MI6 chief, Sir Mansfield Cumming. From Salonika, Hill reported intelligence information to Cumming on the progress of the Bolsheviks plotting for the coming revolution -- *already 10 years in the making*. On Nov. 17, 1917, Cumming ordered Hill to Moscow, where he at once became a personal aid to Leon Trotsky, on the recommendation of Parvus (Alexander Helpland.) Hill drew up a plan for military intelligence which was accepted and became the basis of the GRU, with Hill and Trotsky as its founders.

The CHEKA remained under the control of Dzerzinsky. In later years, according to Whitehall documents, following a request from Jerusalem, Hill was sent to the Middle East where he set about organizing and training the Jewish Irgun and Stern gangs, with the vast majority of officers and rank and file came from Bolshevik Russia. The intelligence service Hill set up for the Irgun was later adopted by the Israeli secret service, which became known as the Mossad.

The British Secret Intelligence Service is the most expert at covert operations. Sir Stewart Menzies, MI6 wartime chief, once described Allen Dulles as lacking the necessary acumen to really understand covert operations. Be that as it may, MI6 formed and trained the OSS, forerunner of the Central Intelligence Agency (CIA.) Covert operations may be described as perhaps the most sensational part of intelligence work, which generally speaking, includes fairly routine activities like monitoring economic activities all over the world, preparing reports which go to national policy makers who are allegedly that part of government which decides what course of action, if any, should be followed.

MI6 and the CIA are, by law, not allowed to meddle in domestic affairs or spy on their citizens, their duties confined to foreign matters. But in the past three years, these lines have become very blurred, which ought to be cause for serious concern, but, unfortunately, no positive action is being taken to curb this phenomenon. Covert action walks a tight-rope between diplomacy and deception, and sometimes, when the walker slips, the results can be very embarrassing if the covert action is not deniable, as was the case with the Iran/Contra affair.

Covert actions calls for an intelligence agency to draw up a program to achieve a particular foreign objective. This often impinges on foreign policy, which is outside the realm of intelligence. A good case in point is the paranoia expressed by President George Bush in his desire to literally destroy Iraq's President Hussein, covert action taking both economic and military avenues.

A total of $40 million was wasted by Bush in his failed endeavor to kill Hussein, in which every trick was tried, including sending HIV viruses in vials to be secreted into the headquarters of the Revolutionary Command. In the end, Bush, overcome by his hatred of Hussein, unleashed 40 cruise missiles against Baghdad and Basra, under the flimsiest pretext of attacking "nuclear arms plants" and anti aircraft sites, both patently absurd.

One cruise missile was deliberately programed to hit the Al-Rasheed hotel in downtown Baghdad, where a conference of the heads of Moslem states was in progress. The idea behind the Al Rasheed attack, (the missile was tracked by Russian satellites from the moment of launching until it hit the target area) was to kill several of the Moslem leaders, thereby turning their countries against Iraq and helping through a backlash against President Hussein to topple the Iraqi leader.

Unfortunately for Bush, the missile fell 20-30 feet short of the actual building, shattering doors and windows up to three stories, killing a female receptionist. None of the Moslem delegates were hurt. The feeble and childish excuse made by the Pentagon and the White House that the missile was "knocked off course by Iraqi anti-aircraft gunners," was so absurd, that DGSE (French intelligence) was highly skeptical about whether the report was genuine or the work of some crackpot private agency.

The Russian military, secure in the data provided by their satellites, told the U.S. government its explanation was false -- and that they had the evidence to prove it. At $1 million per missile, Bush's paranoid behavior cost the American taxpayers $40 million dollars-on top of the covert price tag of $40 million. It is apparent that some mechanism is urgently needed to curb future presidents who in their last days in office, might seek to follow the shocking example set by Bush.

Covert action can often be taken by a government against its own people. Take the case of Alger Hiss and Rockefellers. As the petroleum companies said, they "owed no special obligation to America." This is true in the context of the arrangements made with the Bolsheviks by David Rockefeller and British oil companies. The United States ended up promoting socialism and communism to reward the Bolsheviks for oil concessions given to Rockefeller and Armand Hammer. Certainly, that proved their contention that the petroleum industry was not necessarily loyal to the United States.

In 1936, Alger Hiss was invited by Francis B. Sayre, Woodrow Wilson's son-in-law, to enter the State Department. The RIIA and the CFR decided Hiss was a good man who would do what he was told, regardless of whether it was good for America or not. Actually, Hiss was Rockefeller's first choice, not Sayre's, but Rockefeller stayed in the shadows. At that point in 1936 when Sayre made his approach, Hiss was already deeply involved in espionage for the USSR, and the fact was well known to his law professor at Harvard.

When Hiss was promoted to the position of assistant supervisor on political relations in the State Department, Chambers and a man named Levine blew Hiss's cover reporting that he was active in working for the Soviet Union. The man Chambers went to with his allegation was Marvin McIntyre, who failed to give the information to Roosevelt who was his boss. Instead, he sidetracked Chambers to Adolph A. Berle, who at the time was Assistant Secretary of State in charge of State Department Security. Berle went to Roosevelt with the story, only to be abruptly dismissed by the President.

Undaunted, Berle took his information to Dean Acheson, but exactly nothing happened to Hiss, He was not called on for an explanation; instead he was promoted by Roosevelt, a Rockefeller-CFR puppet, as was Roosevelt's entire staff. In 1944 Hiss received another boost with a promotion to the post of special assistant to the Director of Far Eastern Affairs, where he was well placed to serve Soviet expansionist plans in Asia.

To demonstrate the arrogance of Rockefeller, all the time Hiss was a rising star at State, the FBI had a file on him. He was denounced by Soviet defector Igor Gouzensky, who worked in the office of the GRU (Soviet military intelligence) in Ottawa, Canada. The State Department heads knew all about Hiss and his Soviet connections, as did President Roosevelt, but made no move to oust him.

While Rockefeller was planning the United Nations, he and Stalin agreed on a deal in which the U.N. would not interfere in Russian affairs in exchange for Soviet oil for the Rockefeller oil companies. Nor would the Bolsheviks meddle in Saudi Arabia, and make no further attempts to get into Iran. The man nominated to represent Rockefeller at the U.N. was Alger Hiss. His immediate superior was Nelson Rockefeller, who gave orders to John Foster Dulles. Roosevelt, Dulles, the FBI and Rockefeller all knew that Hiss was working with the Soviet Union.

Following the modem of Standard Oil, the mechanism for controlling the United Nations was taken out of American hands. The Secretary General was given the power to appoint whomever he pleased. For his treason, Hiss received a special staff appointment to the Carnegie Endowment Fund for International Peace at a salary of $20,000 per annum, a very good income for those days. The idea was to place Hiss above the law.

In fact, Hiss was above the law, because he got away with treason and treachery. Hiss was not charged with treason, but with perjury. However, powerful people immediately rushed to his defense. Supreme Court Justice Felix Frankfurter gave Hiss a clean bill of health and Rockefeller paid his legal expenses to the tune of $100,000.

At the time he was confronted by Chambers, Hiss was working as a member of the executive committee for the Association of the United Nations, chief executive for the Institute of Pacific Relations, and was a leading member of the CFR as well as president of the Carnegie Foundation. The House of Hiss was built on the petroleum industry, and never was there such a recorded case of abuse of power by the petroleum industry than as with  Hiss. The petroleum industry showed no fear of the government when Hiss was brought before the court; indeed, the petroleum industry almost pulled their man out of harm's way, and would have done so, had Hiss not tripped himself up. The Hiss case is a good example of diplomacy by deception by government against its own people.

In Iran, the United States is currently engaging in covert action against the government, using local groups inside the country and working with others in exile. The United States has become alarmed at the increasing arms buildup by the Iranian government and has placed a special watch on arms shipments destined for the country.

In addition, there remains a large reservoir of ill will between the two countries over the activities of Hezbollah, and Iran's willingness to give sanctuary to groups regarded as hostile to Israel. Therefore, a danger to the stability of the Middle East has arisen. Iran is becoming increasingly hostile toward the U.S. and its Middle East allies, Saudi Arabia, Egypt and Israel. That there is trouble brewing for these countries is a foregone conclusion, which may be why Israeli intelligence is claiming that Iran will be a nuclear power at a much earlier date than was predicted by the CIA. The Iranians, for their part say this is just another ploy by Israel to get what calls "its big brother to attack us like they did with Hussein."

The Iranian government now has a network of agents all across Western Europe, and is particularly strong in Germany. These agents are also active in Saudi Arabia, where the royal family is regarded with the utmost contempt by Teheran. The Iranian government is the principal financier and logistical backer of ten Islamic fundamentalist camps in Sudan, about which Egyptian President Hosni Mubarak complained to the U.S. State Department in December of 1992. The complaint has not been made public.

The ten training camps in the Sudan are as follows:

*Iklim-al-Aswat.* This is the most important of the ten camps, run by Colonel Suleiman Mahomet Suleiman, a member of the Command Council of the Revolution. Fundamentalists from Kenya, Morocco, Mali and Afghanistan train here.

*Bilal.* Situated at Port Sudan on the Red Sea, the camp is an important training base for Egyptian fundamentalists opposed to Mubarak's regime. At the last count there were 108 men in training, including sixteen Egyptian doctors, under the command of Jihad emir of Tendah.

139

*Sowaya.* Located close to Khartoum, it was reorganized in 1990 and now trains fundamentalists from Algeria and Tunisa under the title of the Popular Defense Militia.

*Wad Medani.* This camp houses African fundamentalists from Kenya, Mali, Sudan and Somalia under the command of Col. Abdul Munuim Chakka.

*Donkola.* Situated in northern Sudan, it is the main camp for Egyptian fundamentalists from Al Najunmin, a group founded by the late Majdi As Safti, who was obliged to flee Egypt in 1988. Also at the camp are members of Egypt's Shawkiun and 40 Algerians from the Al Afghani group.

*Jehid al Hak.* Here the PLO, Hamas and Jihad train under the command of Lt.Colonel Sadiq al-Fadl.

*Omduran.* At this camp 100 to 200 Egyptian fundamentalists belonging to the Islambuly group train and are considered to be more militant than other groups determined to end the regime of Mubarak.

*Aburakam.* This camp is a training base for up to 100 Afghanis, Pakistanis and Iranians.

*Khartoum Bahri.* This is probably the largest of the 10 camps, housing 300 Tunisian, Algerian and Egyptian fundamentalists of the Expiation and Immigration group, who train under the command of Capt. Mahomet Abdul Hafiz, of the Popular Defense Militia.

*Um Barbaita.* Situated in the south of Sudan, it is the base where the military elite is trained in the use of explosives and arms by Iranian and Sudanese experts.

The camps are coordinated at the offices of the Arab Popular Islamic Congress, very close to the Egyptian embassy in Khartoum. It is a very modern facility with the latest communications equipment that allows the Congress to be in contact with leaders of the Islamic fundamentalist movement in other lands. It is known that GCHQ is monitoring communications of this important office from Cyprus, among them communications to the mufti of the Egyptian Jihad, Sheik Omar Abdul Rahman.

Sheik Rahman was found not guilty of conspiring to murder the late President Anwar Sadat of Egypt, and on his release, moved to the United States where he coordinates fundamentalist activities from a storefront mosque in New Jersey. Sheik Rahman is said to have funded several hundred Arabs who were forced out of Pakistan by the United States, which in both overt and covert activities, pressured the Pakistani government to crack down on Islamic fundamentalists in the country. The covert action against Pakistan took many forms, but bribery was the key element.

One of the wildest covert actions going on is centered in the West Bank, Gaza and Israel. Involved are the CIA, Hamas, Syria and Iran. Hamas is the fundamentalist group making it life difficult for Israel. Teheran has taken up where Riyadh left off. In a well-established covert action using diplomacy, the United States persuaded Saudi Arabia that Islamic fundamentalist zealots could and most probably would threaten them in the future.

Using the techniques taught to the late Ayatollah Khomeini by MI6, the Iranians government has adapted the techniques to suit Hamas, which are proving very effective. Accustomed to being able to penetrate the PLO without very much difficulty, Israeli intelligence found it was up against something different with Hamas. The case of Israeli border guard Nissim Toledano illustrates the point. Toledano was murdered on Dec. 14, 1992, and the Shin Beth, Israel's internal security agency still has no clues as to who was responsible.

Then there is yet another unsolved murder, that of Haim Naham, a Shin Beth agent who was killed in his apartment in Jerusalem on Jan. 3, 1993. According to Beirut sources, Israeli intelligence is baffled, and is privately admitting that the expulsion of 415 Palestinians suspected of being Hamas leaders has not stopped Hamas from operating at the same level as before the deportations. The Israelis have found that Hamas is based on the Iranian-MI6 model with widely scattered small cells without any organized links between them, presenting a tough front to crack.

The most likely person at the heart of Hamas is Azzedine al Kassam. According to intelligence sources, there are approximately 100 cells, each with five members. These cells all have autonomy, but a group of seven men, one of whom is Tarek Dalkamuni, may help in coordinating activities. It is believed that Dalkamuni replaced Sheik Ahmed Yassine, who has been in an Israeli prison since 1989.

The rise of Hamas came about through covert action sanctioned by the Iranian government, operating under diplomatic cover in Damascus, Syria. In March of 1987, a meeting was held in the Gaza strip, attended by Iranian and Syrian personnel, at which meeting, the Intifada uprising was born. The Islamic Maijlis as-Choura (consultative council), sent Mohammed Nazzal and Ibrahim Gosche to meet with the Iranian ambassador to Syria, Ali Akharti.

Also in attendance was the head of Syrian intelligence, Gen. Ali Duba. This is a fairly good example of how covert operations are conducted, using diplomatic channels and private parties.

Following a successful meeting on Oct. 21, 1992, the Majlis delegation traveled to Teheran accompanied by Abu Marzuk, a leading fundamentalist, where they met with other fundamentalists leaders from Ahmed Jabril's PLFP, Lebanese Hezbollah, Al Fatah and Hamas. Discussions were held with representatives of the Iranian government, which ended in an agreement that Iran would provide financial, logistical and military personnel to train fundamentalists in the camps in Sudan.

A 12 man leadership council was established, which included Mahomet Siam (Khartoum), Musa Abu Marzuk (Damascus), Abdul Nimr Darwich, Imad-al-Alami, Abdul Raziz al-Runtissi (Gaza) (one of the 415 Palestinians expelled by Israel), Ibrahim Gosche and Mohamed Nizzam (Amman), Abu Mohamed Mustafa (Beirut).This group was trained in MI6 methods used to bring down the Shah of Iran, and to date, it is proving to be a tough job trying to penetrate Hamas.

Iran stepped up an active phase of opposition to what the Teheran government perceives as United States pro-Israel policies when the agreement reached at the time of the hostage crisis was allegedly broken by Washington. Using Hezbollah in covert actions against the United States, was to pressure public opinion in America and make it turn against Israel. Here Iran used the Tavistock of Human Relations methodology handed down to those who overthrew the Shah of Iran.

Tavistock founder and brilliant technician, John Rawlings Reese, then adapted "Operation Research" military management techniques so that they could be applied to "controlling a society, from an individual unit right through to millions of such units, i.e. people and the society and nation they collectively make up." In order to accomplish this successfully, rapid data processing was necessary, and it came with the development of linear programming in 1946 following its invention George B. Dantzig. Significantly, 1946 was the year that Tavistock declared war on the American nation. This set the stage for total people control.

The Teheran government of the Ayatollah Khomeini permitted the establishment of a covert action organization known as Hezbollah. Later, using Hezbollah, a number of American and other foreign nationals were kidnaped in Beirut and other areas of the Middle East and held in secret locations. The 5-man cell system worked to perfection. Neither MI6 nor the CIA were able to break Hezbollah codes and the hostages languished for years until the United States was forced to admit defeat and enter into negotiations with Hezbollah.

An agreement was reached which said that shortly after the release of the last hostage held by Hezbollah, the United States would unfreeze Iranian bank accounts and financial instruments amounting to an estimated $12 billion. The United States would also release military equipment ordered and paid for by the Shah, that it had not delivered, believed to be worth $300 million. In addition, Iran would be allowed to join the Gulf Cooperative Council so that it could join in deliberations about Israel. In addition, the U.S. undertook not to engage in covert activities against Iran inside its national boundaries, nor seek to punish Hezbollah kidnapers who were given sanctuary in Teheran.

However, Teheran said that Washington acted in bad faith keeping not a single one of its promises. The bank accounts were not unfrozen, the military equipment paid for by the Shah was not returned to Iran, the CIA actually stepped up covert activities inside the country, and Iran still remains frozen out of the Gulf Cooperative Council. Teheran points in anger to increased terrorist attacks in Teheran, attacks which began in 1992 after the last hostage was handed over.

The commander of the Pasdarans accused the CIA of building a network of royalists around Massoud Rajavi, leader of the Mujahedines, and Babak Khoramdine, and master-minding attacks on Pasdaran barracks, public buildings -- including a library -- an attack on the funeral cortege of the late Hachemi Rafsanjani and the desecration of the tomb of Ayatollah Khoemini. These attacks have not been reported by the U.S. news media. Officially, diplomatic relations between the United States and Iran are described as good.

To get back to Hamas. Using diplomatic channels, Iran and Syria tried to influence France to secretly back Hamas. Lebanese millionaire, Roger Edde, who served as a go-between for France and Syria, approached Foreign Minister Roland Dumas. Syria put pressure on Dumas about buying a new radar facility which Damascus said would go to Thomson, the giant French conglomerate. It was indicated that payments of Syria's debts to France might be delayed in the event Islamic fundamentalists causes were not seen in a favorable light by the Elysee Palace. However, the French government officially stayed adamant: no support for Hamas. The radar contact was switched to Raytheon, a American company. Debt payments have been held up with great inconvenience to France. Outwardly, diplomatic relations between Syria and France remain cordial.

Iran has an old score to settle with British and American intelligence that dates back to 1941 and 1951, when grosss covert actions were carried out against Iraq by MI6 and the CIA to bring about the fall of Dr. Mohamed Mossadegh. Although it properly belongs in this chapter, the account of how Acheson, Rockefeller, Roosevelt and Truman subverted Iran is to be found in the chapter about Rockefellers oil dealings in the Middle East.

The CIA and MI6 had a second go around with Iran when the Shah began to dig his heels in against barefaced robbery by American and British oil companies with concessions in Iran. The petroleum companies then entered into a conpsiracy with President Carter, and a carbon-copy of the Mossadegh operation was launched. Sixty CIA and ten MI6 agents were despatched to Teheran to undermine the Shah and bring about his downfall and subsequent murder.

Covert action does not always mean intelligence operations and terrorist groups with support of their governments. It can, and does, take the form of technological cooperation, especially in the areas of surveillance, and monitoring of communications. Because they are unspectacular as a rule, this type of "snooping" does not arouse a lot of interest, but it is one of the clearest examples of diplomacy by deception.

Two of the biggest and most comprehensive listening posts in the world are located in England and Cuba. Government Communications Headquarters (GCHQ) in Cheltenhanm, England, is probably one of the worst offenders when it comes to snooping. Although the U.S. Constitution forbids snooping on its citizens, the National Security Agency (NSA), meshes tightly with GCHQ and deceives the people of both nations in their ongoing overall surveillance operations. The U.S. Congress is either unaware of what is going on (unthinkable), or else, very possibly, too intimidated to put a stop to such illegal acts which occur every day at NSA.

In addition to its Cheltenham facility, the British government eavesdrops on the telephone conversations of its citizens out of its phone-tapping facility in Edbury Bridge Road in London. Some agreements were made on a diplomatic level, which did not, however, make them any less of a deception upon the people of the countries who signed. UKUSA is one such agreement. UKUSA is allegedly working only on military intelligence levels, but my source says this is not true. Originally a diplomatic agreement between the United Kingdom and the USA, the pact was broadened to include NATO countries, Canada and Australia.

However, over the last few years it also includes Switzerland and Austria, and now there is evidence that traffic to and from commercial companies is being monitored, even Britain's EEC partners, Japan, South Africa and Iran. MI6 has a separate department for economic intelligence gathering, called the Overseas Economic Intelligence Committee (OEIC). In fact, the expansion of this division is what made it necessary for MI6 to move from the Broadway Building, which backed on Queen Anne's Gate, to Century Building, near the North Lambeth underground station in London.

The United States now has a new intelligence gathering agency called the Information Security Oversight Office (ISOO), which cooperates with its British counterpart concerning industry, trade, and also industrial security. ISOO works with International Computer Aided Acquisitions and Logistic Support Industry Steering Group of the United States. Its business concerns the regulating of commercial technology.

The Committee of 300 controls these organizations and is the powerful unseen force behind the decision to make British and Swiss mobile cellular phones of the next 256 byte algorith generation comply with "snooping requirements" of the Britain and American security services. It is almost certain that only the ASX5 version ,with a 56 byte-easier to listen in on phone, will be allowed. This is one of the methods used by governments to secretly control their people.

In January of 1993, representatives of NSA and GCHQ held a conference at which it was made known that the less complicated AS5X version only would be allowed. No discussions were held with the U.S. Congress, no open forums, as demanded by the U.S. Constitution. Where A5 hard-to-penetrate phones are already in existence, they are being recalled for "technical adjustments." The technical adjustments consists of replacing the A5 256 byte chip with an A5Z 509 byte chip. By this means is illegal snooping becoming increasingly easier to carry out, the American people hoodwinked through diplomacy by deception at many different, yet interconnected levels.

Even public phones have come under a lot of scrutiny by security agencies. In New York, for example, under the guise of allegedly "fighting crime", the pay phone system was rigged so that phones could not receive incoming calls. The New York police department felt it could stop public pay phones from being used to transact business in dope for instance, or prevent organized crime figures from conversing with each other, in private. It didn't work out too well, but there were also successes.

The latest technology is to give all public call phones a special number. In certain countries in Europe, pay phones end with 98 or 99. This allows a quick "fix" on the location of pay phones when they are used for "secure" conversations; only calling from a pay phone is no longer "secure." In genuine cases, such as where a crime is in progress, or kidnappers call to demand ransom money, this is indeed a very useful tool, but what happens to the privacy of the individual in cases where no crime is involved? Do innocent citizens get their phone conversations snooped on? The answer is a very definite "yes."

The public is unaware of what is going on in America, and Congress appears to have fallen down on the job. None of the potentially damaging surveillance going on over a wide front in this nation is legal, so deception continues unchecked. The Congress seems slow to act when it comes to overseeing spy activities abroad, and is not at all inclined to act against the proliferation of snooping on citizens at home.

This apathy by Congress toward the right to privacy guaranteed by the U.S. Constitution, contrasts strangely with concerns whenever external problem areas come up for discussion. CIA director James Woolsey Jr. gave Congress a "threat analysis list", consisting of an evaluation by the CIA of nations who have such items as advanced surface-to-air missiles. Woolsey told Congress that Syria, Libya and Iran have operational cruise missiles capable of detecting "stealth" aircraft and threatening U.S. naval forces in the Gulf.

Pakistan is also known to possess such cruise missiles, and is the most likely to use them against India, if war should break out. The U.S. government has long sought a diplomatic ploy whereby India and

Pakistan are played off against each other. The United States fears that Pakistan might use its rocketry to help Syria and Iran against Israel, and this is very likely to happen if a "Jihad" should erupt. The United States is using every diplomatic deception and covert action to persuade Pakistan not to think about joining forces with Iran in a "Jihad" in which Pakistan would use its nuclear weapons.

Covert Action moves intelligence from a passive to an active role, closely related in nature to the use of force, often times under the cover of diplomacy. In either case, it is means action against a foreign government or a group within its borders. The definition of covert activities or special activities set out in Executive Order 12333 is meaningless and valueless for two reasons:

"Special activities means activities conducted in support of national foreign policy objectives abroad which are planned and executed so that the role of the United States is not apparent or acknowledged publicly, and functions in support of such activities, but which are not intended to influence the United States political processes, public opinion, policies or media, and do not include diplomatic activities or collection and production of intelligence or related support actions."

In the first place, executive orders are clearly illegal, as they are proclamations, and proclamations can only be made by kings. There is nothing in the U.S. Constitution that allows executive orders. In the second place, it is impossible to stay within the guidelines set out above, even if they were legal. Only the very ill-informed would, for instance, believe that the United States was not behind the downfall of the Shah of Iran, or that the CIA played no role in Iran to influence the United States political processes. In today's world, the CIA would be out of business if it observed Executive Order 12333.

But there are other secret weapons available to the CIA and MI6, to which we referred earlier, which can get around any written restrictions at whatever level they are proposed. The system developed at Tavistock is the most widely used one, and as indicated earlier it is the best weapon for mass social control and mass genocide, the ultimate objective of people control.

Assassinations are a part of covert activities, although no government will ever admit to countenancing murder as a way of solving foreign and domestic policy problems deemed not possible to be solved by any other means. It is not my intention to list all the assassinations that have occurred as a direct result of diplomacy by deception, that would take a book on its own to accomplish. I shall therefore limit my account to recent and well known murders in a diplomatic or political context.

The shots that killed Archduke Ferdinand and his wife at Sarejevo echoed around the world, and are generally accepted as the cause of the First World War, although this is not the case, but a prepared perception for public consumption. Tavistock now does "prepared perception" well. British and Russian intelligence were heavily involved in the shootings. In the case of Great Britain, it was a desire to start a war with Germany that was the motivation, and in so far as it involved Russia, the object was to get Russia into such a war, and thereby weaken it for the coming Bolshevik Revolution.

The assassination of Martin Luther King Jr., Negro civil rights leader, is a case worthy of further examination, for it reeks to high heaven of covert activity and diplomacy by deception. The American nation, and more especially, the population, are convinced that James Earl Ray fired the shot that killed King. This is "prepared perception." The trouble with that is no one has yet been able to put Ray in the motel room at the window with the rifle in his hand at 6:01 pm on April 5, 1968.

Ray maintains his innocence, having been set up, he says by Raoul, a mysterious figure whom Ray had met in Memphis to sell guns. On April 5, at about 5:50 pm, Ray says Raoul gave him $200 and told him to go and see a movie, so that he, Raoul, and the arms dealer, when he arrived, could talk more freely than if he (Ray) were present. In examining Ray's claim that he is the "fall guy", let us note the following, which when taken together would appear to support Ray and weaken the King "prepared perception" case.

1) Memphis police officers who were keeping a watch on King, stood under the balcony of the Lorraine Motel on which King appeared. One

149

of the officers, Solomon Jones, said he observed a man with his face covered by a white sheet in a clump of bushes opposite, and directly in front of the balcony. The man was also seen by Earl Caldwell, a New York Times reporter. Caldwell stated: "He was in a stooping position. I did not see a weapon in the man's hands..." Neither Jones or Caldwell have ever been questioned by any police agency about what they witnessed.

2) Willy Green, a mechanic who Ray asked to fix a low tire on his Mustang, clearly recalls talking with Ray a few minutes before King was shot. The gas station where the incident took place is four blocks from the apartment house on South Main in Memphis where Ray stayed. Ray could not possibly have been in two different locations at the same time.

3) The entry angle of the gunshot was consistent with a shot fired from the clump of bushes referred to by Jordan and Caldwell. It is inconsistent with a shot fired from the window of Ray's window.

4) The alleged rifle used to kill King would have had to have been jammed into the bathroom wall if it was fired from the window. The bathroom was not wide enough otherwise, yet when the FBI examined the bathroom, there weren't any marks on the wall, let alone damage which would have been caused by the rifle butt.

5) When sheriff's deputies ran to the apartment from where they thought the shot had come, there was nothing outside the entrance doorway. Deputy Vernon Dollohite was at the door in less than two minutes after the shot rang out. He told investigators there was nothing lying by the door. Yet, in the few seconds while Dollohite went into Jim's Grill, right next door to the apartment, someone left a bundle containing a pair of undershorts -- the wrong size for Ray -- a pair of binoculars and the hunting rifle wiped clean of prints on the sidewalk near the door.

Ray is supposed to have been able to jump out of the bath in which it is alleged he stood to fire the shot, clean the binoculars and the gun of finger and palm prints, drop them in a bag with some cans of beer (also clean) rush 85 feet down the hall, run down a stairway, get into his Mustang which was parked some distance away-all in the space of the less than the 20 seconds Deputy Dollohite was gone from the apartment door.

6) Ray was somehow able to travel to Canada and England only on the $200 he says he got from Raoul, yet when apprehended, Ray had $10,000 in cash on him. One of the names assumed by Ray was Eric Starvo Galt, a Canadian citizen who bore an amazing resemblance to Ray whose name came up in a top secret file. Ray said he found Galt in Canada on his own; no one instructed him or gave him money. The other names that Ray used were the names of people also living in Canada; George Raymond Sneyd, and Paul Bridgman.

7) The register for the rooming house in Memphis vanished and has never been found. The only witness who could connect Ray to the King murder was a drunkard, Charles Q. Stephens, whose wife said her husband was in a drunken state at the time of the shooting and saw nothing whatsoever. At first, Stephens said he saw nothing, then later that evening, he switched to a second version:

"I saw who done it was a nigger, I saw him run out of the bathroom..." Cab driver James McGraw says Stephens was drunk on the afternoon of April 5. Bessie Brewer heard Stephens change his tune and said "he was so drunk he didn't see anything." A press photographer, Ernest Withers said Stephens told him that he hadn't seen anything.

No notice was taken of Stephens by any of the investigating agencies, until he suddenly had his memory refreshed after being shown a photograph of Ray by the police. At that point, Stephens said Ray was the man he had seen running from the rooming house. The FBI put Stephens in a hotel at the cost of $31,000 in order to "protect" him, but did not say from whom. However, Grace Walden, the common law wife of Stephens was mysteriously and forcibly taken to a mental institution in Memphis, by an unidentified employee of the Memphis city government. Could it be that Walden could have wrecked the testimony of the government's only witness against Ray?

Walden was held in the institution and her attorney filed a suit against the FBI, the Memphis police and the county prosecutor charging a conspiracy to deprive Walden of her civil rights. Walden has stuck to her story, even under intense pressure to change it; she says Stephens was about to pass out from drinking when the shot rang out. She says she saw a white man without any weapon in his hands leave the bathroom in the rooming house soon after she heard the shot.

8) That Ray's trial was a mockery cannot be disputed. His attorney, Percy Foreman, in the opinion of many expert lawyers, and in my opinion, turned Judas and got Ray to plead guilty. Foreman had defended 1500 people charged with murder and won nearly all of these cases. Experts say that had Percy not coerced Ray into pleading guilty, due to the lack of evidence, Ray would have been found not guilty. By getting Ray to plead guilty, Forman accomplished the unthinkable, Ray forfeited his right of appeal for a motion for a new trial; appeals to the Tennessee Court of Appeals, appeals to the Tennessee Supreme Court and finally, a review of the case by the Supreme Court. No thinking person would disagree with the verdict of Foreman's peers, viz., Foreman did Ray a total disservice.

The whole truth about who murdered King will probably never be told, and in this, it has powerful similarities to the murder of John F. Kennedy. There is just too much doubt surrounding the death of King, and even the late Jim Garrison, former New Orleans district attorney said he believed there is a connection between the King and Kennedy murders, based on what he learned from Rocco Kimball, who made many phone calls to David Ferrie. Kimball says he flew Ray from the U.S. to Montreal. Ray denies this. The other similarity between the Kennedy and King murders is that both were covert operations, most likely sanctioned by very high-level government officials.

9) Ray says he met Raoul in Montreal, Canada after escaping from the Missouri State Penitentiary. (How the escape was accomplished is also something of a mystery.) Apparently Raoul induced Ray to work for him in a number of areas and then enticed him back to Alabama. While in Montreal, Ray was looking for false identity papers, and was introduced to Raoul who claimed to be able to meet Ray's need,

provided Ray would carry out some assignments for him. Rays says that after a number of meetings, he agreed to work for Raoul.

After several cross-border trips (one such trip was to Mexico), Ray says Raoul wanted him to go to Alabama. After a long discussion, in which Ray says he expressed grave reservations about going to that state, Ray eventually went to Birmingham. Ray did several jobs; delivering packages of unknown content and phoned Raoul from Birmingham quite frequently to get new assignments.

According to Ray, Raoul then told him that his last job was coming up, for which he would be paid $12,000. Again, according to Ray, he was instructed to buy a high-powered deer rifle with a telescopic sight.

10) Ray says Raoul accompanied him to buy a hunting rifle at Aeromarine Supply, and Ray says Raoul later returned alone to the store to exchange the rifle for a Remington 30.06.

11) The Memphis Police mysteriously withdrew King's protection. About 24 hours before he was shot, and the seven-man unit stood down. Memphis Police Director Frank Holloman denies ever having given the order for this, and claimed that he wasn't even aware that such an order had been issued. On the morning of April 5, 1968, four of the Memphis Police special units were ordered to stand down. No one in the Memphis Police Department knows where the order came from.

In one of the most mystifying episodes in this unsolved mystery, Edward Redditt, working as a detective in the Memphis Police Department, was lured away from his post by a series of radio messages that subsequently turned out to be false. According to Redditt, he was watching the Lorraine Motel from a vantage point across the street from the Lorraine Motel, where King was staying, when he was contacted on his radio by E.H. Arkin, a lieutenant in the Memphis Police Department. Arkin told Redditt to stop his surveillance and return to headquarters.

On arrival, Secret Service agents ordered Reditt to check in at the

Holiday Inn in Rivermont, because there was a contract out on his life. Redditt balked, saying he was the only police officer who knew by sight all of the local klansmen and members of King's entourage.

However, he was overruled by Memphis Police Chief Frank Holloman, and accompanied by two police officers, Redditt was driven home to collect his clothes and toilet articles. In a most unusual departure from police procedure, the two officers sat in the front room of Redditt's house, instead of in the car outside. Redditt had not been home for more than 10 minutes when a special emergency radio broadcast announced the murder of King.

12) The Galt wanted poster said that he (Galt) had taken dancing lessons in New Orleans in 1964 and 1965, when in fact Ray was in the Missouri State Penitentiary at the time. Attorney General Ramsey Clark, arriving on the scene after the FBI had pushed all other law enforcement agencies off the case, declared "all the evidence we have is that it is the work of one man." Why the unseemly haste to announce such a far-reaching conclusion, when the investigation was still in its infancy? Readers will agree that there is just too much working against the belief that Ray shot Martin Luther King.

President George Bush also deserves a special mention. Probably Bush is the most accomplished president ever to conduct diplomacy by deception, and there are many case histories to prove the statement. The problem with Americans is that we believe that the United States Government is more honest, moral and open about its dealings than foreign governments. We have been taught this since childhood. George Bush proved this is a one hundred percent wrong perception.

The scenario for the Gulf War was actually drawn up in the 1970s. This was almost blown wide open by several newspaper articles in which James McCartney's reported "A U.S. Secret Agenda." According to McCartney, the secret government of the United States decided early in 1970 to base its policy for the Middle East on the control of oil in the region being wrested from the Arabs. A pretext had to be found to establish a substantial U.S. military presence in that region -- but not in Israel.

Robert Tucker, writing in the Jewish magazine "Commentary" of January 1975, said that the United States must overcome any reticence about armed intervention in other countries, and he specifically mentioned the Persian Gulf region in this context. Tucker said what was needed was a preemptive strike to establish control of Middle East oil, and not wait for some crisis to pop up before acting.

Apparently one of the architects of this brazen notion was Bush, who followed the beliefs of James Akins, U.S. ambassador to Saudi Arabia from October of 1973 to December of 1975. Akins' views formed the basis of the Reagan-Bush administration policies, and it is interesting to note that the script ostensibly written by Akins was followed exactly by George Bush when he engaged America in an illegal war against Iraq.

Subsequent investigations turned up the fact that Akins had merely been reading from a Henry Kissinger script, which Kissinger wrote under the title "Energy Security." Kissinger at first advocated a direct assault on Saudi Arabia, but the plan was modified, and a smaller nation was substituted for Saudi Arabia.

Kissinger reasoned that seizing Middle East oil as a preventative measure would be acceptable to the people of the United States, and an idea that could easily be sold to the Congress. According to my source in Washington, the idea was accepted with alacrity by Bush, who had plenty of experience in deception and his stint at the CIA sharpened his appetite for what some say is his natural bent. The Kissinger "Energy Security" plan was taken up by Bush and applied to Iraq. There is a strong belief that the quarrel between Iraq and Kuwait over the Al Sabah's theft of oil from the Rumalia oilfields, and the sabotaging of Iraq's economy by underselling the stolen oil below the OPEC price, was worked out by the CIA in conjunction with Kissinger Associates.

By pushing Iraq into an open conflict through the treasonous conduct of April Glaspie, Bush saw his plans coming to fulfillment. April Glaspie should have been tried for lying to Congress, but this is unlikely to happen. Just when Bush though he had the game in the bag,

155

King Hussein of Jordan almost threw a spanner in the works. According to my intelligence source, and subsequently confirmed by Pierre Salinger of ABC Television, King Hussein believed that the United States was acting in good faith and would welcome a settlement of the Iraq-Kuwait crisis by peaceful means rather than by armed conflict.

Proceeding on the basis of his belief in the integrity of the Bush administration, Hussein called Baghdad and asked President Hussein to submit the quarrel to the Arab nations for arbitration. King Hussein assured Saddam Hussein that he had the blessing of Washington for such a move. On August 3, the Iraqi military advance toward the Kuwait border was halted so that the proposed arbitration could be given a chance. But Saddam Hussein had one other condition: Egypt's dictator, Hosni Mubarak would have to agree to the arbitration proposal.

King Hussein called Mubarak, who readily gave his assent to the plan. Next, King Hussein called President Bush, who took the call in Air Force I, while en route to Aspen to meet Margaret Thatcher, who was sent to deliver the Royal Institute for International Affairs ultimatum that U.S, military forces attack Iraq. According to intelligence sources, partly confirmed by Salinger, Bush was enthusiastic about King Hussein's initiative and promised the Jordanian ruler that the U.S. would not to intervene.

But once King Hussein terminated the conversatiion, Bush called Mubarak and told him not to take part in any inter-Arab arbitration discussions. Bush is reported to have called Thatcher and advised her of his converastion with King Hussein. Like Chamberlain at the time of Munich, King Hussein was going to find out that a peaceful settlement of the Iraq-Kuwait dispute was the last thing that the American and British governments wanted.

After getting approval from Thatcher, Bush reportedly called Mubarak again and ordered him to do everything possible to derail the Arab mediation effort. The payoff, as we now know, came later, when Bush illegally "forgave" Egypt's $7 billion debt to the United States. Bush did not have the constitutional authority to forgive Egypt's debt. With

Mubarak violently denouncing the mediation proposals, Bush began making threatening noises against Iraq. It was only a few hours after King Hussein told President Hussein that they had both been deceived, that the Iraqi Army crossed the border with Kuwait.

The role of the United States and Britain in starting the war against Iraq is classic diplomacy by deception. While talking peace in the Middle East, our government that we so unwisely trust, had been planning for the war against Iraq since the 1970s. The Gulf War was deliberately contrived in accordance with Kissinger's policy. Thus while Kissinger was not a government official, he still exerted great influence over U.S. foreign policy in the Middle East.

The bombing of Pan Am Flight 103 is another terrible example of covert activity. All the facts are not yet in, and indeed, may never be, but what is known thus far is that the CIA was involved, and that there were at least five top CIA agents on board, carrying $500,000 in traveller's checks. There are reports that the CIA actually videotaped the loading of the bag containing the bomb, but thus far these reports have not been confirmed by other sources.

# Panama: The Naked Truth. VIII.

One of the more recent examples is perhaps also the most blatant diplomacy by deception case on record: The Carter-Torrijos Panama Canal Treaty. The treaty deserves closer scrutiny than it was subjected to at the time it was drawn up and allegedly negotiated. I hope to bring out important implications that were never fully nor properly explored or addressed which now more than ever, need amplification. One of these is the danger that we, the sovereign people, face of being forced under the jurisdiction of the United Nations in the near future. A slippery deal like Carter's Panama Canal give-away, could be sprung on us again if we don't know what to look for.

Not generally known is that Anglo-Persian, a British government-owned oil company, tried to buy a concession from the Colombian government for canal rights flanking U.S. territory, at the time the United States was negotiating with Colombia for these rights. Irving Frederick Yates, a British diplomat, almost pulled off a deal with Colombia that would have thwarted U.S. plans to purchase the land for the canal zone. Yates was stopped at the last minute by a diplomatic incident which invoked the Monroe Doctrine.

A short review of the history of how the United States acquired the land through which the Panama Canal was built, might help us to understand subsequent events:

In the period 1845-1849, the government of Colombia concluded a treaty with the United States, granting the U.S. right of transit across the Isthmus of Panama. In 1855 Panama was given federal status by a constitutional amendment. Prior to the revolution of 1903, Panama had been part of Colombia. On April 19, 1850, the Clayton-Bulwer treaty between Great Britain and the United States was signed, in which both parties agreed not to obtain or maintain any exclusive control of a proposed canal, and guaranteed its neutrality. At the time Colombian oil was the key issue. On February 5, 1900, the first Hay-

159

Pauncefote treaty between Great Britain and the United States was signed. The treaty renounced British rights to a joint construction to build a canal and ownership, and was rejected when it reached the British Parliament.

The second Hay-Pauncefote treaty was signed in November 1901, giving the United States the sole right of construction, maintenance and control of a canal. On Jan. 23, 1903, the Hay-Heran treaty between Colombia and the United States was signed, which provided for the acquisition by the United States of a canal zone. The Colombian Senate did not ratify the treaty.

The Hay-Bunua-Varilla treaty between the United States and the new government of Panama was signed on Nov. 18, 1903: Panama sold in perpetuity a zone five miles wide on either side of the future canal, with full jurisdiction to the United States. The United States gained the right also to fortify the canal zone, and paid $10 million for the rights and futher agreed to pay an annual fee of $250,000. Released from the Clayton-Bulwer Treaty in January of 1903, the United States and Colombia negotiated the Hay-Herran Treaty, which accorded United States sovereignty over the territory five miles wide on either side of the proposed canal. The treaty was signed on Feb. 26, 1904. It is of the utmost importance to take cognizance that the land five miles wide on either side of the proposed canal, was henceforth sovereign United States territory, which could not be given away or otherwise disposed of, save and except by a Constitutional amendment ratified by all of the states.

Ratification of the treaty was delayed by Colombia and it was not until eleven years later, on April 6, 1914, that the Thompson-Urrutia treaty was signed, with the U.S. expressing regret over differences that had arisen with Colombia, and agreeing to pay Colombia the sum of $25 million by which action, Colombia ratified the treaty. On Sept. 2, 1914, the boundaries of the Canal Zone were defined and further sovereign rights of protection were conceded to the United States. The Panama Canal Zone then became sovereign territory of the United States.

The Thompson-Urrutia Treaty was signed on April 20, 1921. The

160

terms of the treaty were that Colombia recognized the independence of Panama. The previously disputed boundaries were fixed, and diplomatic relations established with the signing of various accords between Panama and Colombia. The U.S. Senate delayed ratification for another seven years, but on April 20, 1928, finally ratified the Thompson-Urrutia Treaty with certain modifications. The Colombian Congress similarly ratified the treaty on Dec. 22, 1928.

Previously, in 1927 the Panamanian government said that it did not give the United States sovereignty at the time the treaties were signed. But the League of Nations refused to hear this patently absurd dispute, and the indisputable American sovereignty of the Panama Canal Zone territory was reconfirmed when President Florencio Harmodio Arosemena disavowed the Panama government's appeal to the League of Nations.

It is of the utmost importance for every American, especially in these days, when the Constitution is being trampled underfoot by politicians, to take note of how the U.S. Constitution was scrupulously observed throughout the negotiations with Colombia and Panama. Treaties were drawn up and by the Senate and signed by the President. An appropriate period of time was allowed to pass while the agreement was studied before it was ratified.

Later, we shall compare the constitutional manner in which the treaty between the U.S. and Colombia over Panama was handled, with the slipshod, deceptive, crooked, wreathed in dishonesty, unconstitutional, bordering on fraudulent conduct of the Carter administration in giving the property of the sovereign people of the United States to Panamanian dictator Omar Torrijos, and actually paying him to accept it.

The only major mistake the United States made in 1921 was in not instantly declaring the canal and land sovereign possessions of the sovereign people of the United States and making it a state of the United States, in terms of the Constitution which mandates that a territory become a State once it is a territory of the United States. Failure to make the Panama Canal Zone a state was to invite the

Rockefeller international bankers to come in and steal the Panama Canal Zone from its owners, the sovereign American people, an action aided by President Carter every step of the way under cover of diplomacy by deception.

It is said that if we do not profit from our mistakes, then we are bound to repeat them. This maxim applies to the United States today more than ever when we examine the role of the United States in the Bolshevik Revolution, the First World War, Palestine, the Second World War, Korea and Vietnam. We must not allow the illegal precedents set by the Carter administration and the Senate Foreign Relations Committee to be used against us in any future treaty negotiations, such as those likely to come up with the United Nations in the near future. Such attempts to subvert the Constitution might take the form of subjugating our military forces to the command of the United Nations.

The precedent set by the successful theft of the Panama Canal from the sovereign owners, we the people, has resulted in wars at great cost in lives and money, an assumption of powers not given to the president by the Constitution, and a widening of diplomacy by deception actions leading to contempt for the Constitution by the secret upper-level parallel government such as is occurring in Somalia, Bosnia and South Africa.

This is why I believe it is necessary to ensure that no more Panama Canal give-aways are allowed to occur, and the only way to prevent a repetition of that mass swindle carried out under cover of diplomacy by deception is to examine what happened in the period 1965 to 1973. If we know what happened, then our chances of preventing it from happening again are improved.

To understand how the Carter administration was able to swindle the sovereign people of the United States, one must have at least a working knowledge of the U.S. Constitution. To interpret the Constitution, we also need to know our form of government and understand that its foreign policies are firmly anchored in Vattel's "Law of Nations," which the Founding Fathers used to shape our Constitution. We must also understand treaties and their relationship to our Constitution. There are only a handful of senators and members of the House who have a clear understanding of these vital matters.

We constantly hear the ill-informed referring to the United States as a "democracy." The print and electronic media is particularly heinous at perpetuating this falsehood, I think, of as part of an deliberate deception designed to mislead the people. The United States is not a democracy; we are a Constitutional Republic, or a Confederated Republic or a Federal Republic, or an amalgamation of all three. To fail to understand this is the first step into confusion.

Madison brought out that we are not a democracy. It was controversy over the form of our government that led to the Civil War. Had secession from the Union not come up, there would, possibly, and very probably, not have been a war. President Abraham Lincoln believed that there was a plot that had its origin in England to dismember the United States of America, and make of it two nations, which could then always be played off, one against the other, by the international bankers. The Civil War was fought to make the point that, once sovereign, always sovereign and that the South could not secede from the Union. The issue of sovereignty and sovereign territory was decided once and for all by the Civil War.

In a Constitutional Republic, the people who reside in the States are the sovereigns. In the House and Senate are the representatives or agents- if that is a better description of how they are supposed to function. This is spelt out in the 10th Amendment to the Bill of Rights which states: "The powers not delegated to the United States by the Constitution, nor prohibited by it to the States, are reserved to the States respectively, or to the people."

The president is not a king, nor is he the commander-in-chief of the military, except during declared wars (there can be no other legal kind.) It is his job and duty to uphold the Constitution, which he swears an oath to do. Many of our agents, including the president, have flagrantly violated the Constitution. Perhaps the most flagrant of these occurred when President Carter and 57 senators, under cover of diplomacy by deception, gave away the sovereign people's canal at Panama, i.e., in effect they attempted to dispose of sovereign territory belonging to the United States.

United States territory, under the U.S. Constitution cannot be alienated. The authority for this statement is found in Congressional Record Senate, S1524-S7992, April 16, 1926. The Founding Fathers passed a resolution that U.S. Territory cannot be alienated by giving it away or ceding it to another party, save and except by a constitutional amendment ratified by all of the states.

There is nothing in the Constitution that addresses the question of political parties. As I have so often said in the past, politicians arose because we, the sovereign people, were too soft, too lazy to do the work ourselves and so we elected agents and paid them to do the work for us, leaving them for the most part, unsupervised. That is what the House and Senate are today; unsupervised agents of we the people, who are running amuck and trampling the U.S. Constitution underfoot.

The Panama Canal treaty enacted by President Carter was a much bigger scandal than the Iran/Contra affair and the Tea Pot Dome scandal, referred to in the chapters on Rockefeller oil politics and the petroleum industry. Who makes the laws? The Senate and the House enact legislation that becomes law when it is signed by the President. Are treaties part of the law? First, let us understand that a treaty is defined in the Constitution (under Article 6, Section 2, and Article III,) Section 2 as law after the Senate has written up the treaty, and it has been passed by the House, and signed by the President.

The House plays a crucial role in treaty-making, as it has the power to nullify a treaty because they come under international and interstate commerce regulated by the House. (Article 1, Section 8, Clause 3-"to regulate commerce with foreign nations and among the several States.") The Constitution says in the 13th, 14th, and 15th Amendments that the legislature makes treaties, NOT private individuals which Linowitz and Bunker were, although purporting to represent the United States. Article 1, Section 7: "Every bill which shall have passed the House of Representatives and the Senate shall be presented to the President of the United States..."

Carter, Bush, and now Clinton have acted as if they were all-powerful kings, when they are not. We had Carter dealing in international law and giving away the sovereign people's property to Torrijos, and we had Bush going to war without a declaration of war, and now we have Clinton attempting to make use of proclamations (executive orders) to legislate. The Constitution is clear on these matters; there is only one place in the Constitution where power is given to deal in international law, and that is the Congress. It is not an expressed power of the President, no matter what the circumstances may be. (Part 10, Article 1, Section 8.)

What Carter and Bush did, and what Clinton is attempting to do now, is to compress and squeeze the Constitution to make it fit the desires and aims of the Committee of 300. Two examples that come to mind; abortion and gun control. Carter did this compressing and squeezing in the Panama canal give-away. Carter was guilty of perjury in usurping and claiming he had the right to dispose of sovereign U.S. property in Panama.

Carter's power to act as a surrogate for David Rockefeller and the drug banks allegedly under cover of negotiations over the Panama Canal, are neither expressly stated, implied not incidental to another power in the Constitution, Therefore, Carter's actions over Panama were illegal. But Carter got away with violating and trampling the Constitution underfoot as did his successors Bush and Clinton.

If we read Vattel's Law of Nations correctly, on which our foreign policy was based by the Founding Fathers, we see that it never gave a federal power nor a Congressional power to give, sell or otherwise dispose of sovereign territory belonging to the sovereign people of the United States. Treaty power can never exceed that power found in Vattel's Law of Nations.

Article 9 of the Bill of Rights and a careful reading of the Constitution, makes it perfectly clear that neither the president, the House or the

Senate, is authorized to give, sell, or otherwise dispose of any sovereign territory of the United States, save and except by means of an amendment to the Constitution ratified by all of the States. This was not done in the case of the Carter-Torrijos Panama Canal Treaty: therefore every one of the 57 senators who signed the agreement violated his oath of office, and that also includes President Carter. Because of their treasonous conduct, the United States lost control of a key element in its defense, our canal at Panama.

What are the facts of the so-called Panama Canal Treaty fraudulently signed into law by President Carter? Let us deal with what it means to negotiate a treaty. Negotiate implies that there is a give-and-take objective by the negotiators. Secondly, those who do the negotiating must own the property or money or whatever it is that the negotiations are about, or be duly authorized by the owners to negotiate on their behalf. Also, when one gives something, in law there has to be a "consideration" for what is given. If there is consideration from one side only, then it stands in law that there can be no treaty, and there is no treaty agreement.

As I have said, when negotiating a treaty agreement, it is, paramount that the parties doing the negotiating are legally entitled to do so. In the Panama Canal Treaty, the negotiators were not empowered by the Constitution to negotiate. Neither Ellsworth Bunker nor Sol Linowitz (alleged to be a U.S. ambassador) were qualified to negotiate; for the first reason that the treaty document was not written up by the Senate, and because there was a total absence of objectivity in the alleged negotiating done by Bunker and Linowitz.

Neither Linowitz nor Bunker should have had a vested interest in the Panama Canal Treaty, but both had a very big financial stake in the project: it was to their personal financial benefit that the treaty be successful. This was sufficient reason for the treaty to be declared null and void. The Constitution was trampled underfoot by the Bunker/Linowitz appointments. Article 11, Part 2, Section 2 states that Linowitz and Bunker had to have "the advice and consent of the Senate," which neither of them ever received.

Linowitz was a director of the Marine and Midland Bank with extensive banking connections in Panama, and had previously done work for the government of Panama. The Marine and Midland Bank was taken over by the Hong Kong and Shanghai Bank, the premiere drug money laundering bank in the world. The Midland Bank takeover was carried out with the express permission of Paul Volcker, the former chairman of the Federal Reserve Board, even though Volcker knew full-well that the purpose of the takeover was for the Rockefeller-owned banks in Panama to gain a foothold in the lucrative cocaine-banking trade in Panama. The acquisition of Midland by the Hong Kong and Shanhai Bank was highly irregular, and bordered on a criminal act under U.S. banking laws.

The Bunker family did business with Torrijos and had previously done business with Arnulfo Arias and former President of Panama, Marco O. Robles. No matter that both U.S. negotiators allegedly had broken off these relationships; no matter that a a flimsy and transparent deception was carried out (the six-month waiting period), the Constitution says in Article 11, Section 2, Part 2 that the President will appoint an ambassador or ministers "with the advice and consent of the Senate." There is no talk of a waiting period- which was used to get around the conflict of interest surrounding Linowitz and Bunker. It was all just so a gross deception of the American people.

The appointment of Linowitz and Bunker was clouded and fouled in deception, reeking of dishonesty and broke the sacred fiduciary trust the president is supposed to have with we, the sovereign people. Never was diplomacy by deception quite so artfully carried out than in the appointment of Linowitz and Bunker to be the "negotiators" of a treaty that the Senate never wrote up; in outright defiance of the Constitution by the Senate Foreign Relations Committee. The members of the committee ought all to have been impeached and perhaps even charged with treason at the time they accepted the drug banker's choice of Ellsworth and Linowitz as "negotiators."

We come now to what Bunker and Linowitz negotiated. The Panama Canal and territory could not be negotiated; it was the sovereign territory of the United States which could not be disposed of save and

167

except by means of a constitutional amendment passed by Congress and ratified by all of the States. Also, the two ambassador's credentials, if they had any, were not drawn up by the Senate. Carter and his crooked Wall Street accomplices deceived the American people into believing that Bunker and Linowitz were acting lawfully on behalf of the United States, when in fact they were breaking U.S. law.

The strategy worked out by the Wall Street bankers was to keep the American people in doubt and in the dark making things so hazy that they would say, "well I suppose we can trust President Carter on this one." In this the Wall Street bankers and David Rockefeller were ably assisted by an army of paid, kept and directed political writers; newspaper editors, the major television networks, and, particularly two U.S. Senators.

Sen. Dennis De Concini added reservations to the treaty, which were no more than window dressing to be used to excuse the Senator's failure to uphold the Constitution. The "reservations" were not signed by Omar Torrijos and were of no force and effect, but the action gave voters in Arizona a false impression that De Concini was not wholly in favor of the treaty. This was altogether low political chicanery. Voters in Arizona had informed De Concini that they were overwhelmingly against the treaty.

So what was "negotiated? What was the give-and take, the consideration that must by law be an integral part of treaty negotiations? The startling truth is that there was none. We, the sovereign people, already owned the sovereign territory of the Panama Canal Zone; Torrijos and the Panamanian government had no consideration to offer and gave none to the United States. Thus, the negotiations were patently one-sided, which alone makes the Torrijos-Carter treaty null and void.

If there is no consideration from either side, then there can be no treaty. Contracts often contain a token payment as a consideration to make the contract legal, which it otherwise would not be. Sometimes, as little as $10 is given as a consideration, just to make it legal. It was as simple as that. To repeat, Torrijos gave no consideration to the United

States. When the Senate Foreign Relations Committee said that Rockefeller's hirelings could do what they did, all its members failed in their duty to we, the people, and therefore should have been forced from office.

Before the Senate ratified the misbegotten Panama Canal treaty, it should have been studied for at least two to three years. Consider the length of time taken by the United States and Colombia to ratify the 1903 treaty. That was proper; the rushed study by the Senate Foreign Relations Committee of the Carter-Torrijos treaty was highly improper. In fact, the treaty should never have been allowed to come up for consideration, since the Senate itself did not write up the treaty, and only saw it after it was already negotiated. This is in direct contravention of the Constitution.

Thus, signing of a nullified treaty by Carter was a travesty and a deception by the President, aimed at harming his own people and for the benefit of the drug banks and their Wall Street counterparts. No matter how long it has been in existence, the Carter-Torrijos treaty remains to this day, *null and void*. The document contains no less than 15 gross violations of treaty-making in terms of the U.S. Constitution, and perhaps another five more.

Only a Constitutional amendment, passed the Congress and ratified by all the States would have validated the Carter-Torrijos treaty. But the treaty was so badly flawed that it could have been overturned by the Supreme Court, if the Supreme Court had a mind to do its duty to we, the people.

All definitions of a treaty state that a treaty has to give something on both sides. The Panama canal already belonged to the United States. Of that there is no doubt, but let us retrace our steps and reconfirm this position. The 1903 treaty was signed by both parties, one gave land, the other received a cash consideration. The United States let it be known that, henceforth, the territory it had paid for was sovereign U.S. territory. Not a single one of the debates held during the Carter-Torrijos Panama Canal hearings disputed that the canal was U.S. sovereign territory and had been since 1903.

The wording of the 1903 treaty is very important to introduce at this point: "Article 111´to the entire exclusion of the of the exercise by the Republic of Panama of any sovereign rights, power or authority... are located to the entire exclusion of the exercise of the Republic of Panama of any such sovereign rights, power or authority...and exercise it as if it were American territory.'" This left no room for doubt that this was a treaty that established the Panama Canal Zone as sovereign U.S. territory from Nov. 18, 1903 onwards and in perpetuity.

I have mentioned sovereignty many times herein. A good definition of sovereignty is found in George Randolph Tucker's book on international law. Another good explanation of sovereignty can be found in Dr. Mulford's book "Sovereignty of Nations":

"The existence of sovereignty of the nation, or political sovereignty, is indicated by certain signs or notes which are universal. These are independence, authority, supremacy, unity and majesty...A divisive sovereignty is a contradiction of the supremacy which is implied in all of its necessary conception and inconsistent with its substance in the organic will. It is indefeasible. It can not, through legal forms and legist devices, be annulled and avoided, nor can it be voluntarily abdicated or voluntarily resumed, but involves a continuity of power and action...It works through all members and in all organs and offices of the State..."

What Carter attempted to do on behalf of Rockefeller and the drug banks was to alter the 1903 Panama treaty "through legal forms and legist devices." But the 1903 Panama treaty could not "be annulled and avoided" by such legist devices. That left Carter with a null and void fraudulent document which he passed off on the American people as a genuine treaty, as a new and legally binding treaty, which it was not then, nor can it ever be.

When the Rockefeller drug banks began planning on how to protect their investments in Panama in the 1960s, the cocaine trade in Colombia was booming. Inasmuch as trouble was brewing in Hong Kong – as the Chinese government having demanded control of the island and a bigger share of the heroin trade conducted for centuries by the British

-- the Wall Street international bankers began to regard Panama as a newer safe haven for drug money-laundering operations. In addition, the huge amounts of cash generated by the cocaine trade flowing into Panamanian banks needed to be protected.

But to do this, Panama had to be controlled by a representative of the Wall Street banks, and this would not be easy. History shows that President Roosevelt was the first to try and weaken the 1903 Panama Canal treaties by giving away the area of Colón, which subsequently became a hub of commerce and a drug-trafficking center. President Dwight Eisenhower was the second U.S. official to attempt to weaken the sovereignty of the Panama Canal, when, on Sept. 17, 1960, he ordered the Panamanian flag flown alongside the U.S. flag in the Canal Zone. Eisenhower had carried out this treasonous action on behalf of the CFR and David Rockefeller. However, even Eisenhower's act of treason could not "annul and avoid" the 1903 treaty. Eisenhower had no right to order the flag of a foreign government to be flown in the sovereign territory of the United States; it was in gross violation of his oath to uphold the Constitution.

Encouraged by the treasonous conduct of Roosevelt and Eisenhower, Panama's President Roberto F. Chiari formally requested the United States to revise the Panama Canal treaty. This was one month after the Eisenhower flag incident. If our Constitution means anything, it means that no such action is possible by the United States unless it passes the House and Senate and is ratified by all of the States. In January of 1964, paid agitators stirred up rioting and Panama broke off relations with the United States. This was classic stage-management by the Wall Street bankers.

Then, in April 1964, President Lyndon Johnson, (without the consent of the House and Senate), told the Organization of American States (OAS) that the U.S. "was willing to review every issue involved in the rift with Panama over the Canal" and diplomatic relations resumed. President Johnson had no power to deal in international law, nor did he have the power to do anything to alter the 1903 treaty "by legist" or any other deceptive device.

Johnson actively sought measures that would enable new negotiations over the 1903 treaty to commence. Johnson did not have the power to negotiate on treaties and his actions further attacked the sovereignty of the Canal territory, encouraging the Wall Street bankers led by Rockefeller, to become bolder. Clearly, Johnson's acts were unconstitutional because he was attempting to moderate a treaty covering the sovereign territory of the Panama Canal, which no president has the power to do.

The Carter-Torrijos Panama Canal treaty came about because Panama was in debt to the Wall Street banks for approximately $8 billion. The whole wretched piece of deception was designed to force the sovereign American people to make good on what Panama owed to the Wall Street bankers. This was not the first time that we, the people, were swindled by the Wall Street bankers. It will be recalled that it was the U.S. taxpayers who were forced to pay $100 million for German commercialized reparation bonds in the period 1921 to 1924. As in the case of the Carter-Torrijos treaty, Wall Street bankers were deeply involved in the German bonds, the most notable being J.P. Morgan and Kuhn and Loeb and Company.

Following a carefully scripted Rockefeller scenario, in October of 1968, Arnulfo Arias was ousted by the Panama Defense Force controlled by Colonel Omar Torrijos. Torrijos immediately abolished all political parties in Panama. On Sept. 1, 1970, Torrijos rejected the Johnson draft of 1967 (ostensibly to revise the 1903 treaty) on the grounds that it fell short of complete surrender and control of the canal to Panama.

The stage was set for the Wall Street conspirators to move forward under cover of diplomacy by deception and they began to take steps to put the Panama Canal in the hands of Torrijos, who Rockefeller knew could be trusted not to rip the lid off drug money laundering banks in Panama, as Arnulfo had threatened to do. In return, Torrijos was promised that the Panama Canal Zone would be handed back to Panama.

The new treaty turned control of Panama over to the Torrijos government and was signed by President Carter, who will go down in history as having possibly the worst record of violating the Constitution of any President of this century, with the exception of George Bush. When reviewing the fraudulent Carter-Torrijos treaty, one is reminded of the words of the late, great Congressman Louis T. McFadden. On June 10, 1932, McFadden denounced the Federal Reserve Board as "one of the most corrupt institutions the world has ever known..." The Carter-Torrijos treaty is one of the most corrupt treaties the world has ever known.

The American cocaine trade had far outstripped the Far East trade in heroin, so Panama became one of the most sheltered banking havens in the drug money laundering world. The booze-barons of yesteryear became the dope barons of today. Nothing much has changed except that the mechanics of concealment are a great deal more sophisticated today than they were then. Now it is in the gentlemanly image of the board room and the exclusive clubs of London, Nice, Monte Carlo and Acapulco. The oligarchists maintain a discreet distance from their court servants; untouchable and serene in their palaces and their power.

Is the drug business conducted in the bootlegging manner? Do sinister-looking men travel around carrying suitcases stuffed with $100 bills? They do, but only on very rare occasions. Mainly the money end of the dope trade is transacted with the witting cooperation of internationals banks and their interfacing financial institutions. Close down the drug money laundering banks, and the drug trade will begin to dry up. Close up the rat holes and it will be easier to get rid of the rodents.

This is what happened in Panama. The rat holes were closed up by Gen. Manuel Noriega. The international bankers could hardly take that lying down. When one hits the drug money laundering banks, repercussions are sure to follow swiftly. To give an idea of what was at stake, the Drug Enforcement Agency (DEA) estimated that $250 million per day changed hands through teletype transfers of which 50 percent  was interbank money derived from the drug trade. The Cayman Islands, Panama, Bahamas, Andorra, Hong Kong and the

Swiss banks handle the bulk of it, with a larger and larger volume going through Panamanian banks since the 1970s.

It was increasingly clear to the drug money laundering bankers in the United States that in Panama they had a winner. With that understanding came great concern that the money launderers had to have an asset in place in Panama whom they could control. Arnulfo Arias had shaken them when he began poking around in their banks in Panama City. The DEA estimates that $6 billion a year finds its way from the United States to Panama. Coudert Brothers, the Committee of 300 "mob" lawyers for the Eastern Liberal Establishment, began steps that would ensure that another Arnulfo Arias did not threaten the increasingly lucrative cocaine business bursting their Panamanian banks with cash.

The man Coudert Brothers chose to oversee the Panama negotiations with Torrijos was one of their own, Sol Linowitz, whom we met earlier. A partner in Coudert Brothers, director of Xerox, Pan American Airlines and the Marine Midland Bank, Linowitz had all the credentials needed to pull off what Rockefeller had in mind, i.e.: to seize the entire Panama Canal Zone. The messenger from the "Olympians" (the Committee of 300) found in Omar Torrijos the right sort of stuff for the purposes of the international bankers.

As described earlier herein, Panama was destabilized enough for Torrijos to seize power and abolish all political parties. The jackals of the American news media painted a glowing picture of Torrijos as an ardent Panamanian nationalist, one who felt keenly that the Panamanian people were wronged by the 1903 treaty which ceded the Panama Canal Zone to the United States. The "manufactured by David Rockefeller" brand that Torrijos bore was carefully concealed from the American people.

Thanks to the treasonous conduct of the Senate Foreign Relations Committee, and in particular, the conduct of Senators Dennis De Concini and Richard Lugar, Panama passed into the hands of Gen. Torrijos and the Committee of 300 at a cost of billions of dollars to the U.S. taxpayers. But Torrijos, like so many of us mortals, seemed to lose sight of the fact of his maker, in his case, the "Olympians."

Originally hand-picked for the job by Kissinger and Linowitz, in the manner of all those who serve the secret upper-level parallel government of the United States, whether it be Secretary of State or Defense, Torrijos conducted himself well during the transfer of the Panama Canal from the sovereign people of the United States to the Wall Street bankers, the drug overlords and their executives. Then, to the dismay of his mentors, Torrijos began to take his role as a nationalist seriously, instead of continuing to be Wall Street's ventriloquist dummy.

Panama must be seen through the eyes of Trojan Horse Kissinger, that is to say, we must look at it as pivotal to Central America as Kissinger's future killing grounds for thousands of American soldiers. Kissinger's orders were to get another "Vietnam War" going in Central America. But Torrijos began to get other ideas. He opted instead to join the Contadora Group. While not perfect, the Contadoras were willing to do battle with the drug barons, so Torrijos became a contradiction to his masters, and for that he was "permanently immobilized."

Torrijos was murdered in August of 1981. The aircraft in which he was flying was rigged in much the same manner as the plane that took the son of Aristotle Onasis to his death. The controls were rigged to operate the aircraft's elevators (controlling climb and descent) opposite to what the pilot wanted. Instead of climbing after take off, the plane carrying Torrijos literally flew into the ground.

Panama's banks came under the control of a number of David Rockefeller's Wall Street banks as a convenient depository for dirty drug money, and was soon adjudicated the world's cocaine banking center while Hong Kong remained the heroin banking center. Rockefeller commissioned Nicolas Ardito Barletta, a former director of the World Bank and the Marine and Midland Bank (the same bank on whose board sat Linowitz) to take control of the banking situation.

Barletta was to restructure banking in Panama and alter banking laws to make it safe for the drug money launderers. Barletta was respectable enough to be above suspicion and had the necessary experience in handling vast amounts of dope cash gained from his connection with the Hong Kong and Shanghai Bank -- the premiere drug money laundering bank in the world -- which was later to take over Midland Marine Bank in the United States.

Banco Nacional de Panama had by 1982 increased its cash flow of U.S. dollars by 500 percent over 1980 levels, according to U.S. Drug Enforcement Agency (DEA) documents. Close to $6 billion in unreported money went from the United States to Panama from 1980 to 1984. In Colombia, DEA estimates put cocaine-generated cash at $25 billion for the period 1980 to 1983, with almost the total amount being deposited in Panama City banks. Six months after Torrijos was removed, strong-man Gen. Rueben Parades of the Panama Defense Force, was moved up by the drug bankers.

But like his predecessor, Parades showed every sign of not knowing who his bosses were. He started talking about Panama joining the Contadoras group. Kissinger had to deliver a message to Parades in February of 1983 and the general was smart enough to take notice and do an about-face, kicking the Contadoras out of Panama and pledging full support for Kissinger and the Wall Street international bankers.

Parades took great pains in cultivating the friendship of Arnulfo Arias, who was ousted by Torrijos, lending an air of respectability to his leadership. In Washington, Parades was promoted by Kissinger as a "staunch anti-communist friend of the United States." Not even the merciless execution of his 25-year old son by members of the Ochoa-Escobar cocaine clan deterred Parades; he kept Panama open for the cocaine trade and protected its banks.

Manuel Noriega, who was next in line in the PDF to Parades, had become increasingly concerned about the corrupting of the Panama Defense Force, which he had striven to keep out of the drug trade. Noriega plotted a coup against Parades who was subsequently overthrown by the Panama Defense Force and Noriega assumed the leadership of Panama, becoming commander of the PDF. At first there was little reaction; Noriega had been working for the CIA and the DEA for a number of years and was thought by Kissinger and Rockefeller to be "a company man."

When did doubts begin to arise on Wall Street and in Washington about Noriega? I believe that it was immediately following the stunning success of a joint PDF-DEA anti-drug operation codenamed "Operation Pisces," which was publicly revealed by the DEA in May 1987. The DEA characterized "Operations Pisces" as "the largest and most successful undercover investigation in federal drug enforcement history."

The drug bankers found that they had good reason to fear Noriega and this can be seen from a letter written to Noriega by John Lawn, head of the DEA, dated May 27, 1987:

"As you know, the recently-concluded "Operations Pisces" was enormously successful, many millions of dollars and thousands of pounds of drugs have been taken from drug traffickers and international money launderers. Your personal commitment to 'Operation Pisces' and competent and professional and tireless efforts of the other officials of the Republic of Panama were essential to the final positive outcome of this investigation. Drug traffickers around the world are on notice that the proceeds and profits of their illegal ventures are not welcome in Panama."

In a second letter to Noriega, Lawn wrote: "I would like to take this opportunity to reiterate my deep appreciation for the vigorous anti-drug trafficking policy that you have adopted, which is reflected in the numerous expulsions from Panama of accused drug traffickers, the large seizures of cocaine and precursor chemicals that have occurred in Panama, and the eradication of marijuana in Panama territory."

Gen. Paul Gorman, commanding general of U.S. forces Southern Command, stated during the Senate Foreign Relations Subcommittee hearings that he had never seen any evidence of wrong doing by Noriega, nor was there any hard evidence that Noriega was tied to the drug barons. The committee itself was unable to produce one shred of credible evidence to the contrary. The committee let the American people down by failing to investigate charges made by Noriega, that among his most powerful enemies were the First Bank of Boston, Credit Suisse, American Express and Bank of America.

Adam Murphy, who headed the Florida Task Force under the National Narcotics Border Interdiction System (NNBIS), stated most emphatically as follows:

"During my entire tenure with NNBIS and the South Florida Task Force, I never saw any intelligence that Gen. Noriega was involved in the drug trade. In fact, we always held up Panama as the model in terms of cooperation with the U.S. in the war on drugs. Remember, a grand jury indictment is not a conviction. And if the Noriega case ever comes to trial, I will look at the evidence of that jury's findings, but until that happens, I have no first-hand evidence of the general's involvement. My experience ran in the opposite direction."

It was never brought out that "Operation Pisces" was made possible only through passage of Panamanian Law 29, pushed through by Noriega. This was reported by Panama's largest newspaper, "La Prensa", which complained bitterly that the Panama Defense Force was conducting a publicity campaign against drug, "that will devastate the Panamanian banking center."

No wonder. "Operations Pisces" closed down 54 accounts in 18 Panamanian banks and resulted in the seizure of $10 million in cash and large quantities of cocaine. This was followed by the freezing of another 85 accounts in banks whose deposits were made up of cocaine cash. Fifty eight major U.S., Colombian and some Cuban American runners were arrested and indicted on narcotics trafficking charges.

Yet, when Noriega was kidnapped and then dragged before a federal court in Miami, in a stunning violation of Noriega's civil rights, Judge William Hoevler refused to allow these letters and hundreds of other documents showing the anti-drug role played by Noriega to be admitted to the record. And we dare talk about "justice" in America, and our president talks about "war on drugs." The war on drugs ceased when Gen. Noreiga was kidnapped and imprisoned in the United States.

In the wake of "Operation Pisces," a concerted campaign to discredit Gen. Noriega was launched in Panama and Washington. The International Monetary Fund (IMF) threatened that its loans to Panama would be called unless Noriega stopped his "dictatorial behavior," i.e. unless Noreiga stopped battling the drug banks and cocaine merchants. Noriega advised the Panamanian people in a televised address on March 22, 1986 that Panama was being strangled by the IMF. The IMF tried to pressure the labor unions to force Noriega from office by warning that dire austerity lay ahead for Panama unless Noriega was ousted.

The IMF's position with regard to Panama, Colombia and the Caribbean was made clear by John Holdson, a senior official of the World Bank, who stated that the cocaine "industry" was highly advantageous to producer countries: "From their point of view, they simply couldn't find a better product." The Colombia office of the IMF said quite openly that as far as the IMF was concerned, marijuana and cocaine were crops like any other crop that brought much-needed foreign exchange into the economy of Latin America.

The Wall Street bankers and their Washington allies then brought Dr. Norman Bailey to public attention in support of the Civic Group in Panama and the United States. The Civic Group was formed to lend support to the Wall Street bankers attempts to get rid of Noriega, while making it appear as though it was a matter of public concern in Panama. The following people lent their support to the Civic Group:

| In Panama: | In the United States: |
|---|---|
| Alvin Weedon Gamboa | Sol Linowitz |
| Cesar and Ricardo Tribaldos | Elliott Richardson |
| Roberto Eisenmann | James Baker III |
| Carlos Rodrigues Milan | President Ronald Reagan |
| Lt. Colonel Julian Melo Borbura | Senator Alfonse D'Amato |
| The Robles brothers | Henry Kissinger |
| Jose Blandon | David Rockefeller |
| Lewis Galindo | James Reston |
| Steven Samos | John R. Petty |

General Ruben Darios Parades      General Cisneros.
Guilermo Endara
Billy Ford

After the failure of IMF campaign, the State Department, Coudert Brothers, the New York Times, Kissinger Associates and the Washington Post launched an all-out campaign of slander in the U.S. and the world press to turn public opinion against Noriega. In so doing, the conspirators sought and gained the support of drug dealers, drug bankers, couriers and assorted criminals. Anyone who would accuse Noriega of wrongdoing, or of being a drug dealer, even without proof, was welcome. The cash flow to Panamanian drug banks of $6 billion per annum had to be protected.

The Civic Crusade, the principle vehicle for coordinating the campaign to discred it, was organized in Washington D.C. in June 1987. Its principle backers and financial supporters were the Coudert Brothers, Linowitz, the Trilateral Commission, William Colby (formerly of the CIA), Kissinger Associates and William G. Walker, Deputy Assistant of State for International Affairs of the U.S. State Department. Jose Blandon, the self-described "international representative of Panama's opposition to Noriega," was employed to manage the organization.

Publicity was in the hands of Dr. Norman Bailey, a former Panamanian official of high rank. Dr. Bailey was employed by the National Security Council, whose duties were to study the movement of drug money, which of course gave him first-hand experience on how drug money was moved in and out of Panama's banks. Bailey was a close friend of Nicholas Ardito Barletta. Dr. Bailey collided head-on with Noriega when he tried to enforce IMF "conditionalities" that would have imposed greater austerity measures on the people of Panama. Bailey's partner was William Colby of the law firm, Colby, Bailey, Werner and Associates. It was to this law firm that the panic-stricken bankers and dope barons turned when it became apparent that Noriega meant business.

On taking up his post with the Civic Crusade, Bailey stated, "I began

180

my war against Panama when my friend Nicky Barletta resigned as President of Panama." Bailey had been in a unique position to find out about Panama's bank secrecy laws from Barletta, the man who'd set them up. Why was Bailey angry about Barletta losing his job? The reason was that it robbed the dope barons and their banker allies of having their own "man in Panama," a serious blow to the smooth flow of cash and cocaine in and out of Panama. Barletta was also the IMF's trigger man, and a great favorite of the Eastern Liberal Establishment, especially among members of the Bohemian Club. It was no wonder that Noriega collided head-on with Barletta and the Washington D.C. establishment.

Under Bailey's direction, the Civic Crusade turned the full circle from the cocaine barons of Colombia through the elitists of the drug trade in Washington and London. It was through Bailey that the low-class murdering cocaine mafia as well as the untouchable respectable names in the social and political registers in Washington, London, Boston and New York were made.

Bailey claimed that he wanted to oust the PDF "because it is the most heavily militarized country in the Western hemisphere." Bailey stated that a civilian junta would replace Noriega once he was ousted. We shall come to those whom Bailey proposed would run the post-Noriega Panama. In support of the Civic Crusade, six senate staffers flew to Panama in November of 1987 and remained there for four days. On their return, the staffers said it was essential for Noriega to resign, but made no mention of the staggering amounts of cash and cocaine flowing through Panama, nor of Noriega's efforts to interdict the drug trade. Although it did not spell it out, the Senate in a statement about Panama implied that if "the disorders continue," the U.S. military might have to be called in.

What was the nature of the disorders? Were they spontaneous expressions by the people of Panama of dissatisfaction with Noriega, or were they contrived, artificially created situations to suit the plans of the Wall Street bankers? For the answer, we need to examine the role played in Panama's "disorders" by John Maisto. Maisto was the No. 2 man in the U.S. embassy in Panama. He had served in South Korea, the Philippines and Haiti. Maisto had a history of trouble. After he arrived in these countries, unrest and "disorder" soon followed. According to an independent intelligence source, Maisto's influence was behind 90 percent of the street demonstrations in Panama.

Bailey did not try to hide his backing of Maisto. Addressing a forum at George Washington University, Bailey said that only if the people of Panama took to the streets and got themselves beaten up and shot, would Noriega be budged. Bailey added that unless television cameras were on hand for such events, "it would be a wasted effort. "

The final straw that broke Noriega's back came two years later in Feb. 1988, with an indictment handed down by a Miami Grand Jury. This vendetta by the Justice Department would come to seal Noriega's fate and points up the need to get rid of the archaic grand jury system, a hangover from the days of star chambers. Star chamber (grand jury) proceedings are never fair to the accused. The drug barons and their bankers combined with the political establishment in Washington D.C. to rid themselves of Noriega, who was quite properly perceived as a threat to their multi-billion dollar annual income.

Alarm bells began to sound in earnest and calls for action to remove Noriega became strident in 1986 following the forced closure of First Interamerica Bank and the PDF raid on Banco de Iberiamerica, which was owned by the Cali Cartel. Coupled with the destruction of a cocaine processing lab and a huge stock of ethyl ether in a remote jungle in Panama, the Committee of 300 gave the order to proceed with all possible speed have Noriega killed, or kidnapped and brought to the United States.

The Senate Foreign Affairs Subcommittee on Terrorism, Narcotics and International Operations, chaired by Sen. John Kerry failed to make enough mud stick to Noriega, although buckets of it were slung at him during what was tantamount to a trial of Noriega in absentia. The guardians of the $300 billion dollar off-shore drug trade called for quicker, harsher methods to be used to topple Noriega. Senator Alfonse D'Amato called for direct action: he wanted killer squads to go in an assassinate Noriega. D'Amato also advocated kidnapping

Noriega, which is perhaps where Bush first got the idea.

Then, in response to pressure from Wall Street, President Bush changed the rules of engagement of U.S. forces in Panama; henceforth they were to seek confrontation with the PDF. On July 8, 1989, General Cisneros, commander of the U.S. Army South in Panama, made an extraordinary statement, for which he should have been called to account:

"The OAS has not acted firmly enough to dislodge Noriega. Speaking for myself, I believe this is the moment for a military intervention in Panama." Since when is it permissible for the army to make political agenda? All during October and November of 1989, U.S. military forces in Panama kept up a running harassment of the PDF, which finally resulted in the tragic shooting death of an American soldier at a roadblock. The soldiers were ordered to stop at a roadblock set up by the PDF. An argument broke out and the soldiers drove off. Shots were fired and one of the U.S. servicemen was killed.

That was the signal for President Bush to launch his long-planned assault on Panama. As Panama was preparing for Christmas, on the evening of Dec. 20, 1989, a violent act of aggression against Panama was launched, without first obtaining a declaration of war as mandated by the Constitution. Between 28,000 and 29,000 U.S. troops took part in the attack, which resulted in the deaths 7,000 Panamanian citizens, and the destruction of the entire area of Chorrillo. At least 50 U.S. soldiers died needlessly in this undeclared war. Noriega was kidnapped and flown to the United States in an act of brazen international brigandry, the forerunner of many yet to come.

Why was so much attention paid to Panama by the Bush administration? Why was there so much pressure to topple Noriega? For the United States to go to such extraordinary lengths to get rid of an alleged dictator of a small country ought to tell us something. It ought to make us very curious as to what was behind this saga of diplomacy by deception. It should encourage us to be on the alert, to trust government even less, and not let diplomacy by deception on such a big scale sway us into believing that what the U.S. government does is necessarily right.

Noriega hit the drug oligarchists where it hurts; in their pockets. He cost the dope money laundering banks a large slice of their profits. He brought the bankers into disrepute. He upset the status quo by putting teeth into Panama's banking laws. Noriega got in the way of Kissinger's Andes Plan and upset arms sales in Central America. He trampled on the toes of powerful people. For that, Gen. Manuel Noriega was condemned to spend the rest of his life in an American prison.

In the minds of most Americans, Panama is on the back burner, if in their thoughts at all. Noriega is firmly walled up in a prison, no longer a danger to the lawless Bush administration and the Wall Street bankers, or their drug cartel customers. Diplomacy by deception seems to have worked for Carter, Reagan and Bush. Forgotten is the fact that the blatantly illegal invasion of Panama cost the lives of 50 Americans and 7,000 Panamanians. Forgotten is the man whom the head of the DEA, agent John Lawn, once described as the best antidrug team player he ever had in Panama. The cost to the U.S. taxpayers of keeping Panama open for drug trade business has never been disclosed.

Noriega's crime was that he knew too much about the drug trade and the banks that service it, and in 1989 was a serious threat to Rockefeller's drug money laundering banks. So he had to be dealt with. The neighborhood destroyed by U.S. troops still lies in ruins. In Panama, press censorship is still enforced, even three years after the U.S. invasion force departed. In August of 1992, the mayor of Panama City, Mayin Correa, attacked the editor of "Momento" magazine for publishing an article which revealed the goings-on with the mayor and the "special accounts" in a Panamanian bank.

Opposition to Washington's puppet government is not tolerated. Any person who engages in protest demonstrations in Panama risks arrest and imprisonment. Even "planning" a demonstration is a crime, and the planners can be thrown in jail without trial. This is the legacy left behind by Bush and those in the House and Senate who permitted him to get away with flouting the U.S. Constitution.

Bribery and corruption is rife in Panama, with drug-related accusations flying thick and fast, right up to the top levels in Washington's surrogate "Porky" Endara's government, including Carlos Lopez, Chief Justice of the Panamanian Supreme Court. The mess left behind by the Bush administration cries out to be investigated, but unhappily, no one in Washington is remotely interested in doing anything about it. The Civic Crusade has disappeared. It seems that the only civic crusade concerned the Noriega threat to the Wall Street bankers and their partners in the cocaine trade.

Will Bush ever be brought to trial for war crimes in Panama? Hardly likely, considering how the U.S. Supreme Court threw out a very modest claim by 500 Panamanian families for restitution of losses suffered during the December 1989 invasion. How about the drug trade that the removal of Noriega was supposed to guarantee to stop? The truth is, it has gone nowhere. According to my intelligence source, Colón, Panama's free trade zone, is handling about twice as much cocaine now than it did during the Noriega years. Intelligence reports tell of five to six ships loaded with drugs passing through there every day. Where before, only the top echelon officials were paid off by the drug barons, now it is everybody; drug trafficking in Panama has reached incredible new heights.

Along with the enormous increase in Panama's drug trade has come a corresponding rise in the crime rate: up 500 percent since Noriega was dragged off by his kidnappers in 1989. Gangs of unemployed youths roam once bustling Colón in search of work, only to be repeatedly turned away and left to their own devices, usually crime. With the PDF smashed, streets and highways belong to gangsters, including a few former PDF members, who cannot get work because they are "blacklisted." Several American companies based in the Colón Free Trade Zone were forced to move back to the United States because their executives were being kidnapped and held for ransom, often for as much as a million dollars. This could never have happened while Noriega was in command.

In fear of a greater crime rate than ever pertained during the rule of Noriega, a large army of private guards has sprung up. President Bush told the world that the Panama Defense Force was "a repressive tool" of the Noriega government, and let it be known that, along with his friend Dr. Bailey, he intended smashing the force. That left Panama without its formerly well-disciplined PDF, and in its place came 15,000 private guards and every member of government with his own private army. Lawlessness runs rampant through the streets of Panama.

Corruption is rife. U.S. grants (read U.S. taxpayers money), supposedly to rebuild destroyed neighborhoods, ended up in the greedy grasp of politicians placed in power by Washington. The result: uninhabitable concrete blockhouse-shaped apartments without proper windows, bathrooms or kitchens; unpainted and unfit for human occupation. This is what George Bush's "democracy" accomplished in Panama.

# Yugoslavia in Focus.
# IX.

That Serbia has always been a trouble-maker in the Balkans can be seen from the event that led to the First World War. That event was the assassination of Archduke Ferdinand on June 28, 1914, while on a visit to Sarajevo. The assassin, Gavrilo Pricip, who, together with his accomplices, acted for the Serbian secret society known as "Union or Death" (the Black Hand) was founded in 1911 by Serbia and was used to foment agitation against Austria on behalf of Serbian territorial claims.

The Serbian government knew all about the plot, and did nothing to prevent it. Europe was outraged by the crime, especially in the light of the years of intolerable activity by Serbia. On July 5, 1914, Count Alexander Hoyos was sent to Berlin and said "...I am here to settle for once and for all the problems of constant Serbian agitation and to demand justice for Austria." What was revealed by the Hoyos visit was that Serbia was a real problem, a troublemaker of the first waters, bent on acquiring territory and setting up a Serbian dynasty.

On July 23 1914, Austria delivered a written ultimatum to Serbia:

1) Dissolution of publications and organizations engaged in hostile anti-Austrian propaganda.

2) Dismissal of officials accused by Austria of anti-Austrian activities.

3) Cessation of anti-Austrian propaganda in schools.

4) Collaboration with the Austrian government in fixing responsibility for the assassination of Archduke Ferdinand.

5) Judicial proceedings against those responsible for the plot.

6) The arrest of two Serbian officials known to be involved.

7) An apology from the Serbian government.

It becomes clear upon examining the history of the period that the Serbs were devious to a degree unknown before in the Balkans. Even before making its response, the Serbs mobilized for war against Austria. Their official response looked on the surface to be conciliatory, but upon close examination, was actually a rejection of Austrian demands. Serbia had also secretly obtained assurances from Russia that it would not permit Serbia to be attacked, and privately, Serbia received the same promise from the British government.

On July 28, 1914, Austria declared war on Serbia, followed by a bombardment of Belgrade, with Germany urging occupation of Serbia. There followed declarations of war by scores of other nations:

August 1, Germany on Russia.
August 3, Germany on France.
August 4, Great Britain on Germany.
August 5, Montenegro on Austria.
August 6, Serbia on Germany.
August 6, Austria on Russia.
August 8, Montenegro on Germany.

Afterward, there was an explosion of declarations of war, Japan on Germany, Serbia on Turkey, Bulgaria on Serbia, culminating in 1918 with Guatemala on Germany, Nicaragua on Germany and Austria, Costa Rica on Germany, Haiti and Honduras on Germany. Russia was unfortunately not able to see the broader picture: that it was being set up by Great Britain for the coming Bolshevik Revolution, and Tsar Nicholas walked right into the trap which the devious Serbs and the even more dubious British had laid for him.

On May 7, 1915, at the instigation of Great Britain, the allies gave Serbia a guarantee of the eventual acquisition of Bosnia and Herzegovina, which included a guarantee of "wide access to the Adriatic." Herein lies the root cause of Serbian aggression against these states which, in 1993, is threatening to once again engulf Europe in a devastating war. Throughout the four decades of unrest, terrorism, war and Serbian territorial ambitions can be seen the hand of the British Black Nobility, personified by Sir Edward Grey, the man most responsible for dragging the United States into the First World War. Today the players are Lord David Owen, Lord Carrington, Cyrus Vance and Warren Christopher.

On Dec. 18, 1916, the so-called Wilson proposals were made public, among which was the British government's demand that Serbia and Montenegro be restored. In the light of U.S. intervention on the side of Great Britain in 1916, we should not be surprised at the present agitation to get the United States involved, through the dispatch of the Council on Foreign Relations Secretary of State Warren Christopher, to create a wider war in the Balkans. It has all been done before.

A short history of Yugoslavia reveals the presence of the British oligarchical machinations. On July 20, 1917, under tremendous pressure from the League of Nations forerunner of the United Nations, and from Britain and Italy, the Pact of Corfu was signed by Croatians, Serbs and Montenegrans. To the Serbs, signing the pact meant the first step toward a Serbian dynasty in the Balkans, in which the Hapsburgs would play a crucial role. Croatians, backed by the Catholic Church, opposed the pact, but were powerless to prevent its implementation. Thus a single nation under a Serbian dynasty took a step closer to becoming a reality.

On Nov. 3, 1918, Germany was forced to accept defeat in the First World War, thanks to U.S. military intervention, as planned by Grey, Col. House (Mandel Huis) and President Wilson. At the instigation of the British government, a "Yugoslavian Conference" was held at Geneva, and the kingdom of Croatia, Slovenia and Serbia was proclaimed on Dec. 4, 1918.

The Serbs immediately began acts of aggression against Croatia in attempts to assert their rights to Croatian territory, in spite of what they had signed in Geneva. On Nov. 26, 1917, the Montenegrans proclaimed union with Serbia and Prince Alexander accepted the new state. The history of this region from this point on sets out rather clearly all the deceit, dissembling and outright lying which led to the present conflict, in which the British government played a leading role.

As I have so often stressed, the enemy of free people everywhere is not so much Communism, but the secret all-powerful upper-level parallel government in Washington, which, in fact, has always regarded Communists everywhere as allies, while never admitting that Communism and Socialism were created in Great Britain and the United States.

Nowhere is this more in evidence than in Yugoslavia and South Africa. The Babylonian monetary system, falsely called "capitalism," is a far greater threat to Western civilization than the doctrines of Karl Marx, since it creates global conditions and then manipulates them for their One World Government New World Order masters for the benefit of the international bankers.

This tyrannical oligarchical bloc was established decades ago to strip nations of their sovereignty, cultural heritage and natural resources. In the case of South Africa, the Anglo-Boer War (1899-1902), it took the form of mass genocide and was an attempt to crush the Dutch language and the Christian religion of the people. This was combined with wholesale theft of massive amounts of gold, diamonds, platinum, titanium, iron ore and other metals and minerals.

The wheel of misfortune has gone the full circle in South Africa, with "Judas Iscariot" Pieter Botha selling his soul to the One World Government and "Kerensky" Willem De Klerk, betraying his people in a manner that would have made Benedict Arnold blush. The excuse in the case of South Africa, was "apartheid", the Biblical doctrine which advocated separation of races, while in India, the far worse caste system of separation, instigated by British occupation, was allowed to flourish undisturbed, as it does to this day. "Apartheid" in India is far more rigorous than anything seen in South Africa.

Based on the laughable concern for the welfare of the black population, a convicted felon, Nelson Mandela, whose crimes included burglary, terrorism, making bombs and treason, was suddenly made

192

over into a national hero by the jackals of the media, as was his collection of fellow criminals led by Indian lawyers and Communist Joe Slovo. This will be the new government of South Africa, once De Klerk has handed over power to Mandela. The people of South Africa are only now waking up to the fact, with shock and horror, that Moscow played only a very minor role in their betrayal. The major players are Washington and London.

The supranational government, under the direction of the Committee of 300, uses its agenda on the destruction of the sovereignty of nations directly in Croatia and Bosnia-Herzogovina, and in the United States, where it is busy making the U.S. Constitution subservient to the United Nations Charter, treacherously and treasonably introduced by the CFR and passed by the U.S. Senate in 1945, with only five Senators on record as actually having read the treaty document.

Croatia, a 10,000 year old nation, was a victim of the same conspirators who have so greatly damaged the world. Under the pretext that it had sided with Germany in WWII, Croatia began to feel the heat of the poison-pen writers of the media in the United States. Despite a democratically elected government, despite its accepted sovereignty by the United Nations, the European Economic Community, the secret government of America set out to smash Croatia, which had only very reluctantly accepted the unity forced upon it by the "Allies" on Dec. 4, 1918.

Fully backed by Great Britain and the United States, the Serb plan called for grabbing as much territory as possible so that eventually when the Serbs had what they wanted, the United Nations would be called in to "adjudicate." This would be on the basis of territory held and occupied by Serbian nationals; hence the need to drive out Croatians and Muslims to the fullest extent the Serbs could get away with. Herein is the origin of "ethnic cleansing."

President George Bush made it clear where he stood on Nov. 9, 1991:

"We see in Yugoslavia how the proud name of nationalism can splinter a country into bloody civil war." This was the "line" of the

British government also; national sovereignty must be relegated to the background of history for the sake of the New World Order.

Of all the Christian leaders, only Pope John Paul II had the courage to speak out against the Serbs, less than four days after Bush gave President Milosevic the green light. Many Protestant church leaders remained conspicuously silent:

"An end must be put to this tragedy which dishonors Europe and the world. In the last few days there have been attacks of incredible violence all over Croatia, but especially on Dubrovnik and Vukovar. In Dubrovnik, a hotel and a hospital full of refugees and wounded has been hit, among others. It's aggression, and it must end. I beg the Yugoslavian Army to spare the lives of defenseless civilians." The Belgrade government's response was to escalate the shelling of civilian housing, churches, schools and hospitals, knowing full well that the Bush administration would take no action to stop the violence.

In one of his most insidious moves, Slobodan Milosevic called upon the United Nations to send "peacekeeping forces" to divide the two sides. This was accepted by the United Nations, which, through the stationing of its troops, tacitly accepted the land seized by the Yugoslavian military as now belonging to Serbia. The same treachery was repeated in Bosnia Herzogovina. Lord Carrington, the betrayer of NATO and Rhodesia, obligingly had the United Nations deploy its soldiers in what he called crisis areas thereby neatly fulfilling the Yugoslavian objective.

Ably assisted by Lawrence Eagleburger, Cyrus Vance and the Bush administration, Germany was threatened with economic reprisals if it moved to recognize the independence of Croatia and Bosnia-Herzogovina. Eagleburger, who was castigated by Congressman Henry Gonzalez because of his extensive financial links to the Belgrade Government, said that the United States should never allow any European nation to recognize Croatia and Bosnia-Herzogovina's independence. Vance, fulfilling a role in the plan drawn up by the Inter-Religious Peace Colloquium held in Bellagio, Italy in 1972, announced that it was "too dangerous" to recognize the independence of Bosnia and Croatia, but Vance did not say what he really meant: that it was really "too dangerous" for the New World Order-One World Government.

Pope John Paul II put a spoke in the Bush plan by letting it be known that he would "send a message to the Republics recognizing their independence." The announcement sent shockwaves through the Committee of 300 and the Washington and London establishments, helping persuade Germany to recognize Croatia and Bosnia-Herzegovina.

Serbian leader Milosevic dropped "Yugoslavia" in favor of "Greater Serbia." All Serbian regular and irregular military units are now concentrated on taking over the maximum territory before the United States and Britain are forced by public pressure to make a feeble attempt to call a halt to his villainous actions. The model on which Milosevic based his territorial ambitions is the one formulated by the British during the 1923 Lausanne conference, where a plan for the mass expulsions of the civilian population of Greece and Turkey was accepted and caused thousands of deaths. It is also an almost carbon copy of how Lebanon was carved up.

The Bush administration, fully aware of the Serbian strategy, went along with it. Both Britain and the United States closed their eyes to the slaughter going on in the Balkans, where mass genocide and acquisition of territory is occurring so fast, that unless an immediate stop is put to Milosevic's advance, it will be too late. There have been some changes; whereas in Croatia, most of the population was driven out, now, in Bosnia, especially in the Muslim areas, citizens are being willfully slaughtered.

The refugee problem is being taken care of by death on a scale not seen since WWII. Entire villages and small towns have been destroyed, their inhabitants, old and young, shot down, or deliberately hit by shell and mortar fire. French intelligence sources told me that "almost 68 percent of Bosnia is in danger of being eliminated, people, churches, schools and homes. This is the worst kind of terror we have experienced in the past seventy years."

"What about the U.N. troops" I asked, "what are they doing to protect the Bosnians? Isn't that what they are supposed to be there for?" My source said "U.N. forces are actually working on the side of the Serbs, who are not supposed to be fighting inside captured Bosnian territory, patrolled by the U.N., but the Serbs simply uses U.N. troops as a shield. U.N. forces on the other hand, prevent the Bosnian forces from retaking territory lost to the Serbs; U.N. forces stand in their way, but do nothing to prevent Serbian forces from attacking from behind the blue helmets." The Serbians used the so-called "demilitarized zones" to move in heavy artillery and tanks. Bosnian leaders are now sure that the U.N. forces are promoting Lord Carrington's Lausanne plan: while Lord Owen talks "peace", the Serbs brush past the U.N. forces.

Everything that the United States and Britain have done up to now, including the mockery of so-called "sanctions" against Serbia, has been a plus for Milosevic; he was able to tell Serbians that they are the victim of "British and U.S. aggression," while not suffering any deprivation from toothless sanctions. Even the "Washington Post" admitted that sanctions are not making any difference, and concluded that fighting will not stop until the Serbs have satisfied their territorial ambitions.

As always in the case of world political strategy, the British government leads the way when it comes to inflicting pain and suffering on other nations. Lord Carrington, a former "negotiator" whose black record of treason and treachery could fill two volumes, claims that "both sides are lying," the oldest trick in the book used to distort truth. The London "Daily Telegraph" said that no aid of any kind should be given to Bosnia, not even food:

"It just makes it easier for them to go on fighting. They'd stop sooner if we left them to starve and die of their wounds or disease. You've got to be cruel to be kind. There are times when it's a rough decision to sit by and see others suffer, but it is the right one all the same."

The British government should know. During the Anglo-Boer War (1899-1902), when they were unable to defeat an insignificant irregular Boer force, Lord Kitchener rounded up all Boer women and children, put them in concentration camps, and left them to die of starvation and disease. Some 25,000 Boer women and children perished, which by comparison, would have meant that 17-18 percent of the U.S. population would have succumbed to the barbarity. Apparently, Lord Carrington and Lord Owen are repeating the Kitchener tactic in Bosnia and Croatia.

One thing is sure: a coward at heart like all bullies, Milosevic would never have dared to destroy human life and property unless he knew that he would not be stopped and suffer no reprisals from Britain and the United States. Milosevic has no intention of ending the fighting until he has captured 100 percent of Bosnia-Herzogovina. Unless he is stopped soon, the fighting is likely to spill over into Kosovo, which is an ethnic Albanian region.

Turkey has already pledged to come to the aid of Muslims if Kosovo is attacked. Turkey would use its pact with Albania as a justification of such an action. If this happens, the danger of war engulfing all of Europe will be that much greater, because refugees would flood into Macedonia, which has a substantial Albanian-Muslim population. If Turkey does come to the aid of Muslims, we can expect Greece to object, thus laying the groundwork for rapid escalation into a major war.

Right now, Macedonia is being treated to "Perfidious Albion" strategy, which means that everything that can be done is being done to undermine the Macedonian government, which was democratically elected on Sep. 1, 1991, and received its new constitution on Nov. 17, 1991. From intelligence reports I have been receiving, it appears as though political isolation is being encouraged from London, which will make it easier for the Serbian population to call for help, opening the door for an attack by the Serbian Army on Macedonia. My intelligence source told me "this is almost certain to occur once Bosnia is finished off."

The Owen-Carrington-Vance peace plan for Bosnia is a grisly farce. It will accomplish for the Serbs what they set out to do, without further loss of life to them. The plan calls for the partitioning of Bosnia, giving the Serbs a greater share of Bosnia, without the slightest guarantee that once signed and peace is declared, the Serbs wont return to mop up what is left of the Bosnians and, especially, end its centuries old Muslim presence.

Lord Carrington expressed his disdain for the people of Bosnia-Hezegovina in the "Times" of London on May 13, 1992:

"If people want to fight, there are only two options. Either let them fight, or separate them forcefully." This implies that Bosnia and Croatia elected to fight Serbian aggression for no valid reason, with Serbia as the aggressor, and that this is a family quarrel, or, a civil war." This is not a fight, it is an attempt by Croatia and Bosnia to prevent their land being taken from them and their people and culture obliterated.

We can fairly well deduce that Great Britain has been in charge of Balkans operations since before the First World War. It is said that MI6 actually runs many countries, and this is no exaggeration. How is this done? Mainly through deep cover intelligence work authorized by the British monarch, which at present, is Queen Elizabeth II.

MI6 answers only to the monarch, and Queen Elizabeth II has been far more active than most in the affairs of MI6. Of course she can do this, because the funding comes entirely from her purse. Queen Elizabeth gets briefed by "M" Section of MI6 on a daily basis, which makes her better-informed than the President of the United States. Her interest in the Balkans, as a British operation, is unquestionable.

In the present Yugoslavian operation which began in early 1984, British intelligence is in complete control. In preparation for coming events, large amounts of gunpowder were ordered for Yugoslavia from South Africa which, at that time, made the best quality gunpowder in the world. Much of South Africa's production went to Iran in 1984, but then, on orders from someone in London, Yugoslavia began siphoning off substantial quantities from these shipments for its own use. Intelligence reports to which I was privy revealed that the financial side was handled by Arbuthnot Latham Bank in London, for both the Iranian and Yugoslavian shipments. The build up in arms went on in the years leading up to the "constitutional crisis" in Yugoslavia.

The "constitutional crisis" arose at the instigation of MI6 on May 15, 1991, with Milosevic, his MI6-trained "Bolsheviks" and a militant faction in the Serbian Army blocking the system of collective State Presidents, rotated between Serbia, Croatia, Slovenia, Macedonia, Montenegro and Bosnia. This happened at at the time when it was the turn of Croatia's Stipe Mesiac to take up the post.

This action also blocked the move for a constitutional agreement to be signed by all of the parties to make four separate republics, as demanded by popular elections. Serbia, Croatia, Bosnia and Macedonia had agreed to become a confederation of states. Had this happened, MI6 control would have been considerably weakened. The intention of Milosevic acting on MI6 instructions, was to start a war in which Serbia, with the strongest military, could grab territory which did not belong to it.

Mesic went on Belgrade Radio to denounce the inflammatory move by Milosevic: "This is not an inter-ethnic conflict, but a crisis provoked by Bolshevik-Serbian expansionism." These prophetic words went right over the heads of most Western leaders and the people of the world; to them it was just a storm in a teacup, and not the beginning of the Third World War. Even at that juncture, all was not hopeless; Serbia was isolated with only the support of Montenegro, and it looked as if MI6 might be thwarted.

As has been a Committee of 300 custom for years, the United States stepped into the conflict in order to do the dirty work for the British. Bush intervened in Yugoslavia just as he did in the Gulf War. On May 20, 1991, Bush announced that all U.S. aid to Yugoslavia would be suspended. Bush knew too well that his action would destabilize a delicate situation and bring on a shooting war, yet he persisted on the specious grounds that "Yugoslavia is conducting severe repression in Kosovo." Even the timing of the announcement was highly suspect - - Serbia was then in its third year of violence against the non-Serbians

199

in Kosovo -- a pattern it was to follow in Croatia and Bosnia, and will soon follow in Macedonia.

What was the reason for the created crisis? The British government wanted to prevent German trade expansion into the Danube Basin, as well as bring about a restructuring of the Balkans into small states that would be easy to control. As the crisis widened, Russia issued a warning that the Balkans could once again become the tinderbox that could spark a major war in Europe. Addressing its comments very pointedly toward London, Moscow said "there is a very fine line between good offices and interference in internal affairs."

By now seemingly of little import to the West, Serbian-backed guerrillas began attacking Croatia, with Moscow's blessing. Bluntly stating that Russia would oppose any moves to support independent states, Moscow warned that "to enter on one side of the conflict would mean coming into conflict with others inside and outside of Yugoslavia, a conflict which could grow into an all-European one." Moscow went on supplying military backing for the Serbs.

Germany said that "attempts to change borders by force are totally unacceptable" and hinted that Britain, Russia and the United States were trying to help carve out a Greater Serbia, a very factual observation. Bush had met with Gorbachev just before the German statement was made in August. Yet in spite of every warning that a major war was in the making, the United States and Britain did nothing to so advise their people, nor did they take any action to halt Serbian expansionist acts of war.

On August 6, Dutch Foreign Minister Van den Broek issued a dire warning to his European colleagues:

"Our mission in Yugoslavia has failed. At the moment, there is nothing that we can do here, but we want the world to know that it was the Serbian side that has been responsible for the collapse of the talks. Yugoslavia now faces tragedy and catastrophe." What Van den Broek did not say was that the Serbian intransigence was secretly backed by London, Washington and Moscow. The principal intriguer for the

United States was Vance. The flames of the Third World War were rising higher and faster, yet no one seemed to be paying any attention to the danger.

Top secret intelligence information shown to me describes the Serbian-British expansionist plans more or less as follows:

The Serbians would launch an assault and carve out new borders with Croatia-Slovenia. The town of Vinkovci, an important rail center, would be the focal point of the attack. This would displace 170,000 Croatians and leave room to move in Serbians to expand the existing Serbian population of 29,000. This is what happened: the first "ethnic cleansing" had begun, without any real protest from London or Washington. How could there be any, after all it was done in conformity with U.S.-British strategy for the Balkans.

The British plan, designed by MI6, supports a "Greater Yugoslavia" which would seek a return to pre-1915 borders in the Balkans. I will say that 1915 was the optimum year in the Serbian war against Austria, a war which resulted in considerably expanded Serbian boundaries, and all MI6 is doing is picking up from where it left off in 1915.

British intelligence told Milosevic to drop the Communist label and immediately begin to push a Serbian homeland, which is what the media jackals in the United States also did. In the first step toward implementing the British plan, the towns of Karolbag, Karlovac and Virovitica were overrun by Serbian irregulars under the command of Vojslav Seselij, who committed all kinds of atrocities and then told a London newspaper "... the Croats must move or die...We don't want any other nationalities on our territories, and we will fight for our true borders."

In all of this, the CIA apparently closed its eyes, as did the Bush administration. Had resolute action been taken by the United States at that point, there would have been no further "ethnic cleansing." Can we imagine the CIA and the Clinton administration closing its eyes if White South Africa adopted Milosevic's tactics and drove the black tribes to their homelands with great violence and bloodshed?

No doubt there would be a world-wide outcry, and we would see the United Nations, Britain and the United States rush troops to South Africa, quicker than the blinking of an eye. The hypocracy of these powers in their dealings with Serbia and South Africa is atrocious.

There is no doubt that there was no action to stop Serbian atrocities and land grabbing because of Zionist pressure. The Zionists hope to use mass population transfers to solve what they call "the Palestinian problem." Zionist writer Sholomo Tadmor had expressed such an opinion, and quoted as support for his views, the mass transfer of Hindus and Muslims at the time of the separation of Pakistan and India, overseen by Lord Louis Mountbatten. Mountbatten was assassinated, some say with the foreknowledge of MI5, because his alleged homosexual activities were becoming an embarrassment to Queen Elizabeth. "Uncle Dicky" it was alleged, was coming out of the closet a little too often, and refused to heed the advise of MI5 to be more circumspect about his private life.

Serbian ties with Zionism play an important role in the tragedy prophesied by Dutch Foreign Minister Van den Broek. The savage attacks on Germany and Croatia, specifically the "Nazi" epithets hurled at Croatian President Tudjman and German Chancellor Kohl speak volumes. According to my intelligence contact, European efforts to bring about a workable solution to the problem "were sabotaged from the inside by Britain and sources in Jerusalem." Apparently the British method of a balance of powers in France, Russia, Turkey and the United States is the predetermined course.

By September of 1991, it had become perfectly clear that the Serbs intended carving up Croatia and Bosnia-Herzogovina, which would be followed by an "ethnic cleansing" of Macedonia. British intelligence reports made it clear that the Balkans program was on track and proceeding according to plan. All demands to halt Serbian aggression by European Community foreign ministers in Brussels were studiously ignored by Milosevic, Whitehall and Washington.

My intelligence source said that not one of the European leaders dared to disclose that their hands were tied when James Baker III and British foreign secretary Douglas Hurd gave Milosevic the green light to launch a full-scale assault on Bosnia-Herzogovenia. "The European ministers know very well that it is an exercise in futility to try and stop the Serbians, who know that they are backed by London and Washington, hoot at our proposals. Nothing can be done to stop the Serbian onslaught, unless British and American support is withdrawn."

No doubt this is an accurate statement: without British and U.S. tacit support, Milosevic would not have dared to commit the vile atrocities that have resulted in almost 250,000 dead, 2 million wounded and at least 4 million refugees. The Yugoslavian Serbian position is underpinned by American and British support.

History has proved that the secret government of Britain has an astonishing success record in achieving its goals through diplomacy by deception. I call to mind the negotiations over Palestine, which were fraudulent from beginning and controlled by the head of the Zionist Federation in Britain, Lord Rothschild.

In September of 1991, it was not Lord Rothschild, but his underling Lord Carrington, a confirmed Zionist, who stepped forward to negotiate in Yugoslavia. Carrington had gained excellent experience in wrecking Rhodesia, South Africa, NATO and Argentina. As master deceiver, Carrington's Sept. 7, 1991 European Community peace conference held at the Hague in Holland, was a loaded in favor of Serbia. What the conference achieved was a bolstering of Serbian aggression, allowing Serbia to redraw the boundaries of Yugoslavia to the advantage of a Greater Serbia.

By adopting an embargo in trade and economic affairs with Yugoslavia, the conference left it unstated that Croatia was being punished: the greater part of European trade with Yugoslavia is conducted by Croatia. Seeming to punish Milosevic, it was Croatia that felt the weight of the British-sponsored big stick. The peace conference for Yugoslavia was not supposed to be held unless the Serbs first stopped fighting, but when Milosevic thumbed his nose at the condition, the EC delegates went ahead with it anyway, a real political victory for the Butcher of Belgrade.

After the fraudulent conference, Italian Foreign Minister Gianni de Michelis -- who fervently supported the illegal Bush war against Iraq -- flagrantly backed Milosevic by posing the question: "Would we really go to war in Yugoslavia? Would we die for Zagreb? Surely not." On Sept. 19, Lord Carrington, officially accepted that the conference was a failure. Of course, he did not say that it was planned to fail. How could it have been a success, when Carrington had refused to allow any preconditions to be set for the Serbs to meet with the other parties?

The British-American sponsored conference was designed to give the Serbian aggressors all the time needed to grab more land and kill more Croatians, Muslims and Bosnians. This is precisely what happened. Also, for the first time, the Yugoslavian Air Force launched air raids on civilian cities. Fighting continued throughout the conference without Lord Carrington once chiding Milosevic for his conduct. It was an almost exact replay of conditions in Rhodesia: while Carrington talked "peace" and the Rhodesian forces held their fire, Communist Robert Mugabe continued his murderous assaults on women and children in isolated communities, with never a word of criticism from Carrington.

My intelligence source told me that Carrington threatened Germany with "economic reprisals" if it stepped out of line and offered real support to the Croats and Bosnians. Lord Carrington laid down his own secret ruling for a U.N. "peacekeeping" force. After the conference, Chancellor Kohl requested a meeting with George Bush. His request was granted on the condition that talk of military intervention or financial sanctions against Belgrade not be brought up. The only thing Bush agreed to was that a peacekeeping force be placed along the lines between Croatia and Serbia, thus giving de facto recognition to Serbian occupation of Croatian territory.

Primed by the British, Milosevic rejected even such a meaningless gesture against Serbia, saying that he resented "any foreign military presence." Kohl was warned that if Germany made any waves, it could start a major war in the Balkans that could quickly spread to all of Europe. What Bush did not want to recognize, was that such a war was already well into its stride, and that nothing would be allowed to stop it from occurring.

Thus, as the diplomats jawboned, Croatians, Muslims and Bosnians continued to bleed. Adding his support to the farce, Bush dispatched long-time Illuminati member and top servant of the Committee of 300 Cyrus Vance to negotiate yet another round of peace talks. Arriving in Belgrade on October 9, Vance, an original member of the Inter-Religious Peace Colloquium held in 1972 -- which laid down the basis for the current actions taking place in Yugoslavia -- got maximum peace coverage from the media.

All that transpired from Vance's visit was that the U.S. State Department told Americans in Yugoslavia to leave the country and reduced consular staff at its embassy in Zagreb. Vance's weapons embargo against the Serbs was again, a total fraud, because he knew that the Belgrade government had laid up big stocks of gunpowder for its artillery, and that its own flourishing weapons industry would not be dented by an American-sponsored embargo. As in the case of the economic embargo, it was the Croatians, Muslims and Bosnians who were severely hit by the arms embargo. A more cruel piece of diplomacy by deception would be hard to find.

On Nov. 6, 1991, German Chancellor Helmut Kohl could contain himself no longer. Defying the gag order placed on him by Lord Carrington and George Bush, Kohl told the Bundestag (Parliament) that it was necessary to immediately recognize the independent republics of Slovenia, Croatia and Bosnia-Herzogovina. Kohl was spurred on by the third rejection of a European peace plan by Milosevic.

My intelligence source told me that Kohl was outraged by the tactics of Lord Carrington, whose pro-Serbian edicts got more and more brazen. Carrington had told Milosevic that there would be no demand for Serbia to respect the Albanian-dominated Kosovo region. Carrington there and then gave the green light for the Serbians forces to attack Kosovo, and then march into Macedonia. Kohl had privately discussed with his intelligence chiefs the prospect of freezing all Yugoslavian assets in German banks, and forcing German investors to withdraw their money from banks in Belgrade.

My intelligence source told me that when Kohl's secret discussions were "leaked" to Carrington, he flew into a rage and is reported to have warned Milosevic of what might be coming. Milosevic there-upon issued an urgent decree instructing the Yugoslavian Central Bank to deposit up to 95 percent of its foreign currency -- amounting to almost $5 billion -- in Swiss bank accounts. This was carried out within hours after the Carrington "tip" was received in Belgrade.

Unsatisfied with the damage he had already done to the independent republics of Croatia, Slovenia and Bosnia-Herzogovina, Bush, most probably on the instructions of the Royal Institute for International Affairs, traveled to The Hague. On November 9, he addressed del-egates from the European Community. Declaring "there is no place for these old animosities in the new Europe, and what we see now in Yugoslavia is how the proud name of nationalism can splinter a country into civil war." Bush then berated Croatia for wanting its independence.

Continuing his attack on Croatia, Bush declared, "...while the urgent work of democracy-building and market reform moves forward, some see in freedom's triumph a bitter harvest. In this view the collapse of Communism has thrown open a Pandora's box of ancient ethnic hatreds, resentment and even revenge...All of Europe has been awakened to the dangers of an old enemy -- nationalism -- animated by hatred, unmoved by nobler ends. This nationalism feeds on old stale prejudice teaches intolerance and suspicion, and even racism and anti-Semitism."

The tail-end is the key to the Bush speech: striving for independence must be equated with anti-Semitism. How the connection is made will not be clear to those who are not familiar with codewords and intelligence jargon. What was behind the message? Intelligence con-tacts of mine who specialize in code-words told me that the message was aimed at Germany, as a warning not to come to the rescue of Croatia, Slovenia and Bosnia, lest it be mistaken for a rise in national-ism which would equated German attempts to help with "Nazism."

In the Canadian Parliament, the government was also obliged to show its hand. On Nov. 18, 1991, Foreign Minister Barbara McDougall was forced to announce that there would be no recognition of the independent republics of Croatia and Bosnia-Herzogovina. Amid roars of rage from both sides of the house, McDougall said that she had been convinced by Carrington and Vance that recognition of the republics would be a wrong move. There were angry exchanges as the truly evil, deceptive, backstabbing role of both false "negotiators" was revealed. Incredibly McDougall said "...recognition of Croatia, Bosnia and Slovenia at this time would signal the end of the negotiated process and would leave force and violence to settle the issue." This is precisely the policy of the Serbians, and what they have always desired.

Meanwhile, the arms embargo against Yugoslavia continued to be a joke, as the Serbians kept receiving gun powder from Swedish merchants, and other arms not produced in Yugoslavia. There was no end to the weapons train. The Muslims received no arms and Bosnians received only small amount of rifles and grenades via Iran. These weapons are no match for Serbian artillery and tanks. The heavily-armed Serbian Army proceeded with its campaign of "dead refugees." Croatia and Bosnia who had received 7,000 rifles and enough ammunition to last for 3 months, were pitted against Serbian 155mm artillery, mortars, heavy machine guns, grenade launchers, tanks and APCs.

The Geneva Convention was totally flouted by the Serbians, but then the United States cannot really complain on this score, for we did the very same thing in Iraq, if not worse. I do not know-of any incident to match the barbarous brutality of burying 12,000 Iraqi soldiers alive. Serbian heavy artillery has rained down a deadly barrage on churches (probably the number one target), hospitals, schools and even nursery schools. There was no doubt about the intention of the Serbians to terrorize, murder and maim as many civilians as possible.

The future of Bosnia-Herzogovina is undoubtedly very bleak; already the Serbian aggressors occupy 78 percent of the land mass and are daily driving all before them in a fearsome onslaught, while the

United Nations dashes up and down side roads and does nothing to prevent the wholesale terror and slaughter of innocent people. My intelligence source told me, "[the United Nations is] totally discredited, they do nothing to help the civilian population, less still protect them from Serbian atrocities. The U.N. mission in Bosnia in particular is a sham and a disgrace."

Not satisfied with the havoc it has already wrought in Croatia, Bosnia-Herzogovina and Slovenia, the Council of Ministers of the Europeans Community met in Portugal on May 2, 1992 and immediately issued a statement declining to recognize the independence of the Republic of Macedonia. It was, in effect, the third time that destabilization forces from outside of Yugoslavia had stepped into the arena to ensure that Macedonia is the next target for Serbian aggression.

Macedonia is entitled to independence, as are all the Balkan states. It has territory, a sovereign people, a sovereign parliament, and the overwhelming support for independence expressed by the people in a referendum held on Sep. 18, 1991. The Assembly (parliament) was elected in November of 1990, and a new constitution was promulgated and accepted a year later.

So why is the European Council unwilling to recognize Macedonia's independence? The reason given is that Greece does not like the name "Macedonia," and this could be a cause for future conflict. In the interim, the door is left wide open for Serbian aggression on the grounds that Macedonia is not a republic, but an integral part of Yugoslavia. I expect Macedonia to suffer the fate of Croatia and Bosnia-Herzogovina, with the tacit approval of the United States, Britain and France. President Mitterand of France is determined to play a major role in Yugoslavia, even though he is a lame-duck president.

Thus the stage is set for ethnic cleansing in Macedonia, but this time it will escalate and spread to Albania and Hungary, invoking a strong possibility that Russia might step in which would mean the start of a major European war into which the United States will be dragged. Our forces will carry the main burden in men, equipment and financial costs.

This must not be allowed to happen. The American people must somehow be awakened to the diplomacy by deception which is going on, in spite of which the deception of the media ,has given their full voice of support. There are many other alternatives that can be used to stop the war. Such measures were used successfully to topple the Shah of Iran, put severe pressure on South Africa, and destroy Iraq *after* the shooting had ended.

One principal weapon in the hands of the United States and Britain is financial control. Within a matter of days the Serbians could be forced to halt their aggression by placing a ban on trading in Yugoslavian currency, by freezing all Yugoslavian funds, wherever they are found and by imposing severe penalties (with teeth in them) for any nation trading with Serbian Yugoslavia. These measures, stringently applied, will do far more than any ground forces can do, and can be quickly implemented. Under no circumstances should the United States commit ground forces to the Balkans, as this would herald the start of a major European war.

Coupled with these financial and economic measures, the United States should give Serbia a three day period to remove its heavy artillery and mortars, after which time the United States, upon approval of Congress, should send in fighter-bombers, or retro-fitted cruise missiles to knock out Serbian gun emplacements. The lame excuse that our pilots will not be able to find their targets does our armed services a great disservice. Given the high state of technological advances, especially in infra-red and laser imagery, there is no doubt that our pilots could find their targets in almost any kind of weather, day or night. The only thing that is stopping this kind of action is the unwillingness of Washington to act against the interests of Great Britain. The use of retro-fitted cruise missiles would also eliminate the possibilities of any U.S. casualties in the air.

Defense intelligence experts say that it would take a force of 35,000 to 40,000 soldiers to end Serbian aggression. This is an absolute understatement designed to deceive the American people, who might be willing to consent to such a number of troops, but would balk at a larger force. The grand plan is to get our ground troops involved, either in Bosnia or (most likely) in Macedonia. When the timing is right, we will be told that our ground forces are in danger of being overrun, and that another 50,000 troops are needed. On the face of it, who among us would say "no more troops, enough is enough." In this manner will the war be escalated. Now is the time to say "NO" to ground forces, and "YES" to air or cruise missile strikes to take out Serbian heavy artillery and mortars.

Such action will foil the grand design of British strategists who have long planned to keep Europe in subjugation -- economic and militarily -- using the political and military wings of NATO. There is no longer any need for deception once the game plan is known. It is a matter of putting a bold face on what has to be done. The clear intent of Washington and London is to force the New World Order on Europe, using the Serbians as surrogate terrorists to show other nations that NATO protection is still a vital necessity.

What the New World Order proponents are trying to establish is that there is a long-term trend toward anarchy when nationalist interests dominate. The continuing fragmentation of Europe, according to the IRPC 1972-Bellagio plan, was to show that peoples living together, whether in a majority or a minority, will always have differences and seek to end their differences in violent conflict. Thus it is reasoned, the protection of a non-nationalist New World Order government is absolutely necessary, and indeed desirable.

A balance of power between nations, say the NWO strategists, won't solve the problem, because nations will always be suspicious of each other, fearing the one is trying to secure an advantage over the other. An example of this can be seen in relations between Japan and the United States which have deteriorated sharply over the past five years. A New World Order-One World Government will take care of the tensions and make them vanish, because the root cause of the problem is nationalist rivalry which would be removed.

This idealistic sham proposed by the New World Order will of involve mass transfers of large population groups, which, we are told will not be accompanied by bloodshed. "You have seen what happened in Yugoslavia," the NWO strategists will say, "surely it is better to accomplish such transfers peacefully?" They might point to the peaceful transfers of Hindus and Moslems and the Greeks and Turks; the latter at the end of the First World War. The truth is very different; millions of Hindus and Muslims died as did thousands of Greeks and Turks in these "peaceful" transfers.

"Perhaps" the NWO planners will say, "but the real benefit will come from a turning away from global politics. " In support of their theory, they point to the horrors of Yugoslavia, which they will promise, could never be repeated in a New World Order-One World Government. They point to Europe's inability to bring about a cessation of hostilities in Yugoslavia, promising that under a One World Government, such conflicts would not begin. If by some chance they did, they would be quickly smothered. Europe's gross failure to prevent the Yugoslavian conflict will be held up as a model of how the world should not be allowed to run its affairs in the future.

Under these circumstances, the collapse of Europe into a major war would be a big plus for the New World Order-One World Government. The French rushed to embrace Woodrow Wilson as a peacemaker and a savior when he arrived in Paris with his peace plan, and the deception is about to be duplicated. European nations and America will probably rush to embrace the New World Order-One World Government as the only hope for eternal peace.

Like Wilson's 14-point peace plan, what each of the nations will get is everlasting slavery and barbarity never before seen on earth. The Yugoslavian tragedy is a created tragedy, with much wider goals in the overall strategy. The brutality of the Serbians is all to the good, since daily it causes fear among the nations of Europe that they might be next, and when the moment arrives, they will have been sufficiently "softened up" to embrace their future slavemasters with open arms.

After vacillating for months, President Clinton promised to arm Bosnian Muslims. There were cries of outrage from London. With a single voice, the plan was denounced by Lord Owen, Lord Carrington and Cyrus Vance. My intelligence source said the message received by Clinton from these worthies was that it "would be unwise to arm the Bosnian Muslims, as this would only tend to increase the level of violence that would block a peaceful settlement on which we are working."

As a result of this unseemly pressure on U.S. foreign policy, Clinton delayed the plan to help the Muslims defend themselves, a delay which will make it easier for the Serbian aggressors to go on murdering and land-grabbing. This is what "our" sovereign independent nation has come down to; we bow the knee to every demand that comes from the Committee of 300.

We do not know as yet which of the Black Nobility is controlling the Serbians, but it is a foregone conclusion that there is involvement by some of their top members. Lebanon is a good example of things to come in Bosnia, Croatia and Slovenia. The "civil war" in Lebanon was set in motion and controlled by Black Nobility members Prince Johannes von Thurn und Taxis, Lord Harlech (David Ormsby Gore) and Lord Carrington, acting in conjunction with Alexander Haig, Julian Amery, Henry Kissinger, Sir Edmund Peck, Nicholas Elliot, (MI6 station chief for the Middle East), Rupert Murdoch and Charles Douglas Home, among others.

This crime against Lebanon was characterized by the news media as civil war when it was nothing of the kind. The murderous Serbian onslaught against its neighbors is portrayed in the same way. Only this time the conspirators are being considerably more careful in covering their tracks in view of the way they were followed in Lebanon, which led to their exposure by myself and one other writer. Once I have the names of the behind-the-scenes controllers in Serbia, I will not hesitate to expose them.

As in Lebanon, the plan is to carve up the Balkans into a number of small, weak autonomous states which will not be able to offer any resistance to the plans of the New World Order-One World Government. If American and allied ground troops are sent to Bosnia and

Macedonia, they will perform in the manner of the Allied Expeditionary Force which landed in Murmansk during the closing days of the First World War.

The deviousness of Lawrence Eagleburger and Brent Scowcroft companion in Yugoslavian business enterprises must be exposed, and the importance of Milosevic's Washington connections cannot be overstated. The people of Slovenia, Bosnia-Herzogovina and Macedonia will not receive any help from the world's only superpower, controlled like a wimp by the Committee of 300 and its foreign affairs department, the Royal Institute for International Affairs.

# Anatomy of Assassinations. X.

Assassination has long been a favorite method of getting rid of a political rival or leader whose policies are an anathema to another power, or where a leader appointed by a secret body does not continue to obey their orders, as in the case of President John F. Kennedy.

Assassinations are also carried out to bring about political, economic or religious changes deemed desirable by parties in opposition to a government, ruling body or religious precept. History is filled with examples.

Very often conspiracies surround assassinations which are never uncovered, such as in the murder of Martin Luther King Jr., John F. Kennedy and Robert Kennedy. In these three cases, the alleged murderer was silenced, Oswald before he could get his day in court; Ray by being sidetracked by an unscrupulous lawyer; Sirhan Sirhan committed to prison. This has given rise to the belief very strongly held by millions of Americans that neither Ray, Oswald nor Sirhan Sirhan were the ones who pulled the triggers.

Immediately following the King murder, the Memphis police had a golden opportunity to lift fingerprints from the rooming house where Ray was supposed to have stayed. The rooming house was on South Main Street, in a black neighborhood in Memphis; Ray arrived there at 3pm on April 4 1968. Witnesses said they saw three men coming out of the building, one of whom was Ray. It would be interesting to know why no effort was ever made to locate the other two men seen with Ray.

There was no positive identification of Ray's fingerprints at the rooming house. According to Major Barney Ragsdale, of the Georgia Bureau of Investigation, the Missouri State Penitentiary where Ray had been incarcerated sent the FBI a wrong set of fingerprints. For some reason, as yet unexplained, it took the FBI two weeks to announce that Ray was the killer. This confounded the FBI's long-held claim that it can identify a person by print comparison within 10 minutes. The fingerprint comparison check was taken from Los Angeles records, a departure from normal procedure. Atlanta would have been the logical place to check records. The Los Angeles fingerprints were those of Eric Starvo Galt. A photograph accompanied the prints. Did the delay have anything to do with Eric Starvo Galt? Was "Galt" Ray?

When the Memphis police were shouldered out of the way by the FBI, AP reporter Don McKee wrote: "Federal agents have scoured the city showing sketches of a man's face and asking about the name Eric Starvo Galt, the mysterious object of a hunt linked to the probe of Dr. Martin Luther King's assassin. What the agents have learned or what they want with Galt is a tightly kept secret."

Gaylord Shaw, also an AP reporter sent a dispatch which stated: "the FBI is withholding nationwide distribution of a composite drawing of Dr. Martin Luther King's assassin. When the white Mustang, which Ray was said to have used to make his getaway after the shooting, was found in Atlanta, it was traced to Eric Starvo Galt. The FBI issued a bulletin for the arrest of Galt for 'conspiring with another man he alleged was his brother to injure, oppress, threaten, intimidate Dr. King.' The bulletin was at first withdrawn, and then reinstated. Among other things, it stated that Galt had taken dancing lessons in New Orleans in 1964 and 1965. James Earl Ray was in the Missouri State Penitentiary at the time.

Two weeks after King's murder, J.Edgar Hoover announced that Galt was in fact James Earl Ray. Hoover did not say what became of Galt's brother. Why was no investigation conducted into the whereabouts of Galt's "brother?"

The mysterious removal of Detective Redditt of the Memphis Police Department from the area of the Lorraine Motel has yet to be explained. After Redditt was escorted home, Lieutenant Arkin of the Memphis Police Department received a message from the Secret Service said that "a mistake had been made" concerning the "contract on Redditt's life." Detective Arkin then drove to Redditt's home for an unknown purpose. Arkin still won't talk to anyone about this strange episode.

Redditt was actually accompanied on his surveillance detail by W.B. Richmond, a fellow detective. Richmond testified that he was not on surveillance duty at the time that King was shot, but that he was at the Memphis Police Department headquarters and knew nothing of the actual murder. Later, Richmond did a complete about-face and admitted that he was at a fire station directly across the street from the Lorraine Motel at the exact time King was shot. Why the contradiction? Did Richmond testify to this fact under oath to the Justice Department, and if so, why was he never indicted for perjury?

When Scotland Yard arrested Ray at London's Heathrow Airport, he told the officers that his name was "Ramon George Sneyd." Once again, the FBI did something strange; the Los Angeles fingerprints of Galt were sent to Scotland Yard, rather than the ones in FBI records in Washington.

The now-famous photograph of King lying dead on the balcony of the Lorraine Motel shows Jesse Jackson and Andrew Young pointing not at the window of the rooming house, but to the knoll where witnesses said they saw a man covered with a towel hiding behind some bushes. The directional track of the wound in King's body indicates beyond a reasonable doubt that this was most likely the area from where the shot was fired, rather than from the bathroom window of the rooming house.

That Ray's trial was a mockery of justice cannot be doubted. Ray was not allowed to mention the word "conspiracy" which appeared in his original pleas a number of times. The judge also refused to let Ray discuss his conspiracy statement and his lawyer Percy Foreman, agreed with the judge. On Foreman's advice, Ray pleaded guilty, which doomed his chances of obtaining a full and fair trial.

In October of 1974, Ray was granted a retrial hearing in Memphis Federal District Court, but after eight days of hearings, his plea was dismissed. Ray continued to proclaim his innocence and told his family he was determined to have the truth come out. Perhaps that is why in 1977, while in the Brushy Mountain State Prison, an attempt to murder him was made. Although he suffered serious stab wounds, Ray survived. There are just too many loose ends lying around for a convincing case to be made that Ray fired the shot that killed King.

The Committee of 300 is constantly striving to control all natural resources in all countries. Their position has been stated and restated by H.G. Wells and Lord Bertrand Russell. Nowhere was this position more strongly enforced than in the Congo and South Africa.

Known as the Belgian Congo, this huge country, the second largest in Africa, was for decades ruthlessly stripped of its natural resources: copper, zinc, tin, rubber, ivory and agricultural products such as cacao, coffee and palm oil. Belgian King Leopold II often said that everything of value in the Congo belonged to him. This was certainly true, as the Belgian government ran the country's railroads, mines, smelters, cacao and palm oil plantations, factories, hotels through front corporations. The corporations answered to King Leopold II, in essence, to the Committee of 300. It was Committee of 300 policy at its best.

Congolese workers received little pay, and what they did get was largely in the form of free housing, medical benefits and clothing. All that was threatened by an aspiring political leader by the name of Patrice Lumumba who, in 1959, announced the formation of a national political party to oppose Belgian rule of the country. The Belgian authorities tagged Lumumba a "communist" and a danger to the welfare of the country. He was arrested and then released. Lumumba was in fact not concerned with communism, but directed his efforts at bettering the life for the Congolese people.

In 1960, great unrest occurred as Lumumba called for independence from Belgium. Lumumba asked for help from the United Nations and the United States, but was refused. He was dubbed a "man who plays with Marxist verbiage" by the State Department which, by the way, did not offer proof of its contention. Lumumba's amazing gift of oratory was creating such an impression with the Congolese people that the Committee of 300 began to sit up and take notice.

In August of 1960, two CIA officers, both with criminal records, were ordered by Allen Dulles to murder Lumumba within 3 months. Lumumba's gift of oratory was noted by CIA reports from the Congo and also described Lumumba's alleged communist connections. The following month, the CIA ordered Joseph Schneider, a bacteriological scientist, to the Congo with a diplomatic bag containing a vial of a lethal virus to be used to kill Lumumba. Dulles ordered the elimination of Lumumba after consulting with Eisenhower, but the virus carried by Schneider could not be administered because Lumumba was constantly on the move.

The Senate Committee overseeing intelligence operations chaired by Frank Church, reported that the CIA was in touch with elements in the Congo who wanted Lumumba killed. The implication of the Church report was that these were Belgian government officials. Fearing for his life, Lumumba sought protection from the United Nations, but was turned away. Instead, the United Nations placed him under house arrest, but he managed to escape in a car provided by his brother, and with his wife and one of his children, Lumumba fled to Stanleyville, where he enjoyed strong support.

CIA reports in 1960 tell of how the agency helped to recapture Lumumba by showing the Congolese military how and where to set up roadblocks. The puppet leader appointed by the Committee of 300, one Joseph Mobutu, oversaw the search. When Lumumba was caught by Mobutu's men on Dec. 1, 1960, he was held prisoner until Jan. 17, 1961.

On Feb. 12, 1961, Mobutu announced that Lumumba had escaped from a house in a remote area where he was being held and that he had been killed by hostile tribesmen. But the CIA's John Syckwell said that a CIA agent drove the body of Lumumba around in the trunk of his car while deciding what should be done with it. It was never disclosed as to exactly what was done with it. However, the United Nations reported that two Belgian mercenaries, Col. Huyghe, and Capt. Gat, were the killers. The Justice Department ended its inquiries by concluding that there was no evidence to support any CIA involvement in Lumumba's murder.

The murder of Pope John Paul I can also be classified as a political assassination if we take into account that the Vatican is a state and that its titular head, the pope, can and does wield enormous power which has changed the course of history. From the documents I studied, it is certain that four popes have been murdered, all of them by the administering of poison.

The recorded history of Pope Clement XIII (Carlo Rezzonico) is well documented, if not proven. At the urging of royalty in Europe, Clement decided to put an end to Jesuit subversion inside the Catholic Church hierarchy. After months of delay, Clement's proclamation suppressing the Jesuit Order was ready. But he never got a chance to read it into canon law. After a night of terrible convulsions and vomiting, Clements died on Feb. 12, 1769. Clement's proclamation vanished, never to be found again, and the Jesuits grew stronger than ever.

Pope Clement XIV (Lorenzo Gananelli) took up where Pope Clement XIII was forced (by death) to leave off. On Aug. 16 1773, Clement issued the Bull, "Dominus ac Redemptor" which declared the Jesuits as enemies of the Church. Immediate action followed with the arrest and imprisonment of the Jesuit general and his hierarchy, seizure of Jesuit property and the closure of its learning institutions. It was the greatest blow ever struck against the Jesuits. Immediately thereafter, sinister whisperings against Clements began to circulate in the Vatican.

On Oct. 2, 1774, Pope Clement XIV became violently ill, and, after hours of horrible suffering, he passed away. A potent poison, administered by persons unknown, ended his life. So potent was the poison that it caused an immediate collapse of his internal organs, followed by an amazingly swift decomposition of his entire body. His face was completely unrecognizable and his body could not lie in state. The message was clear, leave Freemasonry and the Jesuits alone, or suffer death.

When Albini Luciani reluctantly accepted the papal crown and became Pope John Paul I, he immediately realized the extent of the Freemason/Jesuit influence in the highest councils of the Vatican. An excellent scholar with a remarkably quick mind, he was completely misread by his enemies; his meek humility mistaken for servility. It was perhaps, for this reason, that among the 99 cardinals who voted for him, were prominent supporters of Freemasonry and the Jesuits.

But Pope John Paul's demeanor hid an iron will and determination of a man who, once his mind was made up, could not be dissuaded from carrying out what he believed he should do. The liberal cardinals who voted for him in the mistaken belief that Pope John could be easily manipulated where shocked to hear that he intended exposing the Freemasons in the Vatican hierarchy, and intended to terminate the big business inside the Church.

Pablo Panerai, editor of "Il Mondo," a leading newspaper in Rome had specifically attacked what he called "Vatican Inc." Panerai named Menini and Paul Marcinkus and criticized their links with Sindona's and the Continental Illinois Bank of Chicago. Panerai shocked the Vatican by sharply attacking Bishop Marcinkus for sitting on the board of the Cisalpine Overseas Bank of Nassau, Bahamas.

This was enough for Pope John Paul I to take action. On August 27, 1978, he invited his Secretary of State, Cardinal Villot, to have supper with him in his private apartment. There is one loose end here that is bothersome: Pope John knew that Villot's name appeared on Gelli's P2 list of more than 100 Catholic Freemasons in the Vatican. This list was seized when the Italian police raided Gelli's villa. Why then, did the pope forewarn Villot of what he was about to do?

That evening over supper, Pope John Paul I ordered Villot to prepare a list of the Freemasons in high places in the Vatican. He told Villot that it was beyond the pale for Catholics to belong to a secret organization which, he said, was dedicated to the destruction of Christianity, as recorded by three previous popes and confirmed by Weishaupt, founder of the Illuminati.

221

He then ordered that once Villot completed his task, there was to be a spectacular reshuffling of the Freemasons; they were to be scattered abroad where they could do less harm to the Church. According to my Vatican intelligence sources, Villot was at first angry, then stunned arguing that such sweeping changes would only bring chaos. But like so many others, Villot underestimated the iron-willed determination of his Pope. Luciani remained adamant; his order stood. Villot was to have the list ready without delay.

Those who had the most to lose were Marcinkus, Calvi, Sindona, Cody, De Stroebel and Menini in "Vatican Inc.," while leading Jesuits stood to lose all power and influence if their names appeared on the Villot list. Villot himself had a lot to lose as a member of the exclusive financial club in the Vatican, the Administration of the Patrimony of the Holy See. He would lose his position as its head, as well as his position as Vatican Secretary of State. For Villot, perhaps even more than the others, it was absolutely necessary to prevent Luciani's order from being carried out.

One month later, on Sept. 28, 1978, Villot was again invited to supper at the Pope's private apartment. Luciani sought to calm Villot's fears, speaking in French, one of the many languages in which he was fluent. According to Cardinal Benelli, who was present, it had no impact on Villot's icy demeanor. In a firm voice, Luciani demanded that his orders for the list of Freemasons be carried out forthwith. The pope said he was disturbed by reports from Cardinal Bennelli that Institutompoer la Opera di Relione (OPR, the Vatican bank) was involved in improper business dealings. He wanted Monsignor de Bomnis, Marckinkus, De Stroebel and Ortolani dismissed, and OPR's links with Sindona and Calvi severed immediately.

Luciani had unleashed a chain of events that would lead to his undoing. Others, who imagined that their power was enough to override the power of Freemasonry, failed to realize how flawed their beliefs were. Pope Clement XIV may have been aware of his fate when he whispered, "I am undone," as he signed the Bull to break up the Jesuits.

The details of what Luciani proposed to do were given to Cardinal Benelli, and the Pope called his close friend, Cardinal Colombo, in Milan and confided the details in him. This was confirmed by Father Diego Lorenzi, who made the call for Pope John and heard what passed between them. But for this, there would have been no record of what Pope John Paul I demanded of Villot; the papal document containing instructions to Villot to deliver the names of the Freemasons was never found.

Shortly after his meeting with Villot, on the evening of Sept. 28, 1978, Pope John Paul retired to his study. Curiously, that night there was no medical doctor on duty in the Vatican, and even more curious, no guard was posted outside Pope John's apartment. Between the hours of 9:30 p.m., that evening and 4:30 a.m., the next morning, Pope John Paul I was murdered. A reading lamp that burned the whole night was seen by a Swiss Guard, yet nothing was done by Vatican security to check up on the unusual circumstance. Pope John Paul I was the first pope to die unattended, but not the first to die at the hands of poisoners.

Villot featured prominently in the cover up of the death of Luciani. When called by Sister Vicenza, who attended to Luciani's simple needs, and was the first to discover the Pope's body on September 29., Villot slipped a bottle of Efortil, a medication prescribed for Pope John that was on the nightstand, into his pocket. He then removed Luciani's glasses and slippers. Next, Villot went to Pope John's desk and removed the last will and testament of his Pope. He then walked out of the apartment without saying a word to Sister Vicenza, who was present. Sister Vicenza described Villot's peculiar behavior to Cardinal Belleni. When queried about his actions by Belleni, Villot denied Sister Vicenza's report. He also lied about the circumstances in which Luciano's body was found.

Others who perished at the hands of a poisoners were President Zachary Taylor, who paid with his life for refusing to carry out orders of Freemasonry. The orders were issued by Mazzini's representative De Leon, founder of Young America, a Freemasonic movement. On the evening of July 4, 1850, Taylor took ill and began vomiting up a thick black substance. He died a slow and painful death, which doctors put down to "drinking too much cold milk and eating too many cherries." But this did not explain the thick, black substance. Vomiting of such a severe nature would indicate the presence of a deadly poison. As in the case of Pope John Paul I, no autopsy was performed on Taylor, and the manner of his death was most casually described by doctors who could not possibly have known its exact cause. In this regard, the death of Pope John Paul I was similarly handled in a most cavalier fashion by the Vatican physician, Dr. Buzzonnetti, who should have had the utmost suspicion of foul play.

The murder of Congressman Louis T. McFadden came as a result of his frontal assault on the Federal Reserve Board and the Federal Reserve Banks, the most sacred cow of many sacred cows of the secret government of America. McFadden was chairman of the House Banking Committee in 1920. He openly attacked the governors of the Federal Reserve Board and accused them of causing the 1929 Wall Street Crash.

McFadden's war on the Federal Reserve reverberated throughout Washington. George Stimpson, founder of the National Press Club, said that McFadden's charges against the governors were incredible and that the community could not believe what McFadden was saying. But when McFadden was accused of being mad, it was Stimpson who said he didn't believe it for a minute.

McFadden waged a tireless war against the Federal Reserve for more than 10 years, exposing some of the most vile crimes of the 20th Century. One of McFadden's most stinging charges was that the Federal Reserve system treasonably conspired to destroy the constitutional government of the United States. He also attacked President Roosevelt and the international bankers.

On Friday, June 10, 1932, speaking before the House, McFadden made the following statement:

"Mr. Chairman, we have in this country one of the most corrupt institutions the world has ever known. I refer to the Federal Reserve

Board and the Federal Reserve banks. The Federal Reserve Board, a government board, has cheated the United States and its people out of enough money to pay the national debt...This evil institution has impoverished and ruined the people of the United States; has bankrupted itself and has practically bankrupted our government. It has done this through the defects of the law under which it operates, through the maladministration of that law by the Federal Reserve Board, and through the corrupt practices of the moneyed vultures who control it..."

In a fiery and impassioned speech before the House on May 23, 1933, McFadden said as follows:

"Mr. Chairman, there is not a man within the sound of my voice who does not know that this country has fallen into the hands of the international money changers, and there are few Members here who do not regret it...Mr. Chairman, we are on Concord Bridge today. Our enemy, the same treacherous enemy, is advancing upon us. Mr. Chairman, I will die in my tracks before I yield him a square inch of American soil or so much as one dollar of his war debt to us.

"Mr. Chairman, I demand that the gold stock of the United States be taken from the Federal Reserve banks and placed in the U.S. Treasury. I demand an audit of the United States government financial affairs from the top to the bottom. I demand a resumption of specie payment based on full gold and silver values..."

This denouncement, followed by McFadden's exposure of the Reparation Bonds and Foreign Securities in $100 million worth of German commercialized reparation bonds, so shook the secret upper-level parallel government, that conspiracy watchers believe it was at this juncture that the order was given to permanently silence McFadden.

In all, there were three attempts on McFadden's life. The first one happened when he attended a dinner function and suddenly became violently ill. A medical doctor who sat close to him was able to pull him back from the jaws of death. The second attempt happened when McFadden was alighting from a taxi near the Capitol. Two shots were fired at him, but both missed. The third, attempt which was successful, occurred in New York City, where McFadden was attending another dinner function. Again, he was seized by a violent fit of retching and died before help could reach him. The poisoner succeeded in ridding the international bankers and the Federal Reserve Board of Governors of the one man who might have gone on to fully expose their activities and turn the nation against them, thereby forcing an end to their control over our money system.

Dr. Hendrik Verwoerd was the father of "apartheid" in South Africa. A native of Holland, Dr. Verwoerd strode across the South African political landscape like a colossus. Fearless and scornful of the Oppenheimer machine and the liberal politicians it controlled, Dr. Verwoerd lost no time in attacking the international bankers and their lackeys in South Africa.

Dr. Verwoerd despised the United Nations and sharply criticized its interference in South Africa's internal affairs, particularly its invitation for India to discuss discrimination against Indians in South Africa. The Indians were descendants of indentured laborers brought to South Africa by Cecil John Rhodes. As a class, they had achieved tremendous prosperity, mostly at the expense of the native Bantu, this being attributed to the Jan. 13, 1949 riots between the Zulus and the Indians in Durban, which left 100 dead and more than 1,000 injured. The majority of victims were Indians.

Dr. Verwoerd would not have anything to do with the Indians, claiming that their leaders were all communists. In later years, after his murder, his claim appears to have been substantiated by the fact that legal representation for Indians and blacks accused of political crimes had fallen into the hands of Indian lawyers, all of whom belonged to the Indian Congress, an organization with ties to Communism.

On April 27, 1950, the Group Areas Bill was introduced, the primary purpose of which was to separate the races into different areas. Following rioting in April of 1953, new anti-terrorist legislation was introduced and put into effect. At this point, the Committee of 300 found a stooge in one Alan Paton, an whose book "Cry the Beloved Country" was artificially made into an internationally recognized piece of literature. Paton was a favorite of the liberals, who made something of a hero out of what was a thoroughly disagreeable man. Paton founded the Liberal Party which favored the vote for "all civilized people." In this he had the backing of the mighty Oppenheimer machine. Evidence of these accusations can be found in the files of the "Sunday Times," an Oppenheimer-owned Johannesburg newspaper.

Dr. Verwoerd was elected as prime minister on Sept. 3, 1958. On Oct. 5, 1960, a referendum approved a proposal to establish a republican form of government and end membership in the British Commonwealth. On May 31, 1961, Dr. Verwoerd was accorded a hero's welcome upon his return from London, where he delivered his bombshell withdrawal statement to the British Parliament. The United Nations immediately asked its member-states to ban the sale of military equipment to the Republic of South Africa.

The political lines were drawn as the third Anglo-Boer War got under way. On April 20, 1964, a so-called panel of U.N. experts issued a report calling for a non-racial democracy in South Africa, totally ignoring the caste system which had been in force for hundreds of years in India. The caste system, a strict segregation of social classes, far more severe than anything seen in South Africa, remains in force. Still to this day, the United Nations remains silent on "apartheid" in India.

Dr. Verwoerd ruled the country in an orderly manner and tolerating no black or Indian anti-government groups. On June 12, 1964, Nelson Mandela and seven blacks were caught red-handed manufacturing bombs and in possession of banned Communist literature. Mandela's mentors -- the instigators of these crimes -- Abrams and Wolpe, fled the country, but Mandela and his followers were sentenced to life imprisonment for acts of sabotage, theft, violent crimes and attempts to subvert the government.

The trial was *scrupulously* fairly conducted under South Africa's independent judicial system. Mandela was jailed for common criminal activities, and not for political reason. Records of the case which I studied in the Rand Supreme Court, clearly state the nature of the *civil* criminal acts of which Mandela was found guilty. It is the Western press that has obscured this truth, and made out that Mandela was jailed for political reasons. There was never any attempt by the United States and Britain to be objective about Mandela.

On Sept. 6, 1966, Dr. Verwoerd was stabbed to death by a messenger while Parliament was in session in Cape Town. The messenger was well known as he had worked in that capacity for years, and was a familiar figure as he moved freely around the floor delivering papers and documents to various members. The obvious conclusion that foreign elements were involved in the assassination were suggested by the police. Already, the dark forces were at work to destroy the Republic of South Africa.

The assassin was described as "mentally deranged", but intelligence agents around the world believed that he was programmed to commit the murder, knowing what we know today about intelligence agencies use of hypnotism. The assassin had never previously shown any signs of mental disorder before his attack on Dr. Verwoerd. The question is, "who gave the order to murder Verwoerd and who did the programming?" Only two intelligence agencies had the power at that time to carry out missions involving mind control; the CIA and the KGB. Nothing could be proved, but the consensus of opinion is that the murder was the work of the CIA.

In 1966, secret experiments carried out by the CIA using gigahertz mind-altering rays was not in the public domain and remained secret up until John Markus, in 1977, and Gordon Thomas, in 1990, fully exposed the conduct of the CIA in this field. There are experts today who firmly believe that Dr. Verwoerd was one of the first victims of these CIA experiments.

Like many others, I wrote a substantive work on the assassination of John F. Kennedy. Many of the claims I made could not be substantiated at the time, but now, other independent sources are coming forward to confirm what I said. Thus far, none of perpetrators of these heinous crimes has been caught and it is unlikely that any of them will ever be apprehended. The threat of assassination by whatever method still hangs over all national leaders, especially in the United States, where if someone takes it upon himself to let the truth be known, the possibility of coming to harm cannot be discounted.

One such source is Robert Morrow, a former contract employee of the CIA. Morrow confirms that Kennedy had to die because he was not liked by the CIA and because he had given notice that he would get rid of both Hoover and Lyndon Johnson. Morrow confirmed what I said about Tippit; that he was sent to kill Oswald to stop him from talking, but that Oswald, recognizing him, shot him first.

Morrow also confirmed what I said about Oswald going to a movie house after the shooting for a rendezvous with Jack Ruby. Morrow further confirmed that Oswald never shot Kennedy, and that at the time of the shooting, Oswald was on the second floor of the Texas School Book Depository, drinking a Coke and eating a sandwich.

Morrow also believes that Kennedy was killed by a shot from the front which came from a grassy knoll situated in front of the motorcade. He also confirmed my account of the President's limousine being hustled away from the scene and shipped away for dismantling before anyone could do any full-scale forensic work on it.

Morrow makes some interesting allegations; one in particular has it that George Bush was given the job of Director of Central Intelligence (DCI) for the sole purpose of preventing the Church Senate committee from getting all of the facts about the Kennedy assassination, which he did. Morrow also claims that Bush knows everything there is to know about Kennedy's assassination.

# Apartheid And India's Caste System. XI.

Much has been made by the Committee of 300 about the "evils" of South Africa's separation of races policy. Yet, little or nothing has been said about India's rigid separation of classes in Indian society. Could it be that South Africa is attacked because it has the richest gold fields in the world, while India has only a few natural resources of any real worth?

Actively assisted by master deceiver Cecil John Rhodes, a servant of the Rothschild, began an agitation for "rights" was raised by the carpetbaggers and hordes of foreigners who flocked to the Transvaal when the discovery of gold was announced. What these vagabonds and fortune hunters demanded was the right to vote, the first of the "one man one vote" scams used to separate the Boer people and their descendants from their national sovereignty. The agitation was orchestrated by the Rothschild-Rhodes political machine in Johannesburg and carefully controlled by Lord Alfred Milner out of London.

It was obvious to the Boer leaders that by allowing the newcomers to vote, their government would be swept aside by the hordes of foreign adventurers who had descended upon them. When it became clear that the Boer leaders were not going to meekly allow their people to become disenfranchised by the political demands for "one man one vote," plans for war, which had been a year in the making while Queen Victoria's ministers and emissaries talked peace, burst on the scene.

Queen Victoria sent the mightiest army ever assembled up to that time to do battle with the tiny Boer Republics. It would take the most vivid imagination to believe that the Queen of England was concerned about non-voting rights for the fortune hunters and carpet-baggers swarming over the Boer republics. After three years of the most brutal conflict during which the British showed no mercy for Boer women and children, 25,000 of whom perished in the first concentration camps ever to be established. The Boers, largely undefeated on the battlefield were obliged to come to the conference table. At Vereeniging, where the conference was held, in an elaborate piece of deception, the Boers were stripped of everything that they stood for, including the vast riches that lay beneath the barren soil of their republics.

It is important to remember that the Boers were a devout Christian nation. Queen Victoria's Illuminati-Gnostic-Cathari-Bogomil ministers and counselers were determined not only to defeat the Boers militarily, and take over the mineral wealth of their republics, but to crush them and wipe out their language and culture. Chief architect of this criminal enterprise was the haughty, aristocratic Lord Alfred Milner, who in 1915 financed the Bolsheviks and made possible the "Russian" revolution. The British banished Paul Kruger, the venerable State President of the Transvaal along with most of his ministers and those who had led the armed struggle against British imperialism. This was the first recorded instance of such barbaric treatment carried out by a supposedly civilized nation.

The reason why blatant, rampant apartheid was, and still is, allowed to flourish in India, is because India is the home of the New Age religion, which is favored by the Black Nobility of Venice and the oligarchists of Britain. The New Age religion is squarely based on the Hindu religion. Theosophist high-priestess Annie Besant, is credited with having adapted the Hindu religion to New Age ideas after going to India in 1898.

The idea of "one man, one vote," in which apartheid is cast as the villain, has no place in United States history. It was merely a ruse to convince the world that the United Nations was concerned about the welfare of the South African black tribes. (The blacks are divided into 17 tribes and are not a homogeneous nation of united people.) The anti-apartheid clamor was raised to cover the real goal, that being to seize full control of South Africa's vast mineral riches, which will now pass to the Committee of 300. Mandela will be cast aside as a worn out tool which has served its purpose, when this has been accomplished.

232

The U.S. Constitution does not provide for "one man, one vote" an observation that may be lost in the shouting over the "evil of South Africa's apartheid" as Mandela likes to call it. Representation in the U.S. Congress is determined by population counts taken by the Census Bureau in given areas once every ten years, and not on the basis of "one man one vote." That is why there is widespred gerrymandering of boundaries every four years. It is the number of people within these boundaries who then choose their representative.

It may be that liberal politicians desire a black or Hispanic representative for a given area; one they hope will vote with them on their liberal agenda. But their may not be enough black or Hispanic voters in the area to make the necessary change, so liberal politicians will try to get boundaries altered, even by the ridiculous subterfuge of linking two areas separated by as much as 100 miles through a narrow corridor between the two areas. The idea is that if blacks or Hispanics in the targeted area are in a minority, then create a majority by linking two areas, who will elect a black or Hispanic representative beholden to the librals in the House and Senate.

All during the clamor over apartheid the British press took good care to conceal a far greater apartheid which preceded South Africas by hundreds of years: the Indian caste system which remains in place to this very day and is still rigidly enforced.

Beginning with the British incursion into India in 1582, the Sufis were used to split the Moslems and Sikhs and set them against each other. In 1603, John Mildenhall arrived in Agra seeking concessions for the English East India Company, founded in London on Dec. 31, 1600. The company changed its name to the British East India Company, and used its agents to break the power of the Sikhs, who opposed the caste system, In 1717, BEIC bribery and deceptive diplomacy and gifts of medical supplies were enough to secure vast concessions from the Moguls, who also exempted the BEIC from taxation on revenues derived from poppy-growing and raw opium making.

By 1765, Clive of India, a legendary figure in the British occupation of India had taken full control of the richest poppy fields in the world in

DR JOHN COLEMAN

Bengal, Benares and Bihar, exercising control of the collection of revenues from the Moguls. By 1785, the opium trade was firmly in the grip of the BEIC under Sir Warren Hastings. One of Hastings's Indian "reforms" was to secure all poppy-growing lands and bring them under his control. This included the making of raw opium.

The British crown extended the BEIC charter for another 30 years after representations were made in Parliament in 1813. In 1833 Parliament again extended BEIC's charter for another 20 years. Seeing power slipping from their grasp, the Indian upper caste began to rebel against British rule through the BEIC. To forestall this, the British prime minister deceived Indian leaders by having the Government of India Act passed on August 2, 1856. The Act ostensibly transferred all BEIC assets and lands in India to the British crown. This diplomatic move was pure diplomacy by deception, because in essence, nothing had changed. BEIC was the Crown.

Prime Minister Disraeli carried the deception a step further when in 1896, at his instigation, parliament declared Queen Victoria "Empress of India." In the same year, famine killed more than 2 million lower-caste Indians. Altogether, during British (BEIC) rule, more than 6 million lower-caste Indians died of famine. Nothing remotely resembling this disaster ever occurred in South Africa. In the CIA-instigated "Sharpeville" riots, there was world-wide uproar and condemnation of South Africa, when less than 80 black rioters were killed by security forces. The blacks were incited to riot by outside forces, not realizing that they were being used.

The "Jati" caste system operating in India is based 100 percent on race. At the top of the pyramid are the Aryans (white with blue eyes, believed to be the descendants of Alexander the Great's occupation of the country.) Directly under them are the Brahmins in varying shades of white to light brown. Brahmin priests are drawn from this caste. Below the Brahmins come the warriors and rulers, called Kshatriyas, who are also very light-skinned. Below the Kshatriyas are the Vaisyas class, consisting of minor officials, merchants, traders, craftsmen and skilled workers. They have darker skins.

234

Then come the Sudras or unskilled workers, those who don't have a plumbing, electrical, auto mechanic or other trade. Then, at the very broad base of the power pyramid come the "Harijans," literally meaning "outcasts," collectively known as "Pariahs." They are also known as "untouchables", and they have very dark to black skins. The blacker their skins, the less "touchable" they are. In 1946 Lord Louis Mountbatten (Battenburg) directly representing the Committee of 300, offered India full independence, a subterfuge to quell serious rioting over continued famine that took the livers of hundreds of thousands of Harijans. This was largely ignored by the Western press. As a further empty gesture, "untouchability" was declared illegal one year later, but the practice continued as though the law had never been passed.

"Untouchability" was the most cruel of all of India's rigid caste system. It meant that the Harijans were not allowed to ever touch those in other castes above them, even by accident. Should this happen, then the upper class person so offended, had the right to have the Harijan offender killed. The system of rigid separation was not only a class measure, but was also to prevent the spread of diseases rampant among the Harijans.

The Harijans are the largest racial group in India, and for centuries they have been shockingly mistreated and abused. When political changes are desired, this group provides the canon fodder, their lives considered of little or no value. We saw a demonstration of this when the Harijans were used to destroy an ancient Moslem mosque in India to bring about political changes in the Indian government. This evil is seldom if ever mentioned in the Western press or any television programming.

Unfortunately for the blacks, they are but pawns in a game. Their importance will end once the Committee of 300 has achieved its goal and Mandela is cast aside like a worn out tool that has served its purpose. The Global 2000 population reduction program will then be applied to them in earnest. They deserve a better fate than the one planned for them by Mandela's controllers; the Oppenheimers and the Committee of 300.

235

# Notes on Surveillance XII.

The United States and Britain work very closely to spy on their citizens and on foreign governments. This applies to all traffic: commercial, diplomatic and private communications. Nothing is sacred and nothing is beyond the reach of the *National Security Agency* (NSA) and the *Government Comminications Headquarters* (GCHQ) who are in a joint partnership to illegally monitor telephone, telex, fax, computer and voice transmissions on a massive scale.

These two agencies have the expertise to eavesdrop on anyone at any time. Every day 1 million communications are picked up by GCHQ listening posts in Menwith Hill in Yorkshire and Morwenstow, Cornwall, in England. These stations are run by the NSA in order to get around British laws that forbid national security snooping on its citizens. Technically, GCHQ is not breaking British law as the interceptions are carried out by the NSA.

The GCHQ/NSA computers look for trigger words which are flagged and stored. This is a simple procedure, given the fact that all communications come through as digital pulses. This applies to the written and spoken word alike. Then, the flagged messages are analyzed, and if there is anything that interests these agencies, further investigations are launched. The fact that the entire operation is illegal, does not stop either agency from their self-appointed task.

The NSA's "HARVEST" computers can read 460 million characters a second, or the equivalent of 5000-300-page books. Presently it is estimated by intelligence sources that the "HARVEST" computers used by GCHQ and NSA intercept more that 80 million calls per year, of which 2.5 million are flagged and stored for additional scrutiny. The two agencies have a large staff of specialists who scour the world, finding and evaluating new products that could be used to safeguard individual privacy, which they then find ways and means to break down.

A big challenge came with the advent of cellular phones. At present cellular phone traffic is "tapped" by listening to cell signals (which are designed for billing purposes) and the various cell codes which have their own identification, are backtracked so that the origin of the call can be traced. But the new generation A5 cellular phones pose a serious problem for government snooping.

These new phones have an A5 scrambling code which is very closely related to military scrambling systems, which makes it virtually impossible for government agencies to decipher messages and to trace the origin of the call. At present it would take surveillance teams at GCHQ and the NSA 5 months to unscramble messages transmitted via A5 cellular phones.

The government say this will seriously hamper its efforts to fight the drug trade and organized crime, a lame old excuse that few people accept. Nothing is said about the fact that in the course of such anticrime measures, the rights of citizens to privacy are grossly violated.

Now the NSA, the FBI and GCHQ are demanding that cellular phones with the existing A5 scrambler be recalled for "modifications." Although they do not say so, government needs to have the same accessibility to private transmissions that it has had up to the advent of the A5 scrambler system. So, government agencies in Britain and America are demanding that the A5 cellular scrambler system be replaced with an A5X system, giving them a "trapdoor" into formerly secure cellular phones.

Phone calls by landline (local calls) are easily intercepted by being "switched " to a clearing house run by the NSA and GCHQ. Long distance calls do not present a problem, as they are generally relayed by microwave towers and can readily be plucked out of the air. In addition, the NSA also has its RHYOLITE satellites which have the capability to pick up every conversation being transmitted by telex, microwave, radiotronic wave, VHF and or UHF signals.

Bruce Lockhart-MI6 controller of Lenin and Trotsky.

Sydney Reilly-economic specialist MI6.

Somerset Maugham-MI6 special agent to Kerensky.

MI6 Headquarters London.

Former U.S. President Bush and Emir Al-Sabah.

## Saudi Arabia: The Wahabi Dynasty (1735–    )

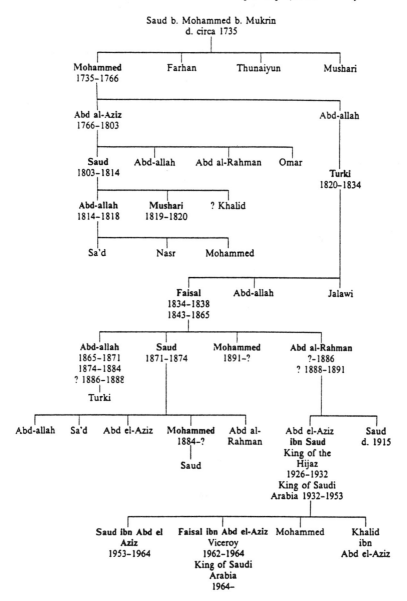

The Saudi-Wahabi Dynasty.

# Source Notes

The source on Martin Luther king Jr's assassination came from an Associated Press report from Memphis April 9,1965. There were two further Associated Press reports from Memphis, one filed by Don McKee and the other by Gaylord Shaw on April 14, 1965. The actual assassin was seen by New York Times Reporter Earl Caldwell, who was never questioned by any law enforcement or investigative agency.

Private Papers Vittorio Orlando.
Private Papers General Anton Denikin.
Minutes of Meetings San Remo Conference.
U.S. Congressional Record, House and Senate.
Minutes of meetings, Lausanne Conference.

Wells. H.G. "After Democracy."

Russell. Sir Bertrand. "Impact of Science on Society."

British East India Company (BEIC). India House, London.
Wilson, President Woodrow .

Congressional Record, House and Senate.

Treaty of Versailles Documents, Paris, France.

Jan Christian Smuts. Boer War Memorial Archives, Pretoria.

Allied Demands for Reparations. Versailles and San Remo Conference.

The Collected speeches of Congressman L.T. McFadden.
League of Nations Documentation, Geneva.

Royal Institute for International Affairs.
Dr.Coleman, "Committee of 300."

Socialism: F.D. Roosevelt "Our Way."

Communist Manifesto of 1848.

"Fabian Freeway High Road to Socialism In America." Rose Martin.

Dr.J.Coleman "Committee of 300"
"   "    "      "Is the U.S. a Member of the U.N.?"

Senator Walsh. Big Five Dictatorship at U.N. Congressional Record, Senate pages 8165-8166.

Dr.J.Coleman. "Gulf War Aims Examined."

Public Law 85766 Section 1602. Public Law 471, Section 109.

John Rarick. "U.N. a creature of invisible government." Congressional Record, House, pages E 10400-10404, December 14, 1970.

Debate Senator Allen and Senator Teller Congressional Record (Senate) 6586-6589 July 1, 1898.

Dr.J.Coleman. "Not a Sovereign Body." United Nations Charter, so-called "Charter." Pages 2273-2297 Congressional Record, House February 26,1900.

Rep.Smith. Limits of presidential power Congressional Record Page 12284.

Allen Dulles. Pressures Congress, Congressional Record Pages 8008-80209, July 25, 1945.

Leonard Mosley. "Dulles; A Biography of Eleanor, Allen and John Foster Dulles."

Constitutional Law. Judge Cooley. Constitution does not yield to treaty or enactment.

Professor van Halst. "Constitutional Law of the United States."

House, Colonel. CFR and controller of Wilson and Roosevelt, documentation from British War Museum,and British Museum, London.

Dr.J.Coleman "Foreign Aid is Involuntary Servitude."

Land of Arabia. British Museum,and Cairo Museum.

Tenets of the Koran. From the Koran.

Lawrence of Arabia betrayed. Sir Archibald Murray Arabian papers. British Foreign Office dispatches, British Museum, London.

Balfour Declaration. Sir Arthur Balfour Papers, British Museum, London.

General Edmund Allenby, Palestine Papers, British Museum, London.

Louis Fischer."Oil Imperialism: the International Struggle for Petroleum."

Independence for Iraq. Protocol 1923. League of Nations documents, Geneva.

L.M.Fleming, Oil in the World War.

Annals of the American Academy of Political Science. Supplement May 1917, "the Mexican Constitution."

Washington Soviet Review, January 1928.

London Petroleum Times, Nov.26, 1927.

Dr.J.Coleman "William K. D'Arcy. Mysterious New Zealander who opened the way for Committee of 300 oil companies. The Committee of 300."

Turkish Petroleum Company. Papers, Sir Percy Cox, London Petroleum Institute, Foreign Office, London.

Status of Kuwait and Mosul left vague. Minutes of meetings San Remo and Lausanne Conferences, 1920 and 1923.

Status of Palestine. British White Paper by the Passfield Commission.

U.S. State Department Consular Directive August 16, 1919. Stressed the vital necessity for U.S. to secure foreign oil concessions and encouraged consular staff to spy on foreign agents competing with.S. for control of oil.

State Dept. "Foreign Relations of the United States." 1913 pp820.
   "      "         "            "      "  "      "         "    1914 pp44.

Federal Trade Commission supra pp XX-XXI, 69th Congress, State Dept. Doc. vol 10 p 3120.

Mohr, Anton. "The Oil War."

Eaton, M.J. "The Oil Industry's Answer Today."

Commerce Dept T.I.B No.385 "Foreign Combinations to Control Prices Raw Materials.

Bertrand Russell. "One of the most important raw materials is oil." Statement made in 1962.

Coolidge. Federal Oil Conservation Board. Federal government "open door" policy for oil. Statements made by Charles Evans Hughes before this board.

Oil and Land Concessions with Mexico: Taken from Congressional Library Records of Treaty of Guadalupe and Hidalgo, 1848.

"Rockefeller Internationalists" Emmanuel Josephson describes R Rockefeller's international oil policies.

Teapot Dome Scandal. The role of Albert B. Fall and the origin of the term "fall guy". Records consulted were obtained from British Museum sources, the Congressional Record, House and Senate and newspaper reports of the day. Senate Foreign Relations Committee hearings on "Revolution in Mexico" 1913. In 1912, President Wilson got the American people fired up on talk of the "Huerta menace" as a danger to the Panama Canal.

Henry, J.D. "Grab for Russian Oil, Baku and Eventful History."

La Espagnol de la Tramerga, Pierre. "The World Struggle for Oil."

Soviet Union Review, Jan.1928.

McFadden, L.T. The Huerta Thomas Lamont Agreement.

Soviet Union Information Bureau. "Russian Economic Conditions 1928."

Partition of Palestine."Jews and Arabs cannot live together." The Peel Commission Report, British Foreign Office documents.

State Department Memo to James Baker III Oct. 1989. "Wall off Agricultural Department" in reference to BNL scandal.

National Security Directive 26 re Iraq and BNL authorizing extended credits to Iraq.

New York Federal Reserve Bank memo February 6. Reveals machinations over BNL's Iraq loans coverup.

Interagency Deputies Committee of National Security Council memo calls meeting at White House for BNL-Iraq damage control.

President Bush falsifies Iraqi troop strength. Joint Session of Congress, Congressional Record September 11, 1990.

Henry Gonzalez asks embarrassing questions: Congressional Record,

House and letters to Attorney General Thornburgh September 1990. Copies of letters House, Congressional Record.

William Barr, Attorney General Refuses cooperation with Congressman Gonzalez. Letters May 1992.

Court Records, Judge Marvin Shoob, Christopher Drougal, BNL case, Atlanta. Judge Shoob asks Justice Department to appoint special prosecutor.

Copy-letter from Senator Boren to Attorney General Barr, demanding appointment special prosecutor.October 14, 1992.

"Off book sales" to Iraq and Iran. Testimony Ben Mashe at his 1989 trial, from court documents.

Dr. John Coleman. "Cecil John Rhodes, Conspirator Extraordinary."

Dr.J. Coleman. "No law 'one man one' vote expressed in Constitution."

British Opium Trade with India.

India House Documents on British East India Company, India House, London. Mentioned are John Mildenhall, who sought first concession from India. Also details work of "Clive of India" and how various opium "charters" were negotiated with Indian Moguls.

Disraeli. Speeches in the House of Commons on Indian policy, "Hansard" 1896.

Thomspon-Urruttia Treaty April 20,1921. Documents in British Museum and Congressional Record, House and Senate.

Vattel's "Law of Nations" on treaties and agreements.

Dr.Mulford. "Sovereignty of Nations."

John Lawn. Director of U.S. Drug Enforcement Agency (DEA.) Letter to Manuel Noriega May 27 1987.

British Secret Intelligence Service. Earliest beginning, Sir Francis Walsingham, Queen Elizabeth 1 spy master, documents in the British Museum, London.

George Bernard Shaw. "Notes on the Fabian Society."

# Index

## C

# H

# N

# O

# W

Wahabi family   32,  34
Walsh, David I.   8
Walsh, Lawrence   59
Walsingham, Francis   127,  129
war, declaration of   26
Wauchope, Arthur   104
Webb, Sydney & Beatrice   17
Weinberger, Caspar   59
Wells, H.G.   1,  6
White, Edward   83
Whitney vs. Robertson   17
Wilson, Woodrow   2,  18,  115
Wiseman, William   131
Woodhead, John   105
Woolf, Leonard   17
Woolsey, R. James   61
World Bank   175,  179
world revolution   23
World Zionist Congress   101

# Y

Yates, Irving Frederick   159
Yeutter, Clayton   48
Young America   223
Young, Desmond   78

# Z

Zapata Oil Company   69